The Business Benefits of GIS

An ROI Approach

David Maguire • Victoria Kouyoumjian • Ross Smith

ESRI PRESS
REDLANDS, CALIFORNIA

ESRI Press, 380 New York Street, Redlands, California 92373-8100

10 09 08   2 3 4 5 6 7 8 9 10

Printed in the United States of America

Library of Congress Cataloging-in-Publication Data

Maguire, D. J. (David J.)
    The business benefits of GIS : an ROI approach / David Maguire, Ross Smith, Victoria Kouyoumjian.
      p. cm.
    ISBN 978-1-58948-200-5 (alk. paper)
    1. Management information systems. 2. Geographic information systems. 3. Information technology—
Management. I. Smith, Ross, 1970– II. Kouyoumjian, Victoria 1968– III. Title.
    HD30.213.M335 2008
    910.285—dc22   2008020610

Ask for ESRI Press titles at your local bookstore or order by calling 1-800-447-9778. You can also shop online at www.esri.com/esripress. Outside the United States, contact your local ESRI distributor.

ESRI Press titles are distributed to the trade by the following:

In North America:

Ingram Publisher Services

Toll-free telephone: (800) 648-3104

Toll-free fax: (800) 838-1149

E-mail: customerservice@ingrampublisherservices.com

In the United Kingdom, Europe, and the Middle East:

Transatlantic Publishers Group Ltd.

Telephone: 44 20 7373 2515

Fax: 44 20 7244 1018

E-mail: richard@tpgltd.co.uk

Cover photos (left to right): Photo by Keith Brofsky/Photodisc/Getty Images; photo by Comstock Images/Jupiterimages; photo by Scott T. Baxter/Photodisc/Getty Images; photo by Sami Sarkis/Photodisc/Getty Images; photo by PhotoLink/Photodisc/Getty Images.

Cover design	Donna Celso (ESRI) and Kristen Anderson (PA Consulting Group)
Editing	Arthur Gelmis
Copyediting and proofreading	Tiffany Wilkerson
Permissions	Kathleen Morgan
Printing coordination	Cliff Crabbe and Lilia Arias

Contents

Preface

Geographic information systems (GIS) has come a long way as a discipline since its humble beginnings in the 1960s. Today the technology is well developed, and there are strong techniques and methodologies for scientific and technical project implementations. In contrast to the maturity of GIS technology, the related business-based return on investment (ROI) aspects are much less well developed. We have found that there are very few examples of the measurable business benefits delivered by GIS projects, and that there is no standardized technique for estimating the value or return on investment of using GIS within organizations.

Although executives are always faced with pressure to justify their expenditures, in recent years, given the number of high-profile economic and accounting offenses, there have been increasing global and local demands to improve accountability, business efficiencies, competitive advantage, and resource utilization. As a result executives are seeking more sophisticated approaches for prioritizing and targeting investment in GIS technology, and for proving how and when that investment will deliver tangible benefits to their organization.

It is important to recognize that ROI calculations are only one component of a complete process; delivering on the benefits expected in a consistent and complete manner is equally important. To prove the business case for GIS, organizations must be able carry out the following activities effectively: link the business benefits sought via the GIS initiatives to the organization's strategic goals and objectives; build a community of GIS advocates across the organization, moving beyond a single department and into the enterprise; ensure the program is business-led, and not technology-driven; and consistently deliver benefits through a well-structured and well-governed program that seeks to deliver value, not applications.

This book sets out to develop a standardized methodology for calculating the business value of GIS projects. The originating methodology was refined over many years by PA Consulting Group, Inc., a leading international firm of management consultants, and applied by them across a number of disciplines. We use a mixture of tried and proven management science methods, adapted to perform in the context of GIS projects. As such, the intended user of the methodology is a GIS professional manager, business architect, system analyst, etc.—who wants or needs to develop a compelling case for introducing or expanding the use of GIS within their organization. We assume only that the reader has knowledge of GIS, and a basic understanding of business concepts and techniques.

We introduce a 10-step process for completing a comprehensive study, from project inception to a compelling business report. The reader is guided carefully through the process, and each step includes an extensive explanation, documentation, and a series of electronic templates used to collect, manage, analyze, and present the key data elements and ideas.

The approach focuses on six key topics that we believe are critical to creating a defensible position on the value of GIS for any organization: demonstrate the real business value; determine the specific costs; estimate the time frame for delivery of benefits; understand the resource requirements; define the governance and management; and calculate the return on investment. This is accomplished by addressing the primary questions generally asked by senior executives when confronted with a request for funding programs of this nature: Why invest, or reinvest, in GIS technology? What is the level of investment needed? When will the benefits be delivered? Who is going to deliver these benefits, and what resources are required? What is the proven financial case—does the investment in GIS provide the financial or other value to make it worthwhile?

The book begins with an overview of our approach for measuring business value. It outlines the 10-step methodology and describes the structure of the book. It also introduces a case study that runs through every chapter. The case study is a fictitious city municipality that was intentionally chosen because it is broad enough to cover a range of commercial, environmental, governmental, and utility business issues. Each of the subsequent chapters uses a common organizing frame for discussing the steps in the ROI methodology. The tasks for each specific step are first described, using examples for illustration, followed by a discussion of how the reader will carry out the tasks. The tasks essentially involve creating a series of documents based on the digital templates provided. Finally, the relevant case study material is presented.

This is very much a hands-on approach. All the materials described in the book are available on an accompanying Web site (http://gis.esri.com/roi). This site includes digital versions of all the chapters, templates, examples, and other miscellaneous supporting materials. There is also a reader discussion list that can be used to obtain insight from others about their experience in implementing the approach.

The methodology is fact-based and benefits focused. In its design, we have tried to make it as robust, objective, and repeatable as possible. It is our hope that by creating a relatively easy-to-use and standardized methodology, we will encourage organizations to create and share compelling ROI-based case studies that show how GIS can create business value for an organization.

David Maguire
Victoria Kouyoumjian
Ross Smith
June 2008

Acknowledgments

The authors would like to thank the following for their help and support in producing this book: Alistair Davidson, Arthur Gelmis, Chris Steel, Chris Thomas, Jack Dangermond, and Judy Hawkins.

Overview of the ROI methodology

The primary objective of this chapter is to introduce the subject of return on investment (ROI) and the ROI methodology in this book, as well as to offer some practical suggestions regarding application of the methodology within organizations. This chapter offers a broad overview of the methodology in contrast to the subsequent chapters that delve into much greater detail. Finally, a case study is introduced that will be followed through each of the chapters in the remainder of the book.

This return on investment (ROI) methodology was developed to show, in a compelling way, how geographic information systems (GIS) can create business value for an organization. It is an end-to-end process composed of 10 distinct steps that, when taken together, provide a recipe for creating a business-based approach to justifying a GIS. It covers the relevant business benefits, capital and operational budget, benefits delivery roadmap, organizational structure, and ROI financial analysis. Collectively, these can be used to add value with GIS. The methodology seeks to address the primary questions generally asked by senior executives when confronted with a request for funding projects of this nature:

- Why invest, or reinvest, in GIS technology? What value will this investment have for our organization?

- When will the benefits be delivered? This quarter or within the next two years?

- Who will be the recipients of the benefits?

- What is the level of investment needed, both initially and in an ongoing operational basis?

- Who is going to deliver these benefits, and what resources are required—both internally and externally—to realize the expected benefits?

- What is the proven financial case—that is, does the investment in GIS provide the financial or other value to make it worthwhile?

Applicable to both public and private organizations, this methodology answers these questions by using a process based on a series of hands-on tasks that use digital tools and templates located on a Web site that accompanies this book (http://gis.esri.com/roi). Originally developed by PA Consulting Group, Inc. (PA), the methodology has been adapted in collaboration with ESRI in order to combine PA's management experience with ESRI's GIS expertise—the result of which is a unique GIS-specific return on investment methodology firmly grounded in management science.

The methodology is equally applicable to organizations that want to determine the value for a mature GIS implementation already in production, as well as for those organizations that have little or no GIS capability deployed at all and want to evaluate whether GIS will help solve their business problems in a cost-effective way.

INTRODUCTION TO RETURN ON INVESTMENT

For many years IT (information technology) projects have been initiated largely based on qualitative, value-added reasoning; for example, "if we implement this technology, then we will be able to perform these additional services." However, in recent years greater pressure for financial accountability in both the public and private sectors, combined with a better understanding of difficulties associated with implementing enterprise IT systems and processes, and a realization that proper project accountability is a key aspect of good management, have all led to wider adoption of return on investment methods in project planning and evaluation. To be successful, IT strategies must be aligned with business strategies, and IT processes must reflect business processes. IT that exists in a vacuum and is disconnected from an organization's business processes may be more of a business concern than no IT at all.

In this book, the term *return on investment* (ROI) is used in a general sense to describe the success or failure of a project or program of work (a collection of projects). ROI studies use a combination of qualitative and quantitative measures to assess the utility that an organization will obtain from an investment. Although we advocate the use of both these measures, here we place much greater emphasis on the importance of fact-based, quantitative measures given their greater objectivity and persuasiveness as far as senior executives are concerned. Later, in chapter 9, a very precise definition of *Return on Investment* (note capitalization) is introduced and defined formulaically as the ratio of net benefits to total costs expressed as a percentage. There are, of course, many financial measures of project efficiency in use today in the wider IT and business communities under the general heading of "return on investment." In chapter 9, each of the main measures is defined and evaluated as a way of assessing GIS projects.

ROI methods have been in use for more than 25 years and are well tried and tested. Roulstone and Phillips[1] provide a good introduction to ROI for technology projects. They point out the wide-ranging and extensive use of ROI in technology projects in areas such as business intelligence, customer relationship management, enterprise resource planning, information security, process automation, and telecommunications. Although there are many variants (e.g., Cost:Benefit Analysis, the CIO Council's Value Measuring Methodology,[2] and the Investment Evaluation Methodology[3]), the common core principles are accepted and have been well documented.[4] The work reported here has centered on creating an objective, robust, and repeatable methodology and set of digital templates that can be used for calculating ROI across a wide range of GIS projects and organizations. It is hoped that this in turn will lead to publication of a series of reference case studies that show the ROI of GIS in a variety of organizations.

There are a number of useful general reviews of the literature on ROI as applied in a GIS context. Halsing, *et al.*[5], summarize the literature as part of a study of the business case for creating a national map for the United States. Similarly, GITA and AWWA[6] provide an extensive treatment of the subject and review a large number of case studies, especially relating to utilities. Karikari and Stillwell[7] illustrate how to apply business analysis to a land administration project in West Africa. Booz Allen Hamilton[8] presents the case for geospatial interoperability at NASA using return on investment. Meehan[9] discusses how to make an enterprise business case for a utility and presents data for a representative but fictitious utility company. A Web search will also turn up a number of very specific examples that sometimes include all the data used in the calculations.

OVERVIEW OF THE ROI METHODOLOGY

The ROI methodology presented in this book comprises a sequence of 10 interrelated steps designed to be performed by a GIS professional supported by a small project team. Shown in outline form in figure O.1, the methodology begins with a series of *planning and investigation* activities that lay the groundwork for subsequent steps. Step 1, preparing for the ROI project, requires a review of an organization's mission statement(s) and an understanding of its past and present landscape of GIS. Step 2 comprises a series of interviews with key stakeholders to elicit, with guidance, how GIS can contribute to an organization's mission, collecting information concerning the high-level business issues and challenges that it faces. These insights will be organized into a series of business opportunities, which are prioritized in step 3.

The next group of steps is concerned with *GIS program definition.* The information gathered in earlier stages is used to define a program of GIS projects in step 4, and dictates how these projects will be governed and managed in step 5.

The next series of steps form the core of the methodology and are concerned with *business analysis.* In step 6, the defined projects are broken down into constituent parts and the resource costs are determined, from which estimated benefits will be detailed in step 7. Since this is often the most challenging stage for many projects, templates and spreadsheets are provided to calculate costs and model benefits. In step 8, a benefits roadmap is created that shows when the benefits will be realized by an organization. In step 9, the template provided is used to calculate the ROI and other relevant financial metrics that will quantitatively demonstrate the value of GIS to an organization.

The last step encompasses the final account of an ROI study. In step 10, a compelling report is created by aggregating the information and research completed previously. The report will concisely show how GIS can contribute value to an organization, including its cost, benefits, time to implement, resources required, governance, and the return on investment an organization will realize.

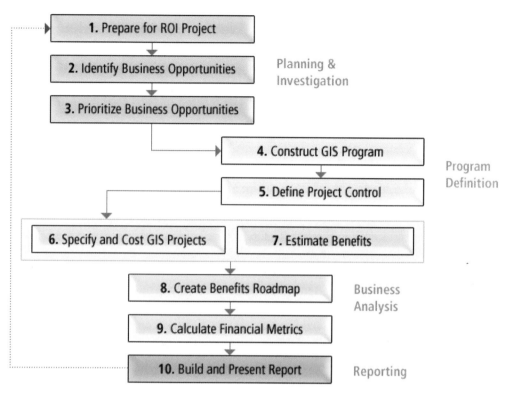

Figure O.1 Overview of the ROI methodology.

In order to use this methodology successfully, a solid understanding of GIS principles and applications is assumed, but the ROI project lead does not need extensive, expert GIS technical skills. Access to the necessary information and people within the organization under study is more important, so that it is possible to collect all of the appropriate data in order to drive the methodology. Experience has shown that this methodology can be completed in about four weeks of continuous effort, but it is expected that the process will typically move forward at an uneven pace, with breaks between the steps so that all participants in the process can continue with other duties and priorities. These intermissions are beneficial in that they allow time for consolidation of information and reflection on what has been achieved, before proceeding to the next step. A good approach is to work continuously on each of the groups of steps—represented by the four different colors in figure O.1—pausing after each completed group of steps. It is usual, therefore, for the whole process to take from four weeks of continuous effort, to twelve weeks averaging two person-days per week.

Although this book presents the methodology as an end-to-end linear sequence of steps, it is not necessary to complete all of the steps in order to obtain useful results. For instance, completing steps 1 through 4 may provide enough information to formulate a qualitative GIS business case, which might be sufficient for some financial purposes. Be advised, however, that providing a comprehensive and convincing case for the key stakeholders in an organization—the CEO, COO, CFO, and CTO—requires complete analysis and reporting on all the steps. In summary, before starting out, it is recommended that the person tasked with conducting the ROI project decides how best to adapt this methodology to the needs and resources available within an organization. The methodology should provide the tools and tasks that can be customized to meet most organizations' requirements to build a robust, convincing, and realizable ROI business justification and a strategic plan for implementation.

Commonly, when starting an ROI project, the focus is solely on the end result: the ROI report, or even more specifically, the "bottom line," which shows the ROI percentage value, money saved, or major business benefits to an organization. However, experience has shown the ROI *journey* to be more important than the destination. During the course of building the ROI project, it is expected that participants will learn more about the people that manage and work in the organization; the important processes and information resources required; how and where business value is generated; and areas that are in need of change.

As the ROI project framework is assembled, using this book as a guide, multiple deliverables will be incorporated into the approach, involving individuals and departments outside normal peer groups. Justifying GIS efforts in order to improve businesses processes and projects must involve other units of an organization, apart from a home workgroup or department. It is important to recognize that working collaboratively is an essential requirement, in order to socialize the ROI objectives, and to gain the buy-in and ownership from those colleagues and stakeholders whose support will foster the eventual success of the ROI project.

1. Prepare for the ROI project

Conducting an ROI project for an organization is an important, time-consuming activity and, consequently, is typically only undertaken for costly, strategic, or mission-critical initiatives. ROI projects tend to be quite high profile, and their results often assume lasting significance. This methodology, therefore, begins with a preparation stage that will build an understanding of an organization's main drivers, business imperatives, stakeholders, and processes. Foremost among the tasks is establishing a small team of committed individuals who will undertake the whole study on behalf of the organization as a whole. The end result will produce a set of materials that will provide a solid foundation for all the subsequent steps.

2. Identify business opportunities

During this step, the ROI team will interview several of the key stakeholders in an organization in order to uncover the key challenges and opportunities to be faced in the future. The purpose of this task is multifold. The key decision makers are most closely aligned with an organization's business processes and are therefore the best qualified to identify the prospective improvements and benefits that a GIS can provide. In addition, gleaning this information directly from senior executives will add significance to the ROI analysis and to the weight of the final ROI project report. Although the ROI team may have exceptional ideas about how GIS can benefit an organization, they are only valuable ideas if the organization's senior executives concur—so it is *the views of the stakeholders* that must be the focus of concern.

The outcomes of step 2 will be GIS awareness from senior executives and a high-level list of business challenges and opportunities. Universal support may not yet be obtained until the executives review the ROI calculations, but by the end of this step, the team should have made some impressions on them by exploring the potential for GIS within the organization.

3. Prioritize business opportunities

This is a relatively short step, but nonetheless important, with the objective of prioritizing the business opportunities obtained in the last task based on a combination of the importance to an organization, and the ease of implementation as a solution.

The team will need to evaluate all the information collected so far to create a prioritized list of business opportunities. The suggested ranking evaluates two variables: the level of value of benefit to the organization, and the level of difficulty involved in delivering the benefit. It is important to make some critical decisions to balance what is important and what is achievable using the GIS resources that are likely to be available.

The output of this step will be a prioritized list of business opportunities in terms of the benefits they will provide and their magnitude of impact on the organization. This list will be used later to scope out a portfolio of GIS projects.

4. Construct a GIS program

The first three steps of the ROI project journey are designed to show how to solve business problems and add value to an organization. The team assessed the current and future organizational challenges and composed a prioritized list of business opportunities. Next, attention turns to converting these business opportunities into a program of GIS projects driven by the business needs of an organization. These projects should be specific, measurable, and achievable using resources that will realistically be made available to the GIS team. Some of the projects might offer "quick wins," some might be foundation projects for the overall program portfolio, while only a few should be challenging but critically important.

For each project, the key objectives, activities, outcomes, deliverables, and time frame for completion need to be defined. Sufficient detail should be provided such that the projects can be budgeted in the next stage. To assist, a project definition template is provided.

The outcome of this stage will be documentation of a completed portfolio of GIS projects.

5. Define project control

Many independent studies have shown that one of the main reasons why IT projects fail is because of lack of good management. This is addressed directly in this step of the methodology. The main task is to define a sound governance and program delivery team. This step is necessary to establish accountability and oversight for the projects and instill confidence in the stakeholders that the GIS implementations will be successful.

A program delivery chart will be completed using the template provided. This chart will outline the key individuals or types of staff who will manage the projects to successful completion—for example, a managing executive, project manager, or solution architect. This step will also identify any differences or gaps between the current and desired capabilities of an organization with respect to successfully implementing the GIS program of work.

The outcome of this step will be a completed model of resource competencies and an organizational design chart of responsibilities.

6. Specify and cost GIS projects

Any ROI project would be incomplete without an assessment of the budget required for a successful implementation. The next activity, therefore, is to assign a monetary cost to each GIS project defined in step 4. In this chapter, several tasks must be completed in order to build a budget. Involvement of the finance department is recommended at the outset to gain approval or assistance before populating a spreadsheet template with information for the budget. The budget is essentially a summary of all the resource costs for each of the projects. The completed template will provide all the information necessary to view the costs for each of the GIS projects, including the magnitude, timing, and duration of resource use. The final budget is presented in both detailed and summary tabular and graphical form.

The overall purpose of this step is to build a well-thought-out budget that will stand up to scrutiny and dissection by the senior executives within an organization. Once completed, the project budget spreadsheet will have a collection of quantitative information used to calculate the ROI figures in step 9.

7. Estimate benefits

There are many benefits of using GIS in virtually all types of organizations. Some benefits are tangible and can be assigned a monetary value, while others are soft or intangible and are difficult to measure. The focus here is primarily on tangible benefits. Estimating the benefits of a GIS program is a little more difficult than specifying the costs, not so much in identifying the benefits, but in translating the benefits into specific, measurable terms that can be ascribed a monetary value. The benefits estimation process focuses on things such as the value added with GIS, the cost avoided, the additional revenue made, and the improvements in efficiency. The process of defining a benefit is broken down into a series of constituent parts to aid in modeling activities so that they can be expressed in a measurable form. The data is then entered into a spreadsheet to provide yearly totals.

The summary benefit data will be used later, along with cost data, to calculate a series of financial metrics in step 9.

8. Create a benefits roadmap

The next task is to assemble the key cost and benefit milestones and project completion dates, as determined in steps 6 and 7, and express them in the form of a benefits roadmap using the template provided. The template is simply a diagram that plots key project elements on a timeline. The dates included in the roadmap do not need to be exact, but they should certainly be realistic and defendable. The benefits roadmap provides supporting evidence that there is clear understanding of the whole end-to-end ROI process. It is used to communicate *when* and *how* the business benefits will be realized by an organization.

The outcome is a benefits roadmap diagram that will act as a useful overview of the whole program of work, as well as a summary of deliverables and the timeline of activity.

9. Calculate financial metrics

Completing the analysis part of the ROI project entails actually calculating some financial metrics, including the return on investment. In this methodology, the focus is on Net Present Value (NPV), Internal Rate of Return (IRR), Payback Period, Maximum Cumulative Free Cash Flow (FCF) Subsidy, and Return on Investment (ROI). The specific definitions for these and all other key terms used in this methodology can be found on the accompanying Web site at http://gis.esri.com/roi/glossary.cfm.

As before, a spreadsheet template is provided to assist in calculating the financial metrics used to support the ROI project. Largely collected from previous tasks, the appropriate financial data is entered into the template. After setting the values for general assumptions—such as the length of the review period, tax rate, and discount rate—all of the key indicator metrics are calculated dynamically by the macros built into the spreadsheet. Both high-level and more detailed outputs are provided, as well as a series of graphs that depict how key indicators change over time.

Once the ROI calculations for the portfolio of GIS projects are completed, attention can move to the final stage, which involves building and delivering a robust and convincing report.

10.   Build and present report

The objective of the final step is to create and present a compelling report that describes a strong ROI-based case for GIS in an organization. This will involve pulling together all of the information created in earlier stages and formulating it as a report and presentation to be delivered to executive stakeholders.

A template is provided to support building the main written report. A successful outcome of this final step, and the methodology as a whole, will be acceptance of the GIS ROI program, with continued and expanded support and funding for the portfolio of GIS projects defined. Although this is not a foregone conclusion, by employing this methodology, the chances of fostering broad ownership of the GIS mission among key members of an organization should be significantly enhanced. This methodology also provides the tools to give the ROI project team the confidence and executive backing to make it happen. Good luck!

Case Study

INTRODUCTION TO THE CITY OF SPRINGFIELD

In this book, the many aspects of the GIS ROI methodology will be conveyed through a case study of a fictitious city. Applied in a "semi-real world" context, the case study illustrates how to complete each of the tasks presented in the 10 steps of the methodology. The case study is designed to show both how to complete the methodology and how to interpret the results. It also illustrates the way to strike a balance between planning, data collection, and analysis, and demonstrates how to apply the material in a real study.

The case study is based on the invented city of Springfield, with an estimated 100,000 inhabitants, located in the midwestern section of the United States. Although entirely invented, Springfield is representative of an average city and provides the usual portfolio of public services to its citizens. The case study is portrayed as realistically as possible, although simplifications have been made in order to focus on the ROI-specific issues. Similar to many cities, Springfield has limited resources and is continually under pressure to improve services, while at the same time reduce costs.

Using the City of Springfield, the methodology is applied with the intention of creating a rigorous and convincing ROI-based case for improving city activities using GIS. A municipality was chosen as the collective example because this type of organization performs a wide range of commercial (e.g., economic development), governmental, utility (e.g., public works) and environmental (e.g., parks and recreation) activities, and is therefore representative of the major GIS application areas and markets. Specifically, the Springfield case study addresses such challenges as improving economic development by increasing inward investment, keeping the city green by planting trees, managing smart growth by redeveloping "brownfield" sites, and reducing the time spent inspecting field assets using mobile technologies. As the case study is being built, chapter by chapter, it will become clear how the City of Springfield can use GIS effectively to improve its activities. While examining the opportunities and constraints on the use of GIS, the ROI business methodology will be applied in a pragmatic manner.

Let us set the stage: Elected officials of Springfield are concerned that, although neighboring cities are making extensive use of new technologies to reduce costs and increase services to their citizens, Springfield has nothing like this established. So, a new city manager, Bob James, has recently been appointed. James has an MBA and comes from a smaller town in an adjoining state that successfully employed technology to improve city services. James hires a new GIS manager, Brian Sobers, who is employed in the Planning Department within the Community Development Division headed by Sue Coldfield (see figure C1.3). This case study is written from the perspective of Brian Sobers, the GIS manager, who is tasked by management with using new technology to improve city services and reduce costs.

The case study sections in each of the following chapters present the materials prepared by Brian Sobers and his ROI project team, who were tasked with spearheading the GIS ROI study at the City of Springfield.

Endnotes

1. Roulstone, D. B., and J. J. Phillips. *ROI for technology projects: Measuring and delivering value* (Oxford, U.K.: Butterworth-Heinemann, 2008).

2. CIO Council. *The value of IT investments: It's not just return on investment.* http://www cio.gov/documents/TheValueof_IT_Investments.pdf.

3. Karikari, I., and J. Stillwell. "Applying cost/benefit analysis to evaluate investment in GIS: The case of Ghana's Lands Commission Secretariat," Accra. *Transactions in GIS* 9(4) (2005): 489–505.

4. NSGIC. *Economic justification: Measuring return on investment (ROI) and cost benefit analysis.* (CBA) NSGIC for FGDC, 2006. http://www.nsgic.org/hottopics/return_on investment.pdf; http://en.wikipedia.org/wiki/Return_on_investment; Roulstone and Phillips, *ROI.*

5. Halsing, D., K. Theissen, and R. Bernknoft. "A cost-benefit analysis of *The National Map.*" U.S. Department of the Interior and U.S. Geological Survey, Circular 1271 USGS, Denver 1–3, 2004.

6. GITA and AWWA. *Building a business case for geospatial information technology: A practitioners guide to financial and strategic analysis.* GITA and AWWA, 2007.

7. Karikari, I., and J. Stillwell, "Applying cost/benefit analysis."

8. Booz Allen Hamilton. *Geospatial interoperability return on investment.* National Aeronautics and Space Administration Geospatial Interoperability Office, 2005.

9. Meehan, B. *Empowering electric and gas utilities with GIS* (Redlands, Calif.: ESRI Press, 2007).

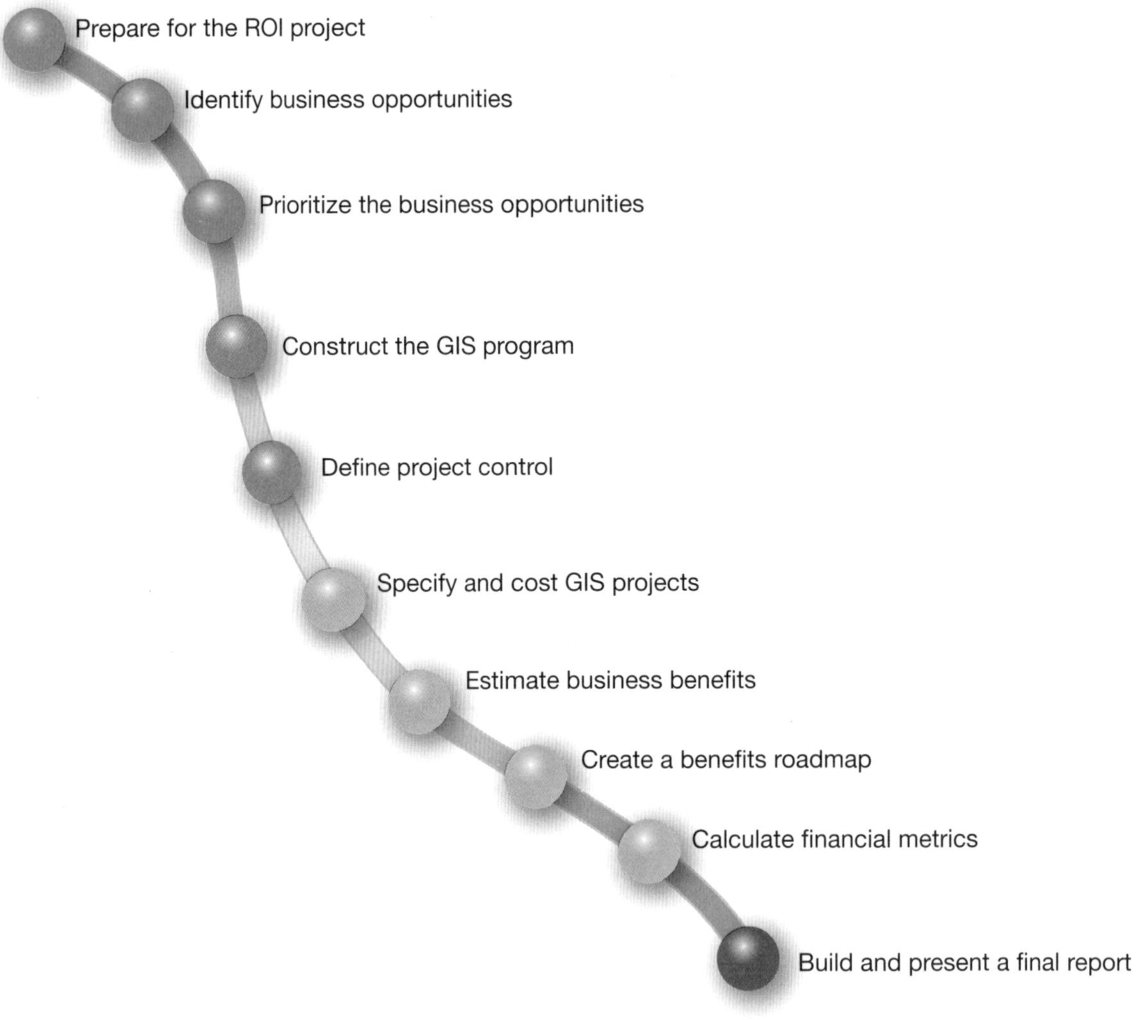

Prepare for the ROI project

Identify business opportunities

Prioritize the business opportunities

Construct the GIS program

Define project control

Specify and cost GIS projects

Estimate business benefits

Create a benefits roadmap

Calculate financial metrics

Build and present a final report

1

Prepare for the ROI project

In order to transform or effect change in an organization, solid research and preparation must first be completed. This ROI methodology begins by reviewing the mission of an organization, assembling a list of key stakeholders, outlining the ROI project schedule, and preparing for briefings to executives. These ideas are put into practice in a case study in the final section.

To determine why and how to define and deliver a business justification for a new GIS implementation in an organization, or to expand an existing one, it is important to have a strategy—a framework that can be followed that goes well beyond simply building a business case for GIS. The proposed methodology provides an achievable, fact-based, and benefits-focused approach that will gain backing and consensus among organization stakeholders, while educating and preparing them for change, to arrive at a quantifiable return on investment (ROI) result. As the framework is assembled, multiple deliverables will be incorporated into the approach, involving individuals and departments outside of just one workgroup. Justifying GIS efforts, in order to improve business processes and projects, must involve many units and departments of a business. Further, understanding the mission and structure of an organization is imperative. To build an ROI strategy, here a holistic approach is adopted, and objectives are focused on determining how GIS technology can be applied to solve problems or create new opportunities and services in an organization. Completing an ROI project will provide the tools to understand and communicate the potential return from a GIS implementation and allow senior management to make the best business decision for one or more departments, and the organization as a whole.

OBJECTIVES

To begin implementation of the methodology for justifying a new or expanded GIS program, there are several tasks that need to be completed by way of preparation. Successfully communicating ideas about the opportunities for a GIS program requires knowledge of the audience, the prospective participants in the program, and the landscape within which the proposal will be introduced. One of the first objectives, then, is to review and understand the role that GIS has played or is currently playing in an organization. An honest and transparent assessment should be made regarding the role of GIS in the organization to-date. A GIS mission statement that supports and is in line with the organization's mission can then be drafted. In order to tune into the "pain points" of the organization, the members of the stakeholder audience must first be identified, and the motivations and organizational objectives of each of these key executives then solicited. Finally, a project timeline will be drafted to estimate when the 10 steps of this methodology will be completed, instilling confidence in the key stakeholders that this approach will result in achievable deliverables.

TASKS

✔ 1.1 Obtain management consent

Before investing time and energy in building a business justification for a GIS program, the GIS advocate should ensure that a supervisor or immediate manager understands and approves of the plan. A short e-mail will provide a briefing and allow him or her to provide feedback and comments (for an example e-mail, see figure 1.1).

Although this step will be quite evident and most likely already achieved, it is used here as an opportunity to introduce the concept of a program "sponsor." The ROI project sponsor, or coach, can act as an executive-level champion for GIS in the organization. As stated, the sponsor will most likely be a supervisor or manager, to whom the ROI project owner is accountable. The sponsor should be kept apprised of the project progress as the ROI-based case for GIS in the organization is built. The ROI project team should also solicit advice from this sponsor on whether or not it is the appropriate time to undertake such project activities in the organization. For instance, perhaps there is a larger, unrelated initiative underway in another division, sapping resources and time from the key prospective stakeholders. Or, perhaps the organization is going through a restructuring or merger of departments and staff, making roles unclear and responsibilities in flux. The current condition of the organization will have a bearing on the success of the ROI project, the initiation of which should be timed appropriately to ensure a smooth launch and to minimize the potential for obstructions.

From: <Your Name Here>
Sent: <Month/Day/Year>
To: <Your Supervisor or Manager's Name Here>
Subject: GIS ROI Project

This e-mail is to let you know that I have started work on the ROI GIS project to investigate the potential for using GIS in <Your Organization Here> to enhance our operations. As I indicated in our recent review meeting, the next step will be to contact department heads to ask for their time to discuss ideas they may have for using GIS in their department. I would appreciate it if you would review the e-mail that I am proposing to send to them, which I have attached.

Many thanks,

<Your Name Here>

Figure 1.1   An example of an e-mail to a program sponsor. The e-mail attachment, referenced in this correspondence, will be completed in task 1.7 (see figure 1.5).

✔ 1.2 Consider the core GIS ROI project team

The GIS advocate, or other individual who is spearheading the ROI project, will find it important to organize a team of individuals who will be supporting this directive. In a large organization, the core GIS ROI team may consist of many members, while for smaller organizations one or two individuals will be adequate to complete the tasks. In forming a team it is important to identify the right mix of people within the organization that have the skills and, more importantly, the desire to participate. It is usually best to identify individuals that see participation as a personal development opportunity or some other type of personal win for them. If they are "volunteered" rather than freely join the team, they will likely not buy-in to the process and generate dedication around the project. It will then be an uphill battle to keep momentum and to push through any hard times during the project.

✔ 1.3 Review and understand the GIS history in the organization

In chapter 2, it is recommended that exclusive time is spent with key executives and other stakeholders to seek their perspective on, among other things, expanding an existing GIS program or possibly initiating a new one. As part of this briefing, a general overview of GIS will be provided, as well as a short discussion of its current involvement in the organization.

Identifying previous and current GIS initiatives—successful or otherwise—is essential to determining the level of GIS involvement, past or present, within the organization. If there has never been a GIS implemented in any department, then most likely the organization and its senior members will not be familiar with GIS concepts, technology, terminology, costs, and benefits. This is an important point to recognize, since the ROI team will need to be prepared to educate and deliver a review or primer on GIS, during the interviews with senior stakeholders, as described in chapter 2. If an organization has an existing GIS, its architecture, applications, ownership, project solutions and challenges must be identified, as well as the objectives for the department(s) or unit(s) that hosts the existing GIS.

There are several avenues for seeking information during this "discovery" phase. These include using online surveys to gather views and comments; e-mail requests for input; conference calls that seek specific information about data, technology, systems, workflow, etc.; site visits to other offices, if geographically disconnected; and interviews with selected key staff.

Insight: Start to collect quantitative as well as qualitative data

Normally during the discovery process, it is relevant to try to quantify both the amount of money spent on projects and the value delivered. Try to look not just for anecdotal evidence of success and failure, but also attempt to understand details about how many licenses currently have been purchased, how much was spent on hardware, how old systems are, and so on.

At first blush, one might assume that if a GIS already exists at an organization, then the task of "winning hearts and minds" would be made easier, since the path has been previously paved. For instance, "GIS" will not be an unfamiliar concept and since buy-in already occurred once before, no trailblazing is necessary. On the other hand, it may be that the previous strategy followed was poorly researched or implemented and, consequently, the GIS implementation is weak and a poor performer. As a result, the senior executives may have a predisposed idea of the benefit and value of a GIS. These precedents can negatively color the introduction and acceptance of a new project and, ultimately, threaten its success.

To communicate a thorough understanding of the existing or past GIS landscape at the organization, a SWOT analysis (**S**trengths, **W**eaknesses, **O**pportunities, and **T**hreats) should be completed (figure 1.2).

The SWOT investigation will entail auditing the organization's GIS environment for the strengths and weaknesses of the program, as well as the opportunities and any identifiable threats. Specifically, all previous projects should be researched and summarized, assessing the causes of the results. Ideally, the individual(s) currently responsible for the GIS implementation should be interviewed and notable successes and failures considered. All of this information should then be presented in the form of a SWOT analysis. Figure 1.2 is an example of a high-level SWOT analysis. More details will most likely be necessary as additional information is gathered during an ROI project.

Strengths	Weaknesses
• Visionary leadership at executive level • Excellent IT infrastructure • Similar organizations and partners already using GIS as good examples	• Inadequate understanding about GIS • Limited funding for putting more money towards GIS initiatives • Lack of human resources

Opportunities	Threats
• Deploy existing personnel more efficiently • Reduce road traffic accidents • Identify high-crime areas and reduce burglaries	• Competition with two other technology projects • Reorganization of division structure in play

Figure 1.2 An example SWOT analysis.

In chapter 2, these completed findings will be presented to each of the stakeholders during the interview process. The SWOT analysis will clearly identify the positive components of the GIS program currently underway, as well as the deficiencies manifested in past GIS implementations. As a result of presenting the SWOT review, it will be evident to the stakeholders that project objectives strive to avoid repeating mistakes and to, instead, reinforce and improve on successes.

✔ 1.4 Draft a GIS program mission statement

In order to properly focus the direction of a GIS program, the objective of the organization as a whole must be clearly understood. Organization mission statements typically communicate the operational purpose and existence of an organization. It is not uncommon for mission statements to be unwritten, but even if this is the case, a mission definition or declaration should still be surmised to baseline the underpinnings of why and how an organization operates.

Studying this mission statement, members of the core GIS ROI team will recognize how select business units, workgroups, or departments are contributing to the organizations' business processes with the aim of furthering the overall goals. The mission statement will also describe the more far-reaching business objectives of the organization from a non-GIS professional perspective. As a result, an open-minded and broad approach to justifying a new or expanding GIS program is important. Stepping back from the daily challenges and tasks, and reviewing the mission statement from a business approach will allow for a better understanding of the extensive goals from a business perspective, disassociated from any GIS or personal ambitions of the ROI project team.

Once the organization's targets and goals are understood, the mission statement should be reexamined, this time from the perspective of how a GIS program could contribute to satisfying this mission. A mission declaration specific to the GIS program should then be drafted, aligning with the official statement of an organization's purpose. Although an organization may have more than one mission statement, the objective should be focused on where the opportunity to benefit from a robust GIS program is the strongest.

For example, the City of Indianapolis and Marion County Geospatial Information Services team mission statement shows how they see the role of GIS:

> The mission of the City of Indianapolis and Marion County is to deliver professional services and decision support systems through robust and accurate spatial databases, innovative geographic information system applications, and strategic partnerships which support Indianapolis/Marion County government and improve the quality of life for all citizens.[1]

Tools: Mission statements

To assist with identifying a mission statement, samples of mission statements and corporate objectives from other organizations are posted on the supporting Web site (http://gis.esri.com/roi). Of course, an easy Web search will result in many more example mission statements.

✔ 1.5 Identify the key stakeholders

After articulating the mission of the organization's GIS program, it is important to identify the various contributors who will play a role in facilitating this mission—or at least to identify the groups or departments, if not the stakeholders themselves. In chapter 2, through the process of interviewing several senior staff members in the stakeholder community, the high-level opportunities for GIS in the organization will be solicited. To prepare for this interview process and identify the individuals who will be influential in fostering the success of the program, it is instrumental to understand the structure of the organization. Clearly identifying the departments and key management personnel is often best expressed through an organizational chart (figure 1.3).

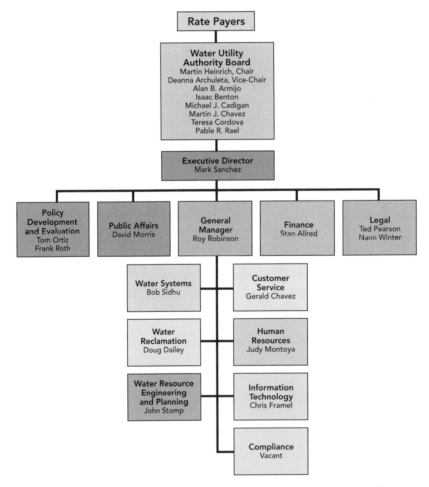

Figure 1.3 Albuquerque Bernalillo County Water Utility Authority.[2]

Courtesy of Albuquerque Bernalillo County Water Utility Authority.

Using the organizational chart, the influential individuals and their respective groups can be located and transferred to a stakeholder engagement table (figure 1.4).

Stakeholder Group	Water Systems	Water Reclamation	Water Resource Engineering	Customer Service	Information Technology	Human Resources
Stakeholder Individual	Bob Sidhu	Doug Dailey	John Stomp	Gerald Chavez	Chris Framel	Judy Montoya

Figure 1.4   A stakeholder engagement table populated with appropriate representatives from the key departments or units.

Insight: The stakeholder engagement table

Four to eight individuals should comprise the group of senior staff members who are considered key stakeholders. When populating the stakeholder engagement table, it is also recommended that the ROI project team weigh the value of the experiences of the seasoned professionals and new employees to ensure an appropriate blend. Of course, the types of stakeholder groups, provided as examples above, will vary by organization. However, the key influential individuals will be identifiable by examining departmental team structures and research derived from the organizational chart.

When composing the table of key stakeholders with the names and departments of each, individuals who may be historically known as critics or naysayers should not be eliminated from the process or avoided. Skipping over the skeptics will only foster their resentment and may, at a future stage, impede the progress of the project. In order to achieve adoption of the GIS program, engagement from a wide mix of staff at all levels of an organization is necessary. If there is no "face time" with these individuals, then they may not feel included in this ROI project, and acceptance and success of the GIS program may become a challenge.

✔ 1.6   Build an executive briefing presentation

As previously mentioned, in chapter 2 the GIS ROI project team will be interviewing the key senior staff members who are likely to be influential in the success of a GIS program. Before meeting with the key stakeholders, a succinct presentation should be built, to be delivered during the executive briefings. This presentation should provide answers to all of the preliminary questions the interviewee might have regarding the ROI project. As such, the presentation will contain a short introduction and background, the primary objectives for conducting the ROI project, and what specifically is required of the senior stakeholder. The GIS mission statement can also be included as part of the presentation, in order to demonstrate that the project aligns with the business mission as a whole. This presentation will be sent to the stakeholders for their reference, at the same time as the e-mail correspondence from task 1.7.

An entire executive meeting will likely be under one hour, so the presentation should be kept at a high level, focusing on the salient points for the executive(s) to take away, and not the low-level details. It is recommended that this presentation limits the references to "GIS-speak," since this is usually not the interest of senior executives.

Tools: Executive briefing meetings

To assist with building a presentation to the senior stakeholders, an outline of a Microsoft PowerPoint presentation, entitled "Executive_Briefing.ppt," containing the topics that will need to be socialized is provided on the accompanying Web site located under step 1 at http://gis.esri.com/ROI. The presentation should provide answers to all of the preliminary questions that the interviewees may have regarding the ROI project.

✔ 1.7 Prepare the stakeholders

Prior to getting one-on-one time with executives (also known as the stakeholders), a short introductory e-mail should be sent that briefly explains what will be asked or required of them. This correspondence will prepare them for the interview, which will be confirmed, following the e-mail. Task 1.7 also prepares for communicating the background, proposed plan, and business benefits of a GIS program to stakeholders and other sponsors who will be involved.

Depending on whether or not a GIS currently exists at an organization, the content of the e-mail to the stakeholders may vary slightly. In sum, however, the purpose of the correspondence is to socialize the proposed ROI project, the aim of which is to seek input on whether GIS technology will add value to the organization. The body of the e-mail should introduce the owner(s) of the ROI project, if necessary, including a brief explanation of the current activities, and an explanation as to why the executive's involvement is needed. An example e-mail is shown in figure 1.5.

To: <Your Stakeholder>
Subject: Request for your involvement & insights
Date: <xx/xx/xxxx>

We are in the process of assessing the value of a GIS at < Your Organization Name >. As you may know, typically, a GIS can be used to manage city assets and integrate data such that we can make educated and informed planning and business decisions.

Currently, GIS is implemented in <Department or Organization name>; however, the quantifiable return on the system has never been measured, and we are unaware of the potential for enhancing and streamlining our operations. As part of our overall strategic business objective, I am investigating the potential for GIS to provide business benefit in the future. In particular, I intend to determine and quantify potential benefits, via a return on investment study, to create a benefits roadmap and budget, to support appropriate investment in GIS software, data, and services.

I am requesting about an hour of your time to outline this initiative, and to solicit your views and insights on how or where you feel that this program of work could add value to your department.

I will be following up this e-mail with a quick phone call to answer any questions and to discuss agreeable dates for an interview. I also enclose a brief PowerPoint presentation that provides further background.

Thank you in advance for your time.

Best regards,

<Your Name>

Figure 1.5 An example of an e-mail to a key stakeholder. This particular correspondence clearly contains language that is better directed at an organization that currently has a GIS implemented (see Task 1.6 for PowerPoint presentation).

In some cases, a strong organizational hierarchy could present a problem when communication with varying levels of management is required. If an organization's structure prevents direct contact with senior executives, the project sponsor should be called on to intervene. In this case, although the e-mail to the stakeholders could be crafted by the ROI project team members, the project sponsor should be the one to send it to the key senior individuals, on the behalf of the ROI project team. This may inspire peer-to-peer discussions between upper-level management tiers, prior to finally settling back to the core ROI team as the GIS evangelists and champions. This communication activity may also be beneficial to initialize stakeholder buy-in, since it will represent the beginning of management endorsement for the ROI project.

✔ 1.8 Estimate project timeline

Finally, before meeting with the key stakeholders, a general time frame for the GIS ROI project should be estimated. This is not a timeline for implementing a GIS, or a specific project, or returning value on an investment. This schedule will cover an estimated time for completing the 10 steps of this ROI methodology. Given the current commitments, priorities, and other business demands of the core GIS ROI project team, a reasonable and palatable time frame for the completion of the GIS justification project should be drafted. Management will, inevitably, want to know how much time this ROI project will occupy, and the stakeholders will need to know when they should expect a completed report showing the results. Impedances should be considered, such as the level of involvement of the core ROI team, the availability of participants, and accessibility of data for costing and calculations, in combination with any other immediate demands and deadlines, if applicable. The timeline is not focused on low-level specifics, but instead, on expressing an estimate or "best guess" such that the entire program becomes a tangible, quantifiable undertaking.

Tools: Project timeline template

To assist with visualizing a time frame for the GIS ROI project, the "ROI_Project_Timeline.ppt" is provided as an example template, located under step 1 at http://gis.esri.com/ROI.

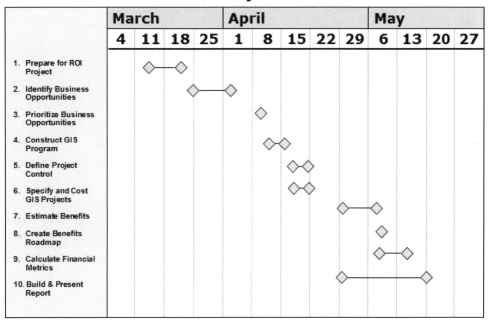

Figure 1.6   Example of a completed project timeline.

Insight: Timing is everything

When estimating a schedule for a proposed GIS project initiative, it is important to think about key organization milestones such as budget submission dates and time frames for budget cycles. Properly timing the proposal around these business milestones can increase chances of approval for moving forward with the GIS program.

OUTCOME

At the end of this stage of the methodology, several tasks are complete, each of which contributes to building a robust ROI project for an organization. First, of course, acknowledgement and approval from immediate management has been obtained, in order to move forward with this project's directive. As such, a comprehensive review of the past and present role of GIS in the organization has been undertaken. The core ROI team should now be familiar with the organization's mission statement, and from this, have derived a GIS program mission statement. A table of key stakeholders has been completed, identifying influential individuals to be interviewed in chapter 2. Lastly, the core ROI team has begun to communicate this ROI project to senior individuals through e-mail correspondence, outlining the proposed program and defining the schedule for the project. In review, the objective of chapter 1 was to collect the information needed to prepare the groundwork and build the critical foundation for an ROI project for GIS at the organization, in order to better embed it within an executive context, completed in chapter 2.

PREPARE FOR THE ROI PROJECT

Before embarking fully on this ROI study for the City of Springfield and engaging with the rest of the organization, some thorough preparation is required. Following the steps in the ROI methodology, Brian Sobers, GIS manager, will ensure that his boss has signed off on moving forward with the ROI project, through a conversation that he follows up on using a simple e-mail. Brian will then form an ROI project team with other colleagues, to define and agree on the project objectives, timeline, and roles. The ROI project team will also review the GIS history of Springfield, to determine the past mistakes, successes, and failures. To ensure that ROI efforts align with the city's overall mission, Brian will draft a GIS program mission statement. Since he has only recently joined the city staff, Brian will rely on the seasoned members of his ROI project team to help identify the executive individuals who will be treated as the key stakeholders for this project. The ROI team will then put together an estimate for the project schedule and include it as part of a presentation to brief influential individuals—a task performed in chapter 2.

C1.1 Management consent

Brian begins by sending the following e-mail to his boss and the senior project sponsor, Sue Coldfield, seeking her approval to proceed with the ROI project. The e-mail attachment referred to in the e-mail in figure C1.1 appears in figure C1.6.

From: Brian Sobers, GIS Manager
Sent: Thursday, January 4, 2008 10:49 AM
To: Sue Coldfield, Head of Community Services
Subject: GIS Project
Importance: Medium

Dear Sue,

This e-mail is to let you know that I have started work on Mr. James's project to investigate the potential for using GIS in the city to improve services and contain costs. As I indicated in our recent review meeting, the next step will be to contact department heads to ask for time to discuss ideas they may have for using GIS in their department. I would appreciate it if you would review the e-mail I am proposing to send to them, which I have attached.

Many thanks,

Brian

Figure C1.1   Letter to Brian's boss at City of Springfield to gain consent before moving forward with the ROI project.

C1.2   Form a team

As a relatively new employee with quite a few tasks at hand, Brian first builds an ROI project team who will work together on this GIS-based ROI initiative. Currently, two staff employed in the Engineering and Library departments, respectively, are familiar with GIS and computer-aided design (CAD) systems, and a business analyst from the Information Systems Department and a member of staff from the Finance Department have all expressed an interest in the project. Brian confers with his boss, and chooses to form an ROI project team with these colleagues. Between the five team members, each of whom will contribute part-time given their departmental commitments, they have adequate skills in project management, business analysis, finance, and technology, and an understanding of organizational workflows and practices.

C1.3   City of Springfield GIS history

With the help of the ROI project team, reviewing existing city reports and talking to key city GIS staff, colleagues and people in the Community Development Division, Brian compiles a brief history of GIS at the City of Springfield. Brian was fortunate to be colocated with all of his colleagues, so he was able to set up brief meetings with people the team had identified as having been involved in past GIS-related initiatives. There was also a healthy amount of documentation available that described the past GIS efforts; and where there wasn't, it only confirmed the challenges and failures experienced.

Like many municipalities, the City of Springfield has been involved in GIS for several years. However, recent developments in the field have gone largely undiscovered or disregarded by the city, primarily because of a lack of awareness of the potential for GIS to contribute meaningfully to the city's portfolio of activities.

A series of largely uncoordinated projects in the Library, Planning, and Police departments, together with the use of CAD systems in Engineering has resulted in a set of digital maps and some good examples of how GIS can benefit the city. A notable example of a good project is the digital zoning map, which is available on the city Web site, maintained by the city library. Unfortunately, the initiative in the Planning Department, which produced the zoning map and some other useful products, came to a halt a few months ago when the GIS manager retired. There has never been a citywide GIS plan and no attempt to quantify the additional value that might be gained through the use of GIS technology, and so the advantages of an enterprise GIS have never been realized.

Presently, Springfield has the following GIS resources:

In the Library Department: A public access site containing selected digital maps and satellite images of the city available via an ESRI ArcIMS Web mapping server. This site serves maps for internal and external use via the city's Web site. The site is maintained using one ArcIMS server license and one ESRI ArcInfo license. The city librarian is trained in basic GIS use, and the library IT administrator is developing and maintaining the system on a part-time basis.

In the Planning Department: A land-use zoning database, current as of the end of last year, is maintained as ESRI ArcView shapefiles. The department has three ArcInfo desktop GIS licenses and two staff users with basic GIS skills.

In the Police Department: Crime incident and beat maps are maintained as ArcView desktop GIS shapefiles. The department has four ArcView desktop GIS licenses and an information technology support officer with solid skills in GIS.

In the Engineering Department: Citywide digital maps are maintained as Autodesk AutoCad CAD system files. There are six AutoCad licenses used for mapping and creating engineering drawings. There is a (relatively) large user community comprising one developer, three experienced CAD users, and four users with basic CAD computer skills.

SWOT ANALYSIS

Using the historical information on GIS at the city, the ROI team builds the following SWOT analysis (figure C1.2). Brian feels more comfortable knowing the successes and failures of technology initiatives at the city, and the SWOT analysis provides a context for understanding the past, present, and future role of GIS. Brian is better situated to fend off any potential naysayer by already knowing the past challenges and being able to acknowledge them. By acknowledging the realities of the past, the conversation can turn toward the future, and how things will be different this time given the lessons learned from past projects.

Strengths	Weaknesses
• High-level executive commitment to using technology to solve problems • Basemap files and widely used online mapping Web site already created • Basic understanding and experience of GIS within multiple departments	• Missing potential of GIS to reduce costs and improve services because not aligned with city IT and business strategy • Limited advanced GIS technical skills among city staff • Existing hardware and software infrastructure outdated • No clear understanding of the potential benefits of GIS

Opportunities	Threats
• Create portfolio of GIS projects to improve services and contain costs • Facilitate collaboration and knowledge sharing among departments • Contribute to green agenda of city	• Competition for funding from other new technology initiatives • Lack of buy-in for GIS from selected executives

Figure C1.2   SWOT analysis for the City of Springfield.

C1.4 GIS program mission statement

Brian knows that his GIS program mission statement needs to build on the key citywide initiatives of using new technology, keeping the city environmentally respectful, and reducing tax rates. Along with the ROI team, he drafts the following program mission statement:

> "The GIS team will use proven GIS methods and technology to improve services and contain and avoid costs for the benefit of all Springfield employees and citizens. We will stay benefits-focused and contribute to the city's green agenda and smart growth initiative."

Brian subsequently sends the mission statement to his boss, Sue, and asks for her comments and views on whether she agrees with the focus and content.

C1.5 Identify key stakeholders

With a little effort, Brian is able to track down an organizational chart from Human Resources showing the main divisions and department heads in the city (figure C1.3).

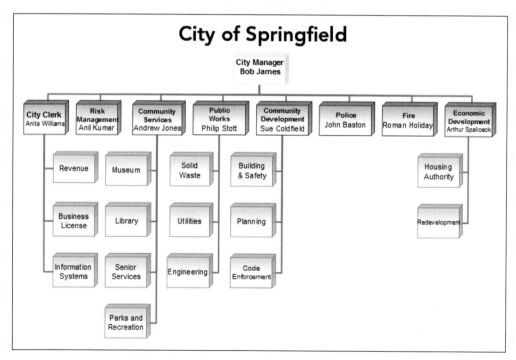

Figure C1.3   City of Springfield organizational chart.

To pinpoint the key executives influential to the success of the GIS program, Brian creates a list of each division head, and associated department, as shown in figure 1.4, using the stakeholder engagement table available on the supporting ROI Web site (http://gis.esri.com/roi). Brian subsequently discovers through his team that the head of the fire department is on long-term disability leave and therefore unavailable to participate in the ROI study.

Stakeholder Group	Community Services	Public Works	Community Development	Police	Fire	Economic Development	City Manager
Stakeholder Individual	Andrew Jones	Phillip Stott	Sue Coldfield	John Baston	Roman Holiday	Arthur Spaliceck	Bob James

Figure C1.4 City of Springfield key stakeholders in the ROI project.

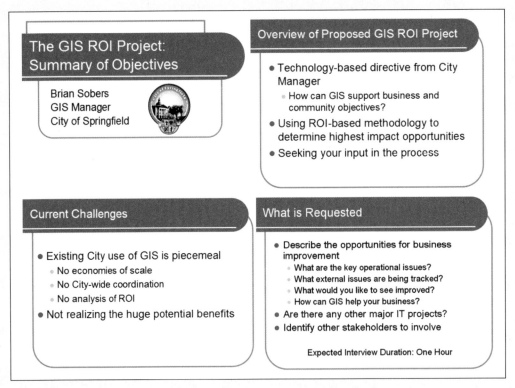

Figure C1.5 Executive briefing presentation for City of Springfield.

C1.6   Executive briefing presentation

Since Brian and the ROI team will be spending time later (chapter 2) with the key stakeholders identified in figure C1.4, he puts together a short presentation of the points he will be discussing at the meetings.

C1.7   Prepare stakeholders

Brian notifies each of the stakeholders via an e-mail asking them for their involvement and input in the ROI project. He attaches a digital version of the PowerPoint presentation for their reference (figure C1.5).

From: Brian Sobers, GIS Manager
Sent: Monday, January 15, 2008 11:20 AM
To: Phillip Stott, Public Works
Subject: GIS Project: Request for your involvement & input
Importance: Medium

Dear Mr. Stott,

At the request of Bob James, I am in the process of assessing the value of our existing geographic information system (GIS) in the city. As you may know, typically, a GIS can be used to manage city assets and integrate data such that we can make educated and informed planning and business decisions. Currently, Springfield has GIS implemented in the Library, Planning and Police departments; however, the return on this system has never been examined and measured. I intend to determine and quantify potential benefits via a return on investment (ROI) study, creating a benefits roadmap and budget, to support further request for investment in GIS hardware, software, data, and services.

I am requesting about an hour of your time to outline this initiative, and to solicit your views and insights on how or where you feel that this program of work could add value to your department.

I will follow up this e-mail with a quick phone call to answer any questions and to discuss agreeable dates for an interview. I also enclose a brief PowerPoint presentation that provides further background.

Thank you in advance for your time.

Best regards,

Brian Sobers
GIS Manager, City of Springfield

Figure C1.6   Example e-mail to Springfield stakeholders.

C1.8   Project timeline

Since Brian expects that the senior stakeholders will need a rough timeline for the entire project, the team estimates a proposed schedule for the City of Springfield ROI study (figure C1.7). He intends to emphasize that this is not the overall GIS program of projects, which will obviously be much longer.

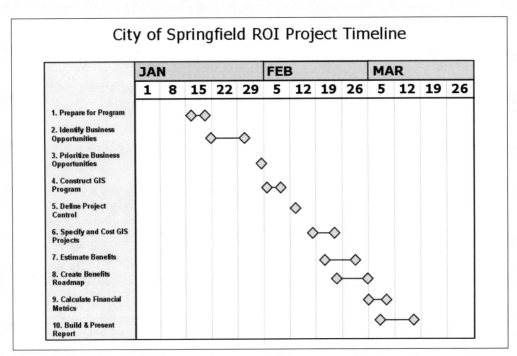

Figure C1.7   Proposed schedule for the City of Springfield ROI study.

C1.9   Discussion of chapter 1 case study

This part of the case study comprised a series of relatively small, simple tasks that are essential preparation for later activities. Perhaps the most important part is the preparation of the material that will be shown to executive stakeholders in chapter 2. It is likely that there will only be one opportunity to solicit information from these key individuals, so it is worthwhile to invest maximum effort into thorough preparation. The timeline for the ROI study should also be taken seriously and should be carefully designed, taking into consideration all the possible risks. Executives will expect the team to stick closely to any plans they develop and share with management.

Endnotes

1. City of Indianapolis and Marion County, Indiana. Retrieved December 2007 from http://www.indygov.org/eGov/County/ISA/Services/GIS/home.htm.

2. Albuquerque Bernalillo County, New Mexico, Water Utility Authority Web site. Retrieved on October 16, 2007, from http://www.abcwua.org/orgchart.html.

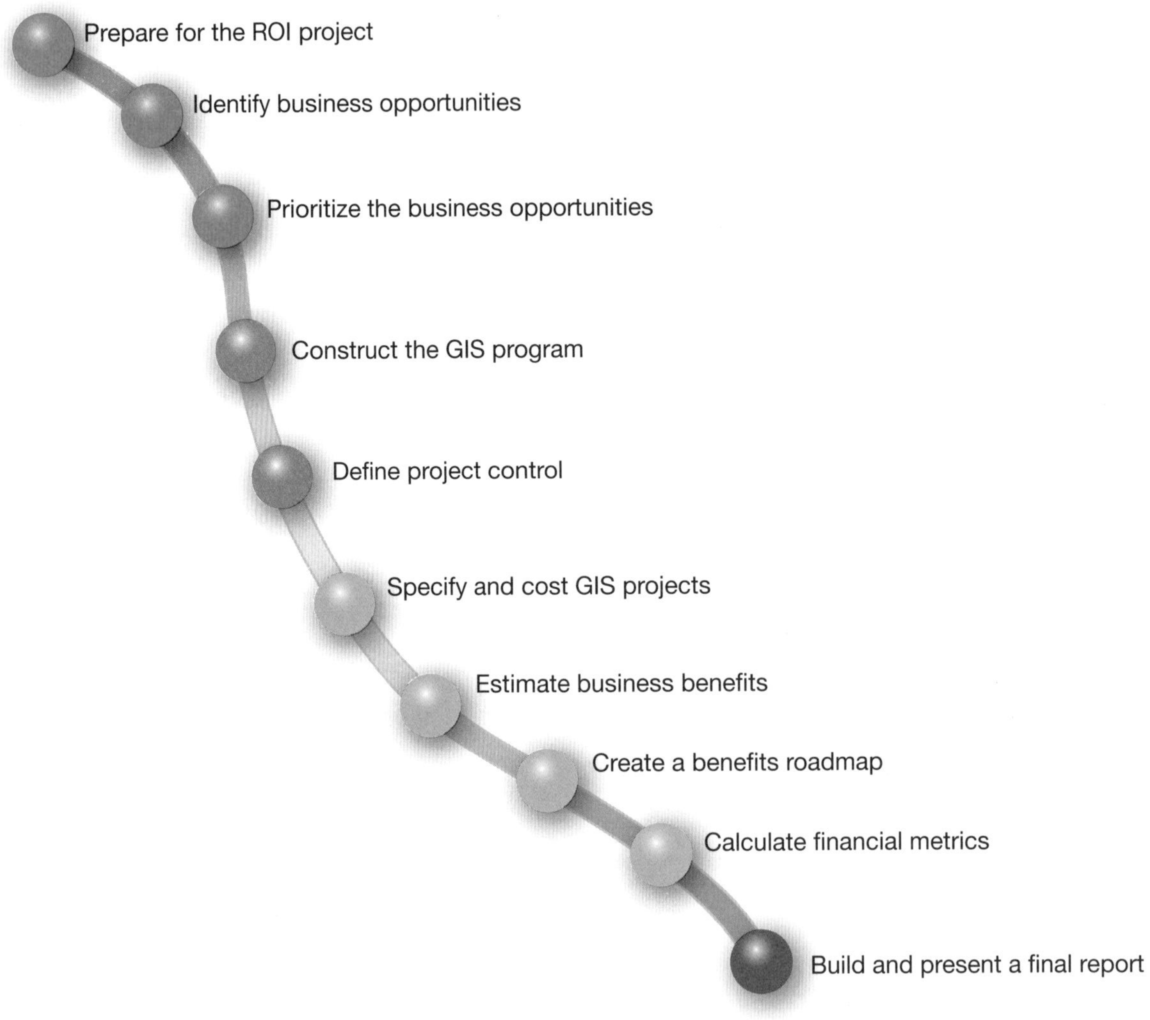

Prepare for the ROI project

Identify business opportunities

Prioritize the business opportunities

Construct the GIS program

Define project control

Specify and cost GIS projects

Estimate business benefits

Create a benefits roadmap

Calculate financial metrics

Build and present a final report

2

 Identify business opportunities

The most powerful arguments for implementing or expanding a GIS will be borne from interviews with the executives who lead an organization. In this chapter, extensive interviews are conducted with the key stakeholders affording these executives the opportunity to articulate their "pain points" and strategic objectives within their respective departments or divisions as they relate to daily business processes, measuring successes and failures, and strategic needs. From these insights, their high-level challenges and objectives will be recorded and examined, exposing the corresponding potential opportunities for GIS.

For many GIS professionals, the value of GIS is very evident. However, for senior management and other members of an organization, the opportunities for GIS may not be obvious at all. Even if a GIS is already deployed in an organization, management and staff may already be conditioned based on the level of success achieved. In these cases, reeducation may be required to erase bias and realign general consensus. Furthermore, the opportunities that the core ROI GIS team believes a GIS affords may not be the specific business benefits that the organization requires or desires. As such, information must be harvested from influential senior executives to discern their unique business challenges and establish the potential for an environment ripe with opportunities for GIS.

OBJECTIVES

To identify the specific business opportunities for GIS, a series of exclusive interviews will be conducted with several senior-level executives in the organization, from a variety of groups and departments. Through a succession of exploratory questions, the opportunities for a GIS program are identified, and the potential benefits to an organization are exposed. Ideally, the ROI team will want to understand if or how these senior managers perceive that GIS can facilitate their business processes. The interviews allow the key stakeholders to articulate how they measure and monitor their existing business performance, define their objectives, and handle perceived challenges. At the same time, by engaging these stakeholders, the ROI team will be building and encouraging support from these individuals to try to "win their hearts and minds" in order to facilitate their acceptance of a GIS program.

TASKS

✔ 2.1   List the potential benefits of a GIS

As a champion of the GIS movement, the ROI team is most likely well acquainted with the high-level benefits GIS can provide: support for better decision making, improving workflow processes, increasing productivity, avoiding costs, saving money, and more. Some stakeholders may need to be informed and educated about the opportunities GIS can provide and the probable benefits that will result. Unfortunately, general lists of this nature usually provide very little detail on how the benefit categories are translated from vague, broad-brush statements, to specific, contextual benefits that would be applicable to an organization. Instead, it is more beneficial to compose a comprehensive list of benefits and assign a specific example that is directly applicable to the industry and organization under consideration.

Here the term "benefit" is used to mean any type of material value obtained from a GIS project. It is useful to distinguish between tangible and nontangible benefits. Tangible benefits, also sometimes referred to as hard or economic benefits, are those that can be precisely defined and to which we can assign a specific monetary value. Examples of tangible benefits include cost avoidance, by increasing the number of valve inspections per route, and therefore decreasing inspection time; increased revenue from additional property taxes as a result of using a GIS to manage land records; and the value of time saved by creating reports more quickly using a GIS. Intangible benefits, also sometimes referred to as soft savings or institutional benefits, are those to which we cannot assign a monetary value. Examples of intangible GIS benefits include increased morale of employees due to improved information systems, improved citizen satisfaction with government as a result of readily available online access to maps and data, and better customer relationships through more efficient information management. Although it is important to include both types of benefits in a GIS business justification, depending on the organization, executive decision makers are usually much more easily persuaded by tangible, measurable benefits rather than those that are intangible.

Figures 2.1 and 2.2 describe some examples of the main types of tangible and intangible benefits that have been used in the past to justify GIS projects for government and utility organizations. Space does not permit us to review other application areas such as business, environment, and education. However, since the general principles are common across all these areas, it should easily be possible to extrapolate from the details presented in figures 2.1 and 2.2 into other industries. These lists are by no means exhaustive, and there is a degree of overlap between several categories (for example, revenue growth, cost reduction, and cost avoidance), but they can be a guide that will help focus the process of researching GIS program benefits. The tables represent facts-based benefits at a high level, without considering details, and can be used as a starting point to express the values of the benefits of a GIS. Since a specific goal of this methodology is to use well-founded benefits that stand up to scrutiny, the next part of this chapter is devoted to identifying specific and measurable benefits.

Benefit type	Government	Utility
Revenue growth—How can a GIS generate revenue (strictly speaking "profit") for the organization?	Property taxes account for a substantial portion of the income for many local governments. GIS is used to accurately assess the size of land parcels and keep an up-to-date record of property improvements. This typically results in additional tax revenue. The benefit is the total additional tax revenue which results from using GIS.	There is great demand for accurate, detailed utility data for emergency management, construction coordination, and other purposes. Utilities sell network data products to other utilities and governments in the same geography for such purposes. The total benefit is the sum of all income.
Revenue protection and assurance—How can GIS help protect revenues or assure the realization of revenue?	GIS, as a communication and collaboration tool, can integrate into an existing business workflow. As a result, interdepartmental staff in, say, health and human services can better collaborate on patient and hospital records management to potentially identify fraudulent behavior, protecting the existing revenue streams through tight monitoring of existing case data.	A GIS can link a map location to utility records in a maintenance management system. Property ownership and all related information can be retrieved to ensure timely billing and payment, delinquency, unusual resource usage or unexpected outages as a result of an accident or other interrupted service issues that can hemorrhage resources if not identified quickly.
Health and safety—How can GIS save the lives (or reduce injury) of employees or citizens? Although some might take the view that lives are invaluable, it is commonplace to ascribe a monetary value to loss of life in, for example, the insurance industry.	The most important role of governments is to protect the lives of citizens. Police forces are usually tasked with monitoring the security of major public events. GIS is increasingly regarded as a key component of emergency operations centers, where it is used to store, analyze, and visualize data about events. Data about, for example, suspicious packages can be used to help support decision making about the evacuating of surrounding areas. The value of the benefit of GIS is based on an estimate of the monetary value of lives saved as a result of using the GIS.	Integrated AM/FM/GIS electric network databases and work-order management systems are being used to create map products for use in call-before-you-dig systems that reduce the likelihood of electrocution from hitting electrical conductors. Before-and-after comparison of lives saved multiplied by an agreed value of a life can lead to large benefits.
Cost reduction—This is different than cost avoidance because here we are assuming that this is an activity that an organization has to perform and the objective becomes how to perform the activity with minimal net expenditure.	Local government planning departments are reducing the cost of creating land use plans and zoning maps by building databases and map templates that can be reused many times. The benefit is the difference in the cost of manual and GIS-based plan and map creation.	Multiple entry of an "as-built" work order by several departments is reduced by centralizing data entry in a single department. The total benefit is the cost of as-built work-order entry multiplied by the reduction in the number of work orders entered.
Cost avoidance—Rather than reducing costs, it is sometimes possible to avoid them.	Local government departments issue permits for many things such as public events and roadside dumpsters (skips). By using GIS a government department can automate the process of finding the location, issuing the permit and tracking its status. The benefit is the reduction in cost of issuing and tracking each permit, multiplied by the number of permits issued. There are often additional benefits of reduced time to obtain a permit and improved tracking.	Forecasting the demand for gas by integrating geodemographics data with a model of the gas network will avoid overbuild of distribution capacity. The benefit is the avoided cost of additional construction and operation.

Figure 2.1   Examples of tangible benefit types for public and private organizations.

Figure 2.1—continued

Benefit type	Government	Utility
Increase efficiency and productivity—How can the organization do more with less resource?	Fire is a major hazard to forests in many drier parts of the world. Firefighters need access in their fire trucks to maps of structures to better fight fires. Field-based GIS are used to map structures more efficiently. These are then transferred to a GIS database and map books produced automatically, thus greatly improving productivity of the surveyors and cartographers (not to mention the firefighters). The benefit of increased efficiency and productivity can be quantified by comparing manual with GIS-based operations. The hours saved can be converted into dollars based on the hourly rates of workers.	Automating map production improves the efficiency and productivity of staff, freeing them up to perform other tasks that improve the customer experience/quality of service. The benefit is equal to the number of person-hours that can be assigned to other tasks, multiplied by their hourly rate.
Save time—If a process is carried out using a GIS, how much faster can it be completed?	Searches are typically performed whenever a property is bought or sold to determine ownership rights and encumbrances (rights-of-way, mineral rights, etc.). This requires a "search" to be sent to many departments. Historically, this has been a manual, paper-based process taking several weeks. By implementing this in a GIS the process can be managed electronically, performed in parallel, and responses automatically produced as a report. The time taken to complete the process can be reduced by several days or weeks. The benefit is the monetary value of the time saved multiplied by the number of searches performed. There are additional benefits of improved service to citizens.	The amount of time it takes to inspect outside the plant will be reduced by providing better routing between inspection sites and field-based data entry tools. The benefit is the additional number of inspections per inspector per day multiplied by the cost of an inspection.
Increased regulatory compliance—If an organization has to comply with mandatory regulations, can it be done cheaper, faster, more quickly with GIS?	Various e-government initiatives around the world mandate that federal/central government agencies expand the use of the Internet for delivering services in a citizen-centric, results-oriented, market-based way. GIS is a cost-effective way to achieve this goal because it is a commercial off-the-shelf system that can be relatively easily implemented across multiple departments. The objective of government is generally to minimize the cost of compliance. The benefit derives from minimizing the costs of compliance and avoiding fines for noncompliance.	Telecom utilities are bound by law to comply with several exacting operating regulations. GIS can be used to maintain a database of the status of resources and to produce timely reports that summarize compliance levels. Given that this is a cost to the utility, the benefit derives from minimizing the costs of compliance and avoiding fines for noncompliance.

When undertaking an ROI study, the GIS ROI team should prepare a list of GIS business described benefits, such as those in figures 2.1 and 2.2, that are germane to the organization under consideration at an operational level. For instance, if the organization specializes in electric or gas resources, the top benefits for a utility should be listed. Categorizing the benefits will allow for better organization and preparation for the discussions with members of the senior management team, who will expect benefits to be articulated and examples to be provided.

Tools: Generic list of benefits

A generic list of GIS business benefits and some examples of their applicability can be found under step 2 of the supporting Web site at http:// gis.esri.com/roi. Many of those listed, and more, can be found in Thomas and Ospina,[1] which covers different benefits of implementing GIS using many high- level case studies; Meehan,[2] and Lerner et al.,[3] provide a similar array of utility case studies.

Benefit type	Government	Utility
Improve service and excellence image—In what ways will use of a GIS cast the organization in a better light (e.g., forward looking, better organized, or more responsive)?	A number of government departments have front desk clerks that respond to requests for information from citizens (e.g., status of a request for planning consent, rezoning request, or water service connection). GIS can be used to speed up responses to requests, and in some cases access can be provided in public facilities such as libraries or on the Web. The benefit is the value of improved organizational image.	By creating a publicly accessible Web site that shows planned electrical network maintenance and outages, an electrical utility can improve its image. The benefit is determined by the value of a page view multiplied by the total number of page views.
Enhanced citizen / customer satisfaction—Can GIS be used to enhance the satisfaction levels of citizens / customers?	Providing access to accurate and timely information is not only a requirement for governments, but it is also desirable because more information generally leads to higher levels of satisfaction. Changes in the satisfaction of citizens can be measured by questionnaires. This is a type of intangible benefit and is difficult to quantify.	Utilities will enhance their customer care capability by providing access to accurate and up-to-date outside plant network information. This is a type of intangible benefit and is difficult to quantify.
Improve staff well-being—Can GIS be used to enhance the well-being and morale of employees?	Staff are generally happier if they can see that an organization is progressive and is improving effectiveness and efficiency, as well as spending public money wisely. GIS is a tool that can contribute to all these and therefore worker satisfaction and well-being. This is also an intangible benefit that is difficult to quantify.	Automating boring and repetitive data entry tasks can increase staff retention. There is a tangible benefit in reducing recruitment costs and an intangible value in having happy and contented staff.

Figure 2.2 Examples of intangible benefit types for public and private organizations.

One or more of the key stakeholders may also find added value in the applicability of these benefits within a real-world example outside the organization. Items in the list of generic benefits should be associated with a compelling example in a like organization or department. For instance, determine if the organization has a strategic partner or alliance with groups similar to yours that have implemented or expanded their GIS program with a successful business return. Such examples can be used as substantive endorsements during interviews with key stakeholders. Providing additional examples will allow a better understanding of where and how benefits are to be measured.

✔ 2.2 Build interview questions

The major task in this chapter is to create a set of interview questions for a meeting with each key stakeholder identified in the last chapter. The executive interviews should have a well-defined structure, with direction, in order to collectively arrive at the business areas of further concern or investigation. For each interview, the goal is to understand the stakeholders' views on the potential benefits of GIS for their business area to build ownership and involvement. The interviews should cover a series of questions, such as the following:

"What are your areas of responsibility in the organization?"

"What are your main technology concerns (if any)?"

"What are the main business issues you face?"

"What would you consider your accountabilities or success criteria to be?"

As discussed previously, the interviewers may need to provide some examples or leading answers to provoke the stakeholder's views and insights. Busy executives may not have a GIS-oriented perspective. As a result, they may need some prompting by providing "for instance . . . " or "have you considered . . . " suggestions. This approach should be tempered, however, since the interviews are an opportunity to listen to the executives, not overshadow the conversation.

Tools: Sample interview questions

The ROI methodology interview template ("Interview_Template.doc") is provided for you on the supporting Web site at http://gis.esri.com/roi. Figure 2.3 shows a snapshot of part of an example set of interview questions. Complete one template per interview, tracking names, dates, and as many notes as can be populated in a document derived from the template. More pages or questions can easily be added for extended interviews. Note: it is important that you build questions around the roles and interests of the interviewee.

Interview Summary

Interviewee: <enter name>   Interviewer: <enter name>   Date: <enter date>

Topic	General Questions	Notes

Introduction		• Use pre-prepared PPT to describe: Who I am and why I am here
		   o What is GIS
		   o Why GIS is important
		• Summarize GIS use to-date in the City

Baseline	What are main activities of the <Fill In> department? Who would you consider as your primary internal customers? What are the main business issues that you face? What are your main technology concerns? What would you consider your accountabilities or success criteria to be? For this particular strategy/roadmap, what are your key objectives that you want to be sure are fulfilled?	
Vision & Goals	What are the key business outcomes you think that a technology solution should deliver?	

Figure 2.3   Snapshot of part of an interview built using the template
provided on the supporting Web site.

✔ **2.3   Conduct the interviews**

After reviewing the organizational chart from task 1.5 (see examples in figures 1.3 and C1.3), the GIS ROI team should have a general understanding of each executive's role. In a sense, the team members are marketing themselves as well as the proposed GIS program. As such, the interviewers should be aware of the key stakeholder's responsibilities and function within the organization. Each of these individuals has a set of issues or topics that are of particular concern to them and their department, so understanding the organizational context is essential in order to formulate how a GIS program will contribute to the organization's value.

The first portion of an interview should be a short briefing, beginning with the PowerPoint presentation created in chapter 1 (see figure C1.5), which was previously e-mailed to each stakeholder. The questions scripted earlier in task 2.2 are then used in the interview.

In sum, there are a handful of topics that should be covered during each of the one-on-one executive interviews:

- Provide an introduction and reason for requesting the executive's time.

- Allow them to articulate their management business goals, objectives, and demands.

- Understand the stakeholder's current situation and strategic needs.

- Identify the performance criteria and indicators.

- Recognize the key information or data requirements for decision making.

- Outline the main business processes that they oversee.

Insight: Interview metrics

It is especially important to try and capture information about metrics during the interviews, since these will define the target for success and will be very useful during the benefits estimation process (chapter 7). Metrics can take many forms, for example, maps created per week, number of miles driven, time for completing a work order, number of people employed on a job, capital expenditure, income from data sales, and so on.

The most important step in the interview is the wrap-up, where it is imperative that each senior stakeholder communicates their critical success factors, distinguishes any impedances or challenges, and expresses their core goals and strategies. The interviewer should allow a stakeholder ample time for this expression, without interruption or interjection.

During the interview, the senior executive may advise that questioning continue with other members of a department or colleagues who work with the stakeholder. As a general rule, it is advisable to interview all references, within reason, and not to assume that they don't have the time or don't want to contribute. One of the objectives of this activity is to socialize the proposed program to as many senior members as possible in order to gain general executive awareness. At this point, as additional references are pursued to collect further information, the interview process may become more iterative, expanding beyond the original list of stakeholders compiled in chapter 1. Of course, there's no need to interview all members of an organization, so the GIS ROI project team should control the scope of the interview process within reason. The project schedule timeline, defined in step 1.7 (figure 1.6) should be frequently consulted in order to remain focused and on track.

By the end of each one-hour interview, the conversations with key stakeholders should have covered all the main topics that concern and affect them. The interview sessions may not have centered around GIS specifically, but should have addressed key areas that affect organizational performance or customer service improvement opportunities, for example.

During the executive sessions, the sample interview questions should be used as a guide, along with the SWOT analysis, and project timeline derived from the work in chapter 1. These items should be left behind with the senior staff members after the meeting concludes as a record of the ROI project's progress.

Unlike a typical needs analysis, which concentrates on examining the gaps in the actual and ideal state of performance, the interviewing step will accomplish several things: a knowledge transfer between the GIS ROI team and multiple user groups; it will generate a consensus among stakeholders with regards to project direction and priorities; it will trigger buy-in among these stakeholders and instill confidence; and it will define accountability and ownership by involving multiple groups and departments.

Insight: Needs analysis versus addressing business needs

A traditional needs analysis seeks to determine the ways in which GIS technology could be applied within an organization. Typical users are interviewed and their needs for automation or productivity gains are generally elicited. Instead, the ROI methodology proposed here advocates assessment of the needs of the business, from a top-down perspective, rather than bottom-up. By ascertaining the business needs that executives feel are critical issues for their organization, you can more precisely target the application of GIS technology, which will in turn carry more weight in a return on investment justification.

✔ 2.4 Extract the business opportunities

Having conducted the interviews and identified the pain points articulated by the senior stakeholders, the GIS ROI team can now recognize opportunities for a GIS implementation. The team will do this by reviewing and summarizing each of the stakeholder interview documents.

Tools: Business opportunities worksheet

To organize the information and focus the topics from the key executive interviews, a business opportunities template (http://gis.esri.com/roi) is provided on the supporting Web site that categorizes the information obtained during the interviews on the basis of stakeholder group, example description, and benefits for the organization (figure 2.4).

Stakeholder Group	Opportunity Description	Opportunity ID	Benefit / Opportunity	Situation	Complication
Police					
	Provide improved emergency service to citizens				
		1	Reduce number of false alarm calls		
			Increase revenue gained from charging for false alarms		
			Increase the number of companies registered with alarms		
			Reduce both personnel and equipment costs for false alarms		

Figure 2.4 Business opportunities for Charles County, Maryland, E911 system.

During the interviews, the key stakeholders were asked specific questions related to their objectives and goals, as well as challenging situations. This data should be used to fill in the columns on the business opportunities worksheet for the "Opportunity Description," "Benefit/Opportunity" and "Metric" sections.

For instance, taking a real-world example of emergency 911 services in Charles County, Maryland, the goals and objectives for the director of Charles County's Department of Emergency Services with respect to false alarm calls are expressed in figure 2.4. The other columns in figure 2.4 will be completed in chapter three.

For each opportunity or benefit, there may be a challenge or impedance that complicates the goal of a senior manager. In the next chapter, the key business opportunities identified during these interview sessions will be examined and the "Situation" and "Complication" columns of the business opportunities worksheet will be completed. In the next chapter, each benefit will be restated as a question and answer to facilitate the process of creating specific GIS projects. There can be one or more business benefits per opportunity, as is shown in the Charles County example.

Question	Answer	Metric
		Nearly 98% of alarm calls are false. Alarm calls account for about 15% of all emergency calls (=9,800 alarm calls per year)
		Revenue Increase
		Number of companies with registered alarms
		More than $2.2m spent per year responding to approximately 9800 calls

Insight: Be prepared for cost and ownership questions

Don't be surprised if questions from your key stakeholders revolve around cost and ownership of the program. You may get questions such as, "What are the costs?" and "Who will be responsible?" Costing projects at a more detailed level and establishing project governance will be addressed in subsequent chapters. Reassure your stakeholders at this stage that you understand their concerns and that answers to their questions will indeed be provided in the final analysis.

OUTCOME

The objectives of chapter 2 revolved around winning over senior executives as the key stakeholders, collecting their input for business benefits, and arriving at a general list of high-level business opportunities and challenges for each stakeholder's department or workgroup. At the conclusion of this chapter, one-on-one interviews with key personnel and influential senior sponsors will have been completed. From these interviews, a list of business challenges and opportunities for each of these stakeholders will have been extracted and summarized. At the same time, the proposed program of work will have been introduced and socialized, in order to arrive at management buy-in from executives. Using GIS professional experience, the next step will be to prioritize the business opportunities so that later they can be defined as GIS projects.

IDENTIFY BUSINESS OPPORTUNITIES

In this part of the case study Brian Sobers, City of Springfield GIS manager, and his ROI team prepare to interview and then meet individually with selected senior executives at the city to get their ideas on where GIS can help them improve their business activities to the benefit of the city as a whole. The team will do this in a professional and structured manner so as to instill confidence in the executives, and to help build the consensus that will be necessary to follow through on delivering the benefits identified.

C2.1   List of potential business benefits of a GIS

The GIS team realizes that it will need to interview senior executives in order to identify their insights, views, and challenges with the intention of identifying the business opportunities that additional spending on GIS might deliver to the City of Springfield. Some of these stakeholders may not have any frame of reference for the value of GIS. So, according to the ROI methodology, Brian and the team build a list of general business benefits of GIS to provide them with some examples during interviews, should questions arise about the uses and potential applications of GIS technology.

Using the resources provided on the supporting Web site (http://gis.esri.com/roi), Brian puts together an easy-to-read table of examples of GIS usage at other similar cities and municipalities (figure C2.1).

Organization	Discipline	Problem	GIS Solution	Return on Investment
Culver City, California	Public Works, Sanitation Division	Desire for increased efficiency in special pickup routing.	Routed trucks more efficiently using ArcLogistics Route.	Decreased overtime and lowered vehicle maintenance costs, producing savings of $15,000 in first six months in addition to improving service to residents.
City of Sacramento, California	Solid Waste Dept. and Admin. Services Dept.	Improve efficiency in routing and balance the workload of the solid waste fleet.	Developed a GIS-based routing methodology.	City reduced the number of drivers and realized an annual savings of $250,000 in fleet and equipment costs.
City of Bartlett, Tennessee	Planning and Finance Departments	A review of the city budget revealed that the city sticker fee of $25 per vehicle was not keeping pace with the estimated number of households in the city.	City staff used GIS to identify a gap between the county and city records caused when a revised annexation was not communicated.	Geocoding 16,000 additional records by ZIP Code yielded 2,100 households that were not paying the required city sticker fee. The inclusion of these households will generate $52,500 annually in revenue.
City of Lincoln, Nebraska	Police Department	Need to identify high crime areas and reduce burglaries in those areas.	Identified problem neighborhoods and trends. Monitored program results. Initiated community outreach programs to targeted neighborhoods.	Crime reduced in target neighborhoods 67 percent in seven weeks.
City of Rancho Cucamonga, California	Redevelopment Agency Department	Encourage business growth. Need to reach businesses.	Web-based available property site search tool for buildings, demographics, business, and maps.	In the first year, 40 percent fewer vacancies, 3 new shopping centers, over 6,000 site visitors, and improved customer satisfaction.
City of Saco, Maine	Finance	Meet GASB 34 requirements and ensure strong bond rating.	A GIS-based asset management system to improve the city's financial position.	Two national agencies upgraded Saco's bond rating, equalling $2 million in savings to citizens over 20 years. Improved working relationships with elected officials, earned national and state recognition.

Figure C2.1 Examples of GIS usage at municipalities similar to the City of Springfield.

C2.2   Interview questions and responses

During the time allocated for executive interviews in the GIS project timeline (figure C1.7), Brian discovers that the director of police, John Baston, is unavailable due to illness, so he can only conduct five out of the six originally planned interviews. During the interviews, Brian plans to use the PowerPoint file (figure C1.5) to introduce the topic and start the discussion. The questions and discussion points that Brian and his team plan to use in the interviews are compiled into interview scripts following the guidelines in task 2.2. Using the templates provided, Brian stores the interview questions and answers in the following digital documents, which are available on the supporting Web site:

- Interview with head of Community Services, Andrew Jones:
  "Springfield Interview_Questions CmSvcs.doc"

- Interview with head of Public Works, Phillip Stott:
  "Springfield Interview_Questions PblWks.doc"

- Interview with head of Community Development, Sue Coldfield:
  "Springfield Interview_Questions ComDev.doc"

- Interview with head of Economic Development, Arthur Spaliceck:
  "Springfield Interview_Questions EcoDev.doc"

- Interview with city manager, Bob James:
  "Springfield Interview_Questions CtyMgr.doc"

By way of example, one of the completed interview templates is reproduced in figure C2.2.

ESRI

Interview Summary

PA

Interviewee: Andrew Jones, Head, Community Services Department	Interviewer: Brian Sobers, GIS Manager	Date: January 22, 2008

Topic	General Questions	Notes

Introduction		• Use pre-prepared PPT to describe: Who I am and why I am here
		  ◦ What is GIS
		  ◦ Why GIS is important
		• Summarize GIS use to date in the City

Baseline	What are main activities of the Community Services department?	Manage library, museum, city-wide senior services programs, and parks and recreation.
	Who would you consider as your primary internal customers?	Work closely with public works for physical plant maintenance, general services for IT support and finances.
	What are the main business issues that you face?	Major business challenges are keeping up with City growth (Springfield's population has grown 30% in the past decade) and plans to implement City Manager's new technology and city greening initiatives. Without a balance between impervious and tree-covered land the city's character is changing. Furthermore, the City's air quality is dangerously close to the Environmental Protection Agency's "nonattainment" designation. If the air quality deteriorates, giving the area a nonattainment status, the region stands to lose a considerable amount of money in federal highway funding, not to mention risking the health of the area's residents. To improve the air, the regional council has agreed on a checklist of a dozen actions, and improving the tree canopy is one of them.
	What are your main technology concerns?	Existing infrastructure is out of date. Reliance on IT department for support.
	What would you consider your accountabilities or success criteria to be?	Manage 2% increase in number of senior citizens without an increase in budget. Increase visits to Library and Museum by 5% per year. Increase the number of trees on city streets and parks by 100,000 per year.
	For this particular strategy/roadmap, what are your key objectives that you want to be sure are fulfilled?	Need assistance in applying appropriate solution(s) to these problems, as well as additional funding to acquire and support systems.
Vision & Goals	What are the key business outcomes you think that a technology solution should deliver?	See above.
	What areas of the business or key functions should be supported?	Need to create a baseline inventory of the number of city trees so that we can monitor future trends. Categorically states that city air quality is just above EPA 'nonattainment' level. Without tree planting could fall below critical level and City will lose federal highway funding of $60,000 per year for three years.
	Is the vision you have common across the business, or is it fragmented, e.g. others 'doing their own thing'?	Most senior people know a bit about GIS, but except for Planning no one has much real experience. "To be honest we are all a bit unsure about why Mr. James (City Manager) has 'a bee in his bonnet' about GIS".
	Are there key metrics, or performance indicators that the technology solution could impact or influence?	No, we don't really operate this way in the City.
	How do you feel the technology should be delivering value in the following areas:	
	Museum: interactive exhibits	Wants to:
	Library: enhanced public access web site	Update and enhance library public access system
	Senior services: trip planning	Create plan to plant more trees
	Parks and Recreation: tree inventory,	Other two are low priority due to inability of staff to accept change and lack of budget.

Topic	General Questions	Notes
Technology - Application development & deployment	Who do you see building the applications and operationalizing them with help desk, support, upgrades, backups etc.?	Would need to be purchased or developed by outside consultants since don't have in-house skills. Similarly will need to be supported by IT staff.
Data	What are the metrics related to data volumes?	Existing web site is receiving 30,000 queries a year.
Process	How do you see the technology applications 'changing how people do their jobs' and what changes do you foresee in process?	Should help people become more productive and get them motivated about their job, except for staff in Senior Services who don't like change and certainly don't like new technology.
Organization / Delivery / Support	Once the technology 'project' has delivered, what do you envisage the team/department composition and function to be? Additional FTEs?	We will need IT support, but this is probably best provided by central IT support staff.
	Executing these types of projects can be challenging without the right governance – do you feel the right control, structure, accountability, timeline/management, milestones etc. are agreed and in place?	We have a new GIS Manager, but it is not obvious who will support him technically. Believes that project governance is critical as 'too many projects have failed at the City due to bad management'.
	It appears that Springfield utilizes contractors and uses internal experts to help shape, guide and manage the delivery of value for vendors...is this accurate?	Yes, city has very limited IT skills.
Wrap-up	What challenges do you for see with the strategy/business case development? Any other topics of concern you think should be covered?	City greening project is important, but it is always going to be difficult to show success. Key requirement is greening city and avoiding a further reduction in air quality.

Figure C2.2 Interview with head of Community Services, Andrew Jones (Springfield Interview_Questions CmSvcs.doc).

C2.3 Extract the business opportunities

Immediately after each interview, Brian and the team extract the key information from the interview templates and enter it into a document derived from the business opportunities template (figure C2.3). They also enlist support from some other trusted advisors in the local GIS community who provide review and comment. The completed business opportunities document provides a summary of the opportunities for GIS at the City of Springfield.

The business benefits are on the Web site under the file name Chptr2_SpringfieldBusinessOpportunities.xls.

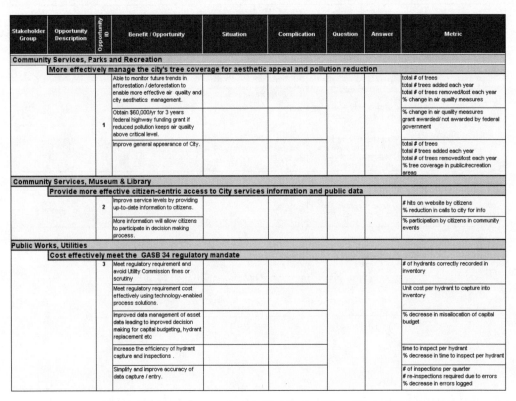

Stakeholder Group	Opportunity Description	Opportunity ID	Benefit / Opportunity	Situation	Complication	Question	Answer	Metric
Community Services, Parks and Recreation								
	More effectively manage the city's tree coverage for aesthetic appeal and pollution reduction							
			Able to monitor future trends in afforestation / deforestation to enable more effective air quality and city aesthetics management.					total # of trees total # trees added each year total # of trees removed/lost each year % change in air quality measures
		1	Obtain $60,000/yr for 3 years federal highway funding grant if reduced pollution keeps air quality above critical level.					% change in air quality measures grant awarded/ not awarded by federal government
			Improve general appearance of City.					total # of trees total # trees added each year total # of trees removed/lost each year % tree coverage in public/recreation areas
Community Services, Museum & Library								
	Provide more effective citizen-centric access to City services information and public data							
		2	Improve service levels by providing up-to-date information to citizens.					# hits on website by citizens % reduction in calls to city for info
			More information will allow citizens to participate in decision making process.					% participation by citizens in community events
Public Works, Utilities								
	Cost effectively meet the GASB 34 regulatory mandate							
		3	Meet regulatory requirement and avoid Utility Commission fines or scrutiny					# of hydrants correctly recorded in inventory
			Meet regulatory requirement cost effectively using technology-enabled process solutions.					Unit cost per hydrant to capture into inventory
			improved data management of asset data leading to improved decision making for capital budgeting, hydrant replacement etc					% decrease in misallocation of capital budget
			increase the efficiency of hydrant capture and inspections .					time to inspect per hydrant % decrease in time to inspect per hydrant
			Simplify and improve accuracy of data capture / entry.					# of inspections per quarter # re-inspections required due to errors % decrease in errors logged

Figure C2.3 Business opportunities for the City of Springfield.

Stakeholder Group	Opportunity Description	Opportunity ID	Benefit / Opportunity	Situation	Complication	Question	Answer	Metric
Public Works, Utilities								
	Enable effective asset management for improved service quality for citizens							
			Improve maintenance work flow scheduling and throughput leading to operational cost reduction and service degradation					# of outages # % decrease in outages # of customer service calls to call center % decrease in number of calls to call center # truck rolls for outages % decrease in truck rolls $ average cost of truck roll # of outage related truck rolls
		4	Optimized and more robust Capital Budget planning process improving the allocation of capital for public works.					$ annual capital budget % improvement in capital allocation OR % decrease in capital misallocation
			Reduction of outages due to unplanned service disruptions					# of service outages % reduction of service outages $ average cost of truck roll # of outage related truck rolls
Community Development, Planning								
	Effectively identify Brownfield sites suitable for redevelopment							
		5	Reduce development of Greenfield sites and increase the likelihood of Brownfield sites being re-developed					# of Brownfield sites # of Brownfield sites suitable for development % of Brownfield sites redeveloped annually
	Improve ability to find new land and properties that could be redeveloped for community housing purposes							
		6	Improve the effectiveness of identifying land/properties in order to reduce operational expenditure					# of temp hours used monthly % decrease in temp hours used $ opex budget spent on temps % reduction in opex budget spend on temps
			Improve the readability and usability of reports by external developers					# of developers # of developers investing or engaged with the city % increase in engagement by developers % increase in investing developers
Economic Development, Redevelopment								
	Promote and enable more inward investment across the City							

			Increase the level of tax revenue generated through new businesses entering the City					$ tax revenue per annum
								% increase in tax revenue due to inward investment
								# of inquires fielded by the Eco Dev team
								% decrease in calls to the Eco Dev team
								# vacant properties in City Center
								% decrease in vacant properties in City Center
								$ medium property value in city center
								% increase in medium property value in city center

		7	Increasing the accessibility of information will improve the 'customer experience' and thus the City's reputation for contributing to the City's image and business community.					# positive survey responses received quarterly # of website hits % increase in website hits # of inquires fielded by the Eco Dev team % decrease in calls to the Eco Dev team
			Increased economic development would positively impact property values and attractiveness to the City.					# vacant properties in City Center % decrease in vacant properties in City Center $ medium property value in city center % increase in medium property value in city center
			Reduce the operational cost of supporting Economic Development activities.					$ operational expenditure on external support for Eco Dev Team % decrease in use of external support
City Manager (Enterprise)								
	Enable more effective cross-collaboration between City departments							
		8	Encourage collaboration, and sharing of data and other resources that will create a type of 'joined up' local government and reduce operational costs.					# of process handoffs % decrease in process handoffs
			Provide better services to citizens by sharing more information, putting information and other services on-line.					# of customer complaints % decrease in customer complaints # of services available 'self-serve' on-line % increase in services available "self-serve" on-line.

C2.4   Discussion of chapter 2 case study

Clearly the success of this part of the case study hinges on crafting good questions that will receive valuable answers, using the time with executive stakeholders in the most effective way. Talking to executives can be quite daunting for middle managers and junior staff. However, fears can be allayed with careful and thorough preparation along the lines suggested here.

Most likely, the information solicited from the stakeholders will be of different levels of generality; possibly there will be conflict between responses, and there may be a number of gaps that will require further investigation. Nevertheless, there will be some pieces of information that will prove very useful in identifying business opportunities in the next stage of the ROI methodology. In addition, gaps can be filled in by talking to other employees in the business who are experts in their own area (e.g., a field crew supervisor, lead planning officer, or manager of economic development).

Endnotes

1. Thomas, C., and M. Ospina, *Measuring up: The business case for GIS* (Redlands, Calif.: ESRI Press, 2004).

2. Meehan, B., *Empowering electric and gas utilities with GIS* (Redlands, Calif.: ESRI Press, 2007).

3. Lerner, N., S. Ancel, M. Stewart, and D. DiSera, GITA and AWWA, *Building a business case for geospatial information technology: A practitioners guide to financial and strategic analysis* (GITA and AWWA, 2007).

4. Korte, G., "Weighing GIS benefits with financial analysis," *GIS World,* 1996, 9(7): 48–52.

5. Smith, D. A., and R. Tomlinson, "Assessing costs and benefits of geographical information systems: Methological and implementation issues," *International Journal of Geographical Information Systems,* 1994, 6(3): 252.

6. Antenucci, J., K. Brown, P. Croswell, and M. Kevany. *Geographic information systems: A guide to the technology* (New York: Van Nostrand Reinhold, 1991), 66.

7. Thomas and Ospina, 10–1.

8. Thomas and Ospina, 16 and 17.

9. Thomas and Ospina, 25–6.

10. Thomas and Ospina, 32–4.

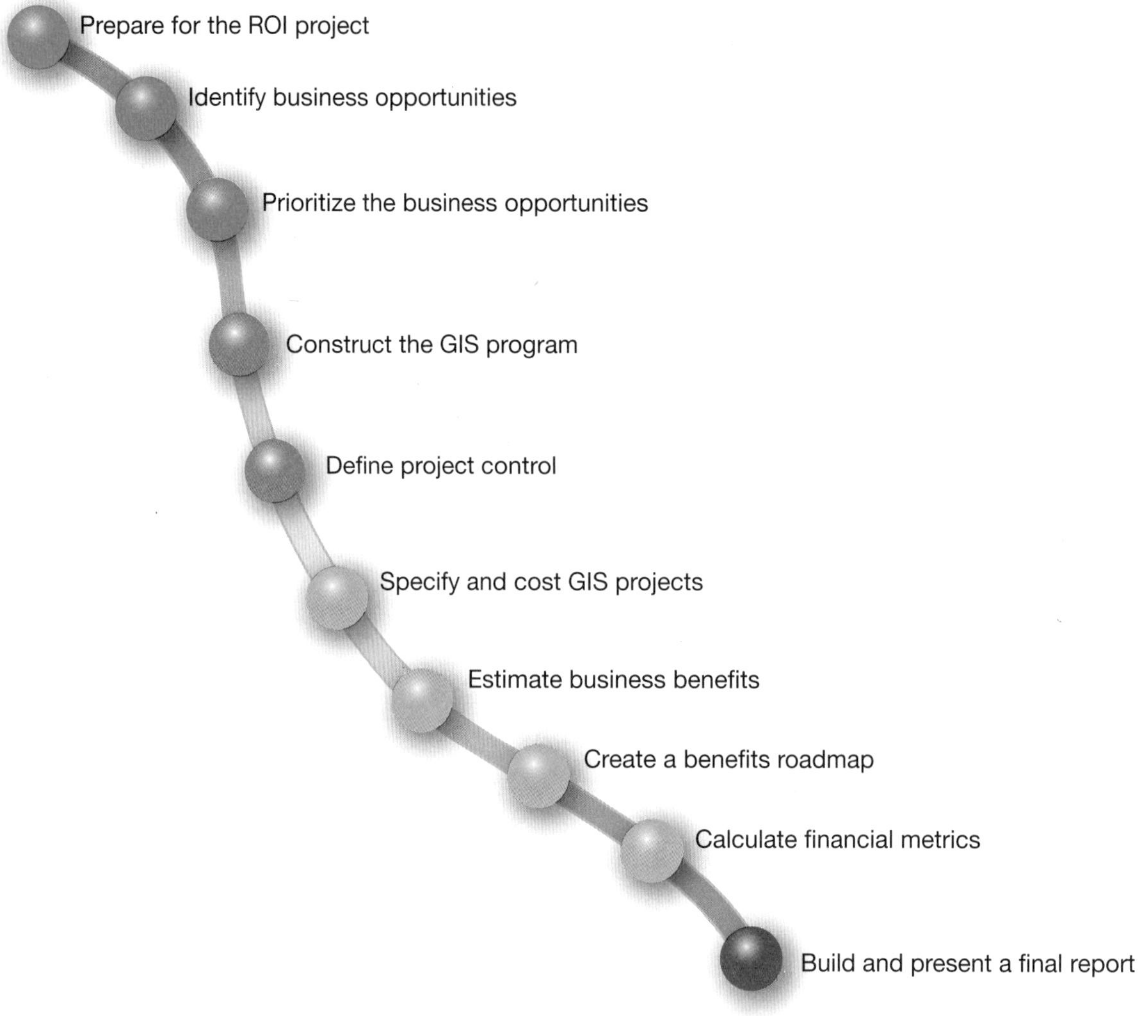

Prepare for the ROI project

Identify business opportunities

Prioritize the business opportunities

Construct the GIS program

Define project control

Specify and cost GIS projects

Estimate business benefits

Create a benefits roadmap

Calculate financial metrics

Build and present a final report

3

Prioritize the business opportunities

The next task is to set priorities for the business opportunities identified previously by the executive stakeholders within an organization. Priorities are set by combining knowledge of the benefit an opportunity will bring, with the ease with which it can be implemented using GIS. This is achieved by completing more of the columns in the worksheet that was started in the last chapter and creating an opportunity prioritization quadrant diagram. This process is carried through the case study in the final section.

Executives are typically very good at generating ideas and opportunities for projects, especially when stimulated by a well-organized ROI team, and there are no resource constraints. It is highly likely, therefore, that a substantial number of potential business opportunities was defined in the previous chapter and entered into the spreadsheet template provided. The tasks in this chapter center around prioritizing the business opportunities so that they can be turned into a collection of GIS projects in the next chapter. Not all of the challenges and stakeholder objectives identified during the interviews will have an associated GIS solution that will deliver a business benefit to an organization. However, those areas where GIS solutions can add value by providing new capabilities or overcoming existing business challenges should be clearly identified and documented. Prioritizing these business opportunities then becomes an iterative process that requires collaboration and consultation, but again is driven by a GIS ROI team. It is an essential prerequisite to building a financial case based on proven, benefits-focused analysis.

OBJECTIVES

In the last chapter, based on the information gathered during the stakeholder interviews, a collection of business opportunities was identified and entered into the business opportunities template worksheet. The tasks here are concerned with prioritizing these opportunities using criteria that will allow them to be ranked in order of importance for consideration as GIS projects. This is achieved by populating a number of additional columns in the worksheet and building a visual diagram of the resulting ranked opportunities. These tasks will define the business opportunities in more detail so that they are clearly understood by all concerned. An important part of this process is gaining consensus on the priority of the opportunity based on the value to the organization examined against the difficulty of delivery, caucusing first within the ROI team, and then consulting with the key stakeholders.

TASKS

✔ 3.1 Provide details about the business opportunities

During the interviews conducted in the last chapter, the key stakeholders were asked specific questions related to their group's objectives and goals, as well as the challenging situations that they face. This information was recorded in documents based on the interview template provided. Key elements of this information were then entered into a business opportunities document also based on the provided template. The task at hand here is to extract additional information from the executive interview documents and organize it in the same business opportunities worksheet from chapter 2. This task begins with completing information for the "Situation" and "Complication" columns (figure 3.1) for each of the business opportunities. The situation is the current state of affairs in the organization—that is, the problem that the executives identified during their interview. The complication is any issue that exacerbates the problem, as highlighted by the stakeholder.

In the last chapter, an example of an emergency (police) service for Charles County, Maryland, was used to illustrate how the ROI methodology can be used, and the same example will be continued in this chapter. The current situation and complication for Charles County have been described as follows:

> . . . emergency service personnel in Charles County, Maryland, knew that the growing number of false alarms was affecting service delivery . . . Charles County's alarm calls accounted for nearly 15 percent of all emergency calls for service, and nearly 98 percent of the alarm calls were false. A 10 percent annual increase in new alarm systems compounded the problem. At a weighted average cost of $225 to respond to a single emergency, the county estimated that it was spending more than $2.2 million a year to respond to approximately 9,800 alarms.[1]

Figure 3.1 shows completed "Situation" and "Complication" columns in addition to those already populated in the last chapter.

Stakeholder Group	Opportunity Description	Opportunity ID	Benefit / Opportunity	Situation	Complication
Police					
	Provide improved emergency service to citizens				
		1	Reduce number of false alarm calls	Vast majority of alarm calls are false alarms	Manual procedures currently in place are inefficient
			Increase revenue gained from charging for false alarms	Currently there is no penalty for excessive false alarm calls	There is no tracking method for specific false alarms
			Increase the number of companies registered with alarms	There is no existing requirement for registering alarms	There is no database for false alarm company registrations
			Reduce both personnel and equipment costs for false alarms	Major cost to respond to the large number of alarms	Reducing staff is not recommended or beneficial to citizens

Figure 3.1 Completed "Situation" and "Complication" entries in the business opportunities worksheet for the Charles County, Maryland, example.

Tools: Business opportunities template

Also used in chapter 2, the business opportunities worksheet template is provided to assist you with task 3.1. This template can be found on the accompanying Web site, http://gis.esri.com/roi, under step 3.

The next part of this task is to populate the "Question" and "Answer" columns in the worksheet document for each of the opportunities. The "Question" posed relates to solving the problem defined by the current situation in order to reap the greatest benefit for an organization. The solution to the problem is provided in the "Answer" column, and it should revolve around a GIS implementation. In the E911 example, the answers shown are based on the actual outcome for Charles County, after a public safety GIS system was implemented (figure 3.2). The question focuses on cost reduction using GIS, which is a very common goal of projects such as this, and one directly amenable to being measured as a business benefit.

Insight: Avoid personnel reduction as a solution

It is not recommended to model head-count reduction as a benefit (e.g., firing or reassigning staff positions) for the purpose of supporting your GIS ROI case because of the difficulties you will almost certainly face in selling this idea to executive stakeholders.

Stakeholder Group	Opportunity Description	Opportunity ID	Benefit / Opportunity	Situation	Complication	Question	Answer
Police							
	Provide improved emergency service to citizens						
		1	Reduce number of false alarm calls	Vast majority of alarm calls are false alarms	Manual procedures currently in place are inefficient	How can the County mitigate costs due to false alarm responses?	Use GIS to eliminate the complexities of tracking and billing alarm calls. Use data on false alarm calls to generate payment notices automatically and send them to owners
			Increase revenue gained from charging for false alarms	Currently there is no penalty for excessive false alarm calls	There is no tracking method for specific false alarms		
			Increase the number of companies registered with alarms	There is no existing requirement for registering alarms	There is no database for false alarm company registrations		
			Reduce both personnel and equipment costs for false alarms	Major cost to respond to the large number of alarms	Reducing staff is not recommended or beneficial to citizens		

Figure 3.2   Completed "Question" and "Answer" entries in the business opportunities template, for the Charles County, Maryland, example.

Insight: Be open to all types of solutions

When populating the "Answer" column of the business opportunities worksheet, be conscious of not falling into a pattern of always arriving at GIS as the solution to the existing situation. You may lose credibility by attempting to force-fit GIS as the solution to all business problems. In other words, be aware that after evaluating the situation, the best answer may not always be GIS.

The business opportunities template also has a column to record specific details about metrics associated with each of the opportunities. These will have been recorded during the executive stakeholder interviews. Metrics are extremely important because they drive several future aspects of the ROI methodology. When designing project implementations in chapter 4, they guide decision making about the GIS approach to be adopted. The benefits estimation process in chapter 7 will also use metrics as the basis for calculation. Finally, the capstone report created in chapter 10 will incorporate metrics as part of the supporting case for funding of the entire program.

Insight: Don't get too hung up on numbers

One of the greatest challenges is actually finding metrics—hard numbers—that can legitimately be used to measure the magnitude of change. Experience shows that it is possible to get caught in an endless search for these numbers, when in fact the most obvious source of a legitimate "best guess" is the executive, or their delegate, who is immersed in the daily business challenges. For example, if a 25-year veteran VP of Sales shares her expert opinion on the GIS yielding a 5 percent increase in sales conversion rates, then most likely few individuals would challenge these figures.

✔ 3.2 Estimate sizes of business opportunities and rank accordingly

Clearly, all of the business opportunities identified cannot have equal weight and be realized at the same time. As a result, they must be prioritized and ranked to provide guidance to the GIS project implementation process that will be considered in the next chapter. Given that each organization and set of opportunities is different, there are no hard ranking rules for prioritization. That said, a ranked priority list can be arrived at using a few basic criteria that are best expressed in the form several questions:

- Is this business benefit opportunity important to the organization and its mission as a whole, not necessarily the objective of one single department?

- Does the organization currently have the talent and resources to undertake the necessary steps to reach this benefit?

- Which opportunity provides the most "bang for the buck"?

- Given the investment required and the organizational change necessary to undertake a project to realize this opportunity, is it too costly?

There is a balancing act to be played when seeking to prioritize the business benefit opportunities that have been identified through the interviews with executives. On the one hand, it is appropriate to focus on delivering the most high-value benefits to an organization, since these will have the greatest impact. On the other, it is often the case that the most high-value benefits also require the most investment, the longest period to realize, or the most organizational change—all of which create challenges for an ROI project.

In the previous task, information about a series of business opportunities was entered into a business opportunities worksheet. The next task is to prioritize these opportunities based on two main criteria: the value to the organization and the ease of implementation. The business opportunities template has two columns for recording the "Organization Value" and "Ease of Implementation" (figure 3.3). Given that a specific solution implementation has not yet been determined for any of the opportunities (this is a task in chapter 4), a best estimate of both these criteria will be the goal here. Clearly there are no right or wrong answers in the evaluation process, and many people may have an opinion of what the best values should be. A two-stage evaluation process is therefore proposed. First, the ROI team should rank the opportunities using the two criteria proposed and create a diagram that illustrates the relative positioning of all the opportunities. Then, the team should consult as widely as possible with key stakeholders and other staff in the organization to obtain general agreement on the prioritization of the opportunities.

"Organization Value" is an estimate of the value or benefit to an organization of implementing an opportunity. Values of 1–3 indicate a low potential benefit to an organization, and it is questionable if such opportunities should be implemented at all. Values of 4–7 indicate a medium potential benefit, and such opportunities are good candidates for implementation. Values of 8-10 indicate a high potential benefit, and opportunities that fall into this range are excellent candidates for implementation.

"Ease of Implementation" is an estimate of how simple it will be to define and carry out a GIS project that meets the business opportunity. Values of 1–3 indicate opportunities that have a low score for an easy delivery or deployment. This score could be low because it is hard to deliver on this benefit with a GIS or because there is a lack of expertise in the organization. Values of 4–7 indicate opportunities that have a medium potential for implementation using GIS. Values of 8–10 indicate opportunities that have very high potential for implementation using GIS. There are many factors that go into estimating the ease of implementation, such as the degree to which an opportunity can be realized using out-of-the-box GIS software capabilities; whether implementation will require acquisition of major amounts of data; the cost of implementing the GIS capability—perhaps it is simply too expensive given the mix of hardware, software, training, and so on; the cultural change in an organization may be too steep—perhaps implementation of GIS capability would face opposition from a union or entrenched workers who have been doing their job the same way for 20 years; and the department head responsible for helping to enable the delivery of a particular benefit may have other priorities or concerns, so gaining their support for resources may be difficult.

Figure 3.3 shows proposed priorities for three business opportunities for the Charles County example. In addition to the police business opportunity already discussed, two other opportunities have been added in the fire department. Using the scales already discussed, values have been added to the "Organization Value" and "Ease of Implementation" columns. The police opportunity has a relatively high organization value, and a medium range ease of implementation value, whereas opportunity number 2 (locate new fire station) has the highest rank for organizational value and a lower-middle range value for ease of implementation.

Stakeholder Group	Opportunity Description	Opportunity ID	Benefit / Opportunity	Situation	Complication	Question	Answer	Metric	Organization Value (1-Low, 10-High)	Ease of Implementation (1-Hard, 10-Easy)
Police	Provide improved emergency service to citizens									
		1	Reduce number of false alarm calls	Vast majority of alarm calls are false alarms	Manual procedures currently in place are inefficient	How can the County mitigate costs due to false alarm responses?	Use GIS to eliminate the complexities of tracking and billing alarm calls. Use data on false alarm calls to generate payment notices automatically and send them to owners	Nearly 96% of alarm calls are false. Alarm calls account for about 15% of all emergency calls (≈9,600 alarm calls per year)	8	6
			Increase revenue gained from charging for false alarms	Currently there is no penalty for excessive false alarm calls	There is no tracking method for specific false alarms			Revenue Increase		
			Increase the number of companies registered with alarms	There is no existing requirement for registering alarms	There is no database for false alarm company registrations			Number of companies with registered alarms		
			Reduce both personnel and equipment costs for false alarms	Major cost to respond to the large number of alarms	Reducing staff is not recommended or beneficial to citizens			More than $2.2m spent per year responding to approximately 9600 calls		
Fire	Locate New Fire Station									
		2	Save lives and reduce property damage by relocating fire station in the best location to serve existing population	County population has grown rapidly in recent years and existing stations needs to be precisely determined	Relocating fire stations is very expensive and existing fire stations?	Where is the best location for all existing fire stations?	Create a location-allocation model using GIS to determine optimum location of fire stations	Statutory requirement defined by National Fire Protection Association (NFPA) to reach 90% of fires within 4 minutes	10	6
	Map incidents									
		3	Maps can be added to existing Fire Chief reports to provide better summary of activity	Existing reports are difficult to assimilate	Creating maps by hand is not feasible	How can simple maps be created for Fire Chief?	Use GIS to create monthly reports of incident data	Average month has 4000-4500 incidents	3	10

Figure 3.3 Ranked business opportunities for the Charles County, Maryland, example.

Once the ROI team has completed its evaluation of the business opportunities based on the value to an organization and the ease of implementation using GIS, it is appropriate to seek consensus among as many stakeholders and workers in an organization as is feasible. A useful way to elicit feedback is to plot the rankings on a opportunity prioritization quadrant diagram and then use the diagram to stimulate discussion. This diagram can be accessed off a second worksheet in the business opportunities template. Once each row is populated with an opportunity and its subsequent ranking values, selecting the "ReCalc Graph" button on the "Input-Data" sheet will redraw the quadrant diagram accordingly.

Figure 3.4 shows the evaluation data for Charles County plotted on an opportunity prioritization quadrant diagram. The numbers on the marker symbols match the "Opportunity ID" from the "Input-Data" worksheet. The diagram is subdivided into four quadrants: the two at the top are high value to an organization, and the two to the right are easy to implement. This means that the best projects are those in the top-right corner (high value, easy to implement using GIS). There is a certain inevitability that the ROI methodology will tend to preselect business opportunities that will provide high value to an organization because executives and the ROI team are unlikely to mention or record low-value or difficult-to-implement projects, and so it is rare that opportunities will be evenly distributed over the diagram. Further, it should be remembered that the quadrant diagram is offered only as a guide. That is, there certainly could be significant business justifications as to why one or more opportunities should become a priority project, regardless of where they are plotted on the quadrant diagram.

When this diagram is shown to stakeholders in an organization, there will likely be considerable and sometimes animated debate about the relative location of business opportunities on the diagram. This discussion is perhaps as valuable as the final result because it will both develop consensus among the stakeholders and get their buy-in to the whole ROI process.

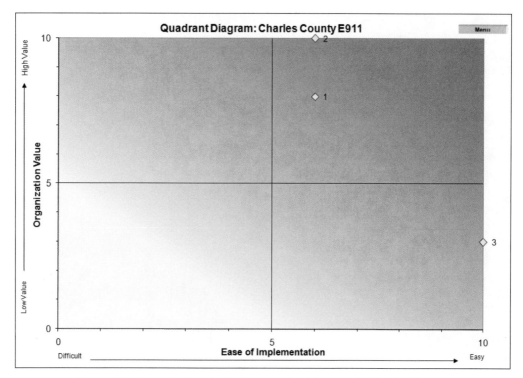

Figure 3.4 Opportunity prioritization quadrant diagram for Charles County.

Once consensus has been reached about the relative importance of the business opportunities, based on the importance to the organization and the ease of implementation with GIS, it is necessary to determine the final overall opportunity priority. The aim here is to have a healthy mix of "quick wins" and long-term benefits. It is better to deliver smaller incremental successes, particularly if the GIS program is new or recovering from past challenges.

Based on this logic and looking at the Charles County example shown in figure 3.4, it would appear to be more apt to seek to deliver opportunities 1 and 2 rather than number 3. The business opportunities template has a column called "Priority," which will automatically calculate and color-code the high, medium, and low values for each opportunity—high is green for go, medium is amber for wait, and low is red for stop. The "Ranking Guidelines" sheet in the templates provides the description for each priority value. Figure 3.5 shows the completed spreadsheet for the Charles County example.

Stakeholder Group	Opportunity Description	Opportunity ID	Benefit / Opportunity	Situation	Complication	Question	Answer	Metric	Organization Value (1-Low, 10-High)	Ease of Implementation (1-Hard, 10-Easy)	Priority
Police											
	Provide improved emergency service to citizens	1	Reduce number of false alarm calls	Vast majority of alarm calls are false alarms	Manual procedures currently in place are inefficient	How can the County mitigate costs due to false alarm responses?	Use GIS to eliminate the complexities of tracking and billing alarm calls. Use data on false alarm calls to generate payment notices automatically and send them to owners	Nearly 98% of alarm calls are false. Alarm calls account for about 15% of all emergency calls (≈9,800 alarm calls per year)	8	6	High
			Increase revenue gained from charging for false alarms	Currently there is no penalty for excessive false alarm calls	There is no tracking method for specific false alarms			Revenue Increase			
			Increase the number of companies registered with alarms	There is no existing requirement for registering alarms	There is no database for false alarm company registrations			Number of companies with registered alarms			
			Reduce both personnel and equipment costs for false alarms	Major cost to respond to the large number of alarms	Reducing staff is not recommended or beneficial to citizens			More than $2.2m spent per year responding to approximately 9800 calls			
Fire											
	Locate New Fire Station	2	Save lives and reduce property damage by relocating fire station in the best location to serve existing population	County population has grown rapidly in recent years and existing stations have suboptimal location	Relocating fire stations is very expensive and needs to be precisely determined	Where is the best location for all existing fire stations?	Create a location-allocation model using GIS to determine optimum location of fire stations	Statutory requirement defined by National Fire Protection Association (NFPA) to reach 90% of fires within 4 minutes	10	6	High
	Map incidents	3	Maps can be added to existing Fire Chief reports to provide better summary of activity	Existing reports are difficult to assimilate	Creating maps by hand is not feasible	How can simple maps be created for Fire Chief?	Use GIS to create monthly reports of incident data	Average month has 4000-4500 incidents	3	10	Medium

Figure 3.5 Complete spreadsheet for the Charles County example.

OUTCOME

The goal of chapter 3 has been to summarize the information collected from the previous stakeholder meetings and distill this data into manageable and quantifiable business benefit opportunities. A business opportunities worksheet will have been completed, which clearly identifies the existing opportunities, situations, and challenges that pervade each of the key stakeholders' spheres of operation. Further, this worksheet identifies the ranked priority of the projects, based upon the positive impact to business level when weighed against the difficulty of delivery.

It would be a good idea at this juncture to review the completed template with the executives involved in order to get their buy-in on the magnitude of the projects as defined. The ROI team should not make unilateral decisions affecting the core benefits of the program without additional external input and, possibly, revision.

Case Study

PRIORITIZE BUSINESS OPPORTUNITIES

Having identified a series of possible business opportunities in the last part of the Springfield case study (see chapter 2), the goal here is to develop the details and prioritize the opportunities, which will then be turned into a series of GIS projects in the next chapter.

The case study results for both tasks in this chapter are in the file: "Chptr3_Springfield BusinessOpportunities.xls" on the accompanying Web site, http://gis.esri.com/roi.

C3.1   Provide details on the business opportunities

Using the Chptr3_SpringfieldBusinessOpportunities.xls worksheet (figure C3.1, pages 80–81), Brian Sobers, GIS manager, and the ROI team continue to populate the worksheet, first filling in the "Situation," "Complication," "Question," and "Answer" columns, along with any metrics that can be extracted from the interview information. The information for these columns is retrieved from the material recorded during the executive stakeholder interviews. Some of this information was also obtained from follow-up meetings with staff in the Utilities and City Manager departments.

C3.2   Sizing and ranking of business opportunities

The process of establishing the priority for the business opportunities begins by the ROI team first determining the organization value and ease of implementation of each opportunity. The ROI team reaches its own conclusions about these values after discussing them for a few hours. Next, in order to facilitate discussion with key stakeholders and their representatives at an open meeting, they create an opportunity prioritization quadrant diagram that shows the relative rank of all eight of the opportunities (figure C3.2). To simplify the benefit ranking, Brian Sobers decides to aggregate the available opportunities based on stakeholder group. In reality, 21 opportunities were exposed during the stakeholder meetings, which Brian distilled into eight groupings (figure C3.1). The open meeting first provided an update on the status of the ROI project to date, and then invited comments on the values assigned to the opportunities as shown in the opportunity prioritization quadrant diagram. Following this meeting the ROI team met again and agreed on the final values for ranking high, medium, and low priorities (figure C3.1).

The business opportunities that the stakeholders identified are plotted on the opportunity prioritization quadrant diagram, labeled using their respective opportunity ID value. Looking at the final prioritized business opportunities for the City of Springfield (figure C3.1) and the quadrant diagram (figure C3.2), it appears obvious that opportunities 3, 6, and 7 should be turned into GIS projects. Opportunities 1 and 5 address satisfying EPA regulations and Green initiatives, which the City of Springfield considers a priority, and so are also to be added to the list. Brian and his team can move closer to meeting opportunity 8 for the city manager, by satisfying the opportunities identified as priorities, above.

C3.3   Discussion of chapter 3 case study

The two tasks in this chapter are fairly self-explanatory. The value derived from the tasks comes in the analysis of the opportunities and completion of the entries in the template worksheets. This is especially true for the opportunity prioritization quadrant diagram, which is often the subject of considerable debate.

It may not always be possible to complete all the fields in the business opportunities template on the first pass, and there may be a need to collect additional data from others in the organization before filling out the whole template. Even after later steps have been completed, Brian Sobers and the ROI team will likely want to return to these templates (and others before them in the methodology) and update various fields. Iteration of the various steps of this methodology and updating of the data in the documents is a standard way of working when conducting an ROI study: no one ever gets it completely right the first time!

Stakeholder Group	Opportunity Description	Benefit / Opportunity	Situation	Complication	Question	Answer	Metric	Organization Value (1-Low, 10-High)	Ease of Implementation (1-Hard, 10-Easy)	Priority
Community Services, Parks and Recreation										
More effectively manage the city's tree coverage for aesthetic appeal and pollution reduction										
		Able to monitor future trends in afforestation / deforestation to enable more effective air quality and city aesthetics management.	Monitor need to keep city air quality levels above EPA nonattainment level.	The lack of a tree inventory prevents the effective and efficient management of tree coverage in the city.	What is the most practical and effective approach to creating a tree inventory and monitoring changes year on year?	Create geographic database of tree cover and assess changes on an annual basis.	total # of trees / total # of trees added each year / total # of trees removed/lost each year / % change in air quality measures			
	1	Obtain $60,000/yr for 3 years federal highway funding grant if reduced pollution keeps air quality above critical level.	Federal Highway Agency provides grants to cities if air pollution is below critical levels.	The lack of a tree inventory prevents us from effectively planning the optimum level of tree coverage that will impact air pollution levels positively			% change in air quality measures / grant awarded/ not awarded by federal government	7	4	Medium
		Improve general appearance of City.	Large number of city trees is a major feature of the City which makes it attractive as a place to live and work.	No means to track or manage tree coverage and therefore limited ability to validate cost/benefit of tree coverage across the city			total # of trees / total # of trees added each year / total # of trees removed/lost each year / % tree coverage in public/recreation areas			
Community Services, Museum & Library										
Provide more effective citizen-centric access to City services information and public data										
	2	Improve service levels by providing up-to-date information to citizens.	Existing on-line public access system has been reasonably well used although it is not seen as a 'one stop shop' for City information.	The existing system lacks a robust and citizen centric user interface; lack of fresh content in an accessible and intuitive form.	How can the City provide more user-centric access to services and data provided by the City?	Update existing system with more robust and intuitive geospatial technology and data.	# hits on website by citizens / % reduction in calls to city for info	2	6	Medium
		More information will allow citizens to participate in decision making process.					% participation by citizens in community events			

Public Works, Utilities

Cost effectively meet the GASB 34 regulatory mandate

#	Business opportunity / benefit	Description / rationale	Current situation	Business question	Solution	Metrics	Priority
3	Meet regulatory requirement and avoid Utility Commission fines or scrutiny	GASB 34 (Government Accounting Standards Board Statement 34) is an unfunded financial reporting method that applies to local government. It requires the development of complete inventories of assets and liabilities for all infrastructure and facilities with maintenance and operational costs, as well as revenues and expenditures.	City of Springfield does not have a complete or consistent asset inventory of hydrants in digital form. Existing records are paper-based and incomplete.	How can a fire hydrant database be created efficiently and effectively to meet GASB 34 requirements?	Equip inspectors with Mobile GIS to record details in field and upload to centralized database.	# of hydrants correctly recorded in inventory	High
	Meet regulatory requirement cost effectively using technology-enabled process solutions.	The need to create an inventory is mandatory per GASB 34	No external funding has been provided and as a result the City needs to meet their obligations while minimizing costs.			Unit cost per hydrant to capture into inventory	10
	Improved data management of asset data leading to improved decision making for capital budgeting, hydrant replacement etc	The City requires a unified citywide database of all assets to improve financial, operational and service management of public works and services, and hydrants are part of that complete	There is currently no citywide database of all assets and no hydrant inventory			% decrease in miscalculation of capital budget	6
	Increase the efficiency of hydrant capture and inspections.	The City currently has 4 inspectors, but one has just retired.	Without technology-enabled process improvements the City will need to replace the retired inspector with a new hire in order to meet regulatory compliance.			time to inspect per hydrant / % decrease in time to inspect per hydrant	
	Simplify and improve accuracy of data capture / entry.	Inspectors are required to inspect hydrants in the field and feed the inspection information back to the office on a daily basis.	Data entry is expensive and error prone, especially existing process which has double entry in field to paper and re-entry in office.			# of inspections per quarter / # re-inspections required due to errors / % decrease in errors logged	

Public Works, Utilities

Enable effective asset management for improved service quality for citizens

#	Business opportunity / benefit	Description / rationale	Current situation	Business question	Solution	Metrics	Priority
4	Improve maintenance work flow scheduling and throughput leading to operational cost reduction and service degradation	Operations and maintenance require quality asset records that are accessible, up-to-date and consistent in order to manage service quality and asset health	Outside plant asset database is only partially complete and is becoming increasingly out of date.	What is the best way to create a complete City-wide asset database that will enable these benefits?	Incorporate technology-enabled processes that are based on mobile and office-centric GIS capabilities in order to build and maintain a consistent and up-to-date asset repository	# of outages / % decrease in outages / # of customer service calls to call center / % decrease in number of calls to call center / # truck rolls for outages / % decrease in truck rolls / $ average cost of truck roll / # of outage related truck	Low
	Optimized and more robust Capital Budget planning process improving the allocation of capital for public works.	Capital budget planning requires a detailed understanding of asset inventories, condition, age etc.	The city lacks a complete and unified set of asset inventory data upon which to base capital allocation decisions.			$ annual capital budget / % improvement in capital allocation OR % decrease in capital misallocation	3
	Reduction of outages due to unplanned service disruptions	Operations and maintenance must respond to unplanned service outages rapidly	Due to a lack of quality asset data, outages are often longer than necessary due to the inability of a truck crew to locate a fault			# of service outages / % reduction of service outages / $ average cost of truck roll / $ of outage related truck	4

Figure C3.1   A portion of the final prioritized business opportunities for the City of Springfield.

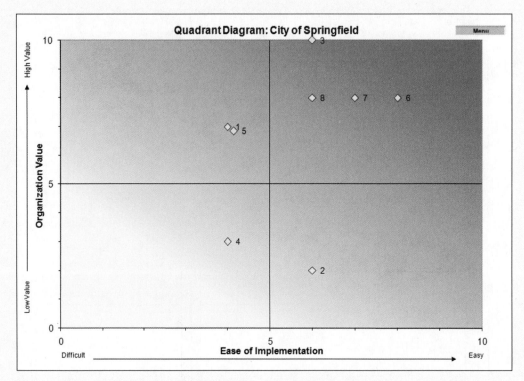

Figure C3.2   Opportunity prioritization quadrant diagram showing all opportunities for the City of Springfield case study.

Endnote

1. Thomas, C., and M. Ospina, *Measuring up: The business case for GIS* (Redlands, Calif.: ESRI Press, 2004).

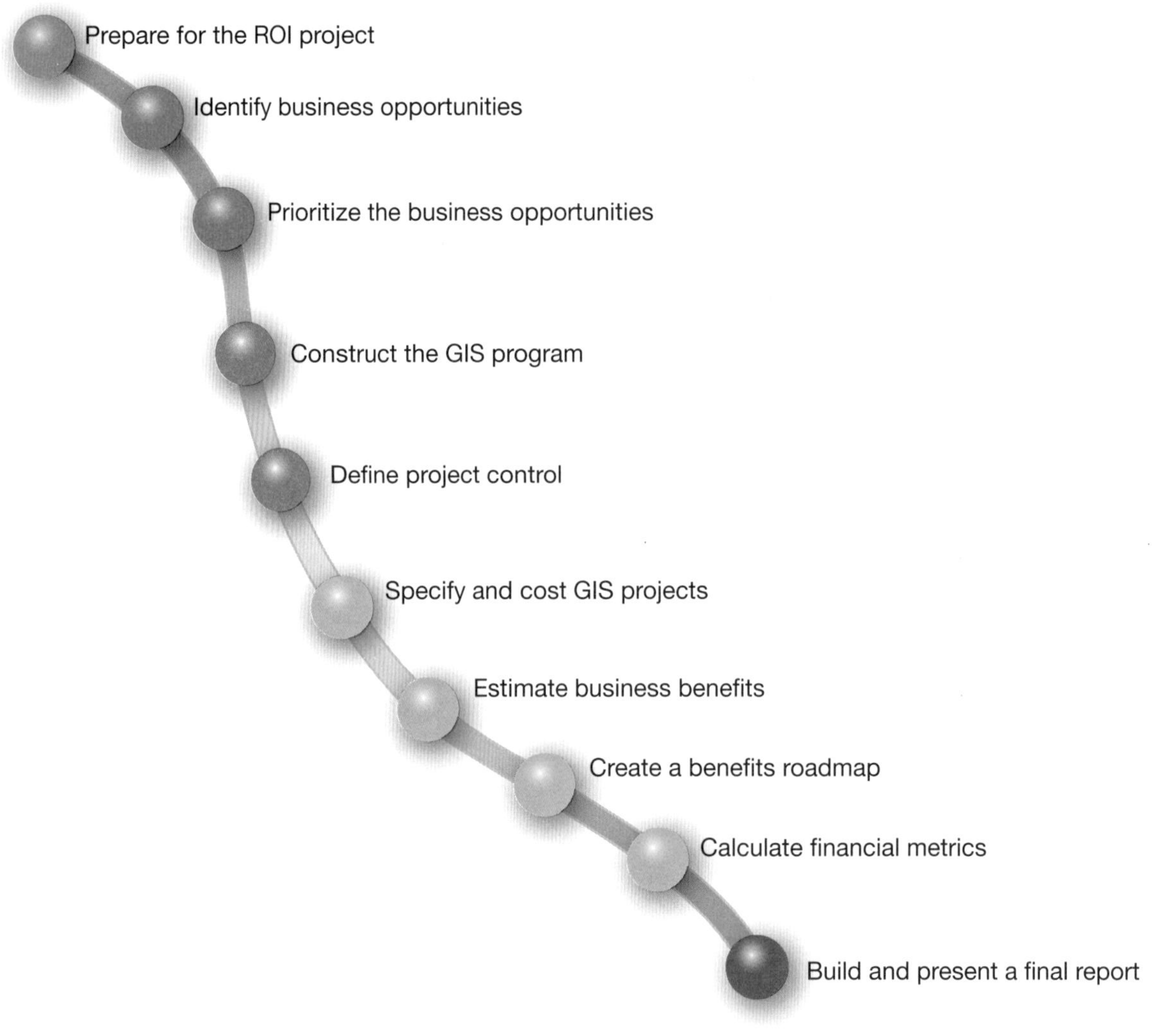

Prepare for the ROI project

Identify business opportunities

Prioritize the business opportunities

Construct the GIS program

Define project control

Specify and cost GIS projects

Estimate business benefits

Create a benefits roadmap

Calculate financial metrics

Build and present a final report

4

Construct the GIS program

Building off the previous interviews and prioritization of business opportunities, this chapter is concerned with defining a series of projects that will successfully deliver some important expected business benefits for an organization. Projects are defined in terms of nine key resource elements: hardware, software, data, process, delivery standards, applications, people, sustainability, and control. A series of example projects is defined in a case study in the final section.

OBJECTIVES

The previous chapters have served to provide the background and planning for justifying new or additional investment in GIS capability at an organization. Among them, highlights of these preliminary steps included gaining a strong understanding of the existing GIS landscape, engaging with key stakeholders to secure their support for the initiative as it moves forward, and identifying and prioritizing the business opportunities identified by senior executives in order to better focus on the areas with the greatest potential for business benefit.

The last chapter defined a collection of business opportunities that set the priorities on where the GIS program should focus delivery effort. This information will be used to define discrete GIS and, possibly, non-GIS projects that will deliver the expected business benefits. These projects, collectively referred to as a program, will consider all the necessary business transformation elements, not just those that are technology oriented.

The process of constructing a GIS program begins with identifying all the project resource elements (for example, hardware, software, data, and people) needed to implement each business opportunity. These elements are then grouped into projects that an organization will need to implement in order to realize benefits from the business opportunities.

PROJECT RESOURCE ELEMENTS AND THE PROJECT DEFINITION PYRAMID

There are nine key business transformation resource elements that need to be considered when defining a program of GIS projects: hardware, software, data, process, delivery standards, applications, people, sustainability, and control. Figure 4.1 shows these elements arranged in a pyramid that communicates how they are all interrelated.

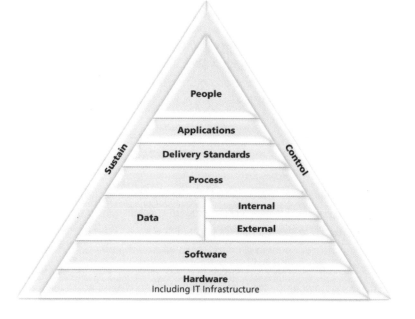

Figure 4.1   The project definition pyramid showing the nine key
GIS project resource elements.

Beginning with the bottom tiers of the pyramid, working upward, the levels are described as follows:

- *Hardware:* All physical devices required within a project's architecture should be considered. This may include workstations, servers, printers, plotters, storage devices, digitizers, and scanners. Both existing IT infrastructure that will be used and new systems should be incorporated into a project definition. It is necessary to decide whether or not a GIS project is best-suited to implementation using a stand-alone desktop, server solution, Web-based client, Web service, or a heterogeneous mix of system architectures.

- *Software:* This tier encompasses the core software systems (e.g., GIS, database management system [DBMS], and Web servers) that will be needed to run the specific applications defined toward the top of the pyramid. Software customization and new software development is considered in the application resource element category. All core software systems should be included in order to obtain an accurate count of licenses.

Insight: Don't omit hardware and software

The required hardware and software elements may already be available in an organization, but new technology solutions and updates to existing systems are released frequently. It is in an organization's best interest, therefore, to ensure that all hardware and software options are properly researched and considered.

- *Data:* There are many facets to consider under the "Data" tier. For instance, an organization will need to decide if data for a GIS project will be provided by internal teams or contracted to external consultants. If the latter, then this will raise questions about whether the data implementation team will be offshore and, if so, whether there are any quality control issues to consider. In addition, it is appropriate to consider things such as data editing, conversion, updating, sanitizing, and maintenance. To assist in addressing these data-related questions and concerns, there may be existing administrative guidelines within an organization that can be followed with respect to data acquisition and consumption.
- *Process:* This tier in the diagram represents the workflow, examined on a few different levels: definition of the current workflow, a statement of what the process should be, and an assessment of the transition, narrating what it will take to arrive at the ideal workflow process. It is in this category that the ownership of various existing projects and services may surface, prompting discussion of the need to identify responsibilities and the presence of checks and balances.
- *Delivery standards:* The most important aspect of standards relates to organizational "change management," considering such things as naming conventions, data protocols, technology rules, and street address standardization. It is likely that an organization's existing change management techniques will be directly involved, and potentially impacted, when defining the standards required for a collection of GIS projects.

- *Applications:* In all but the simplest projects, it will be necessary to develop custom applications that run on top of GIS and other software systems. These applications will need to be outlined so that the time and money required to build them can be considered. As with the "Data" tier, application creation could be an in-house or outsourced activity.

- *People:* The top tier of the pyramid diagram includes all facets of staff and human capital, such as instructors, technical support analysts, database administrators, developers/application programmers, and end users/consumers. By defining the type and number of project participants, it will be possible to estimate, for example, the number of hardware and software licenses, size of servers, and to make an assessment of likely system scalability.

- *Sustainability:* In planning a GIS program, sustaining the projects is as important as the initial setup. It is important to plan for ongoing staffing; hardware, software, and data updates; as well as refreshing some of the other project elements, for example, upgrading an operating system or replacing key staff.

- *Control:* Project governance, or control, is a vital aspect of all IT projects, and GIS is no exception. It is important to define the overarching governance structure that will be needed to manage a project successfully to completion. The topic of control is of such great importance that a whole chapter is devoted to it (see chapter 5).

Insight: Quantifying licenses

When assessing the number of software licenses to purchase, use the "People" category in the top layer of the pyramid in order to identify how many licenses to buy for the optimal level of license management. If senior executives ask you for a justification of the license quantities, you will have valid statistics based on the number of people estimated to be project consumers/users. Ensure you differentiate between licenses required specifically for the GIS projects defined in the current program and those required for other existing or future business operations.

TASKS

✔ 4.1 Define resource elements for each project

The first task on the road to defining a program of projects is to create a brief description of the resource elements that will be required to implement each business opportunity. It should be remembered that great amounts of information are not required, since these descriptions are not being created to define complete project implementation plans, but are simply a mechanism to allow the projects to be easily understood and for the costs to be estimated later (see chapter 6).

For each business opportunity a list needs to be made that defines what is needed to create a project to implement and realize the benefits the business opportunity will bring to an organization. Each project will require hardware, software, data, etc., as described in the project definition pyramid (figure 4.1). A project list will briefly describe each of the resource elements required (e.g., Hardware: A shared server; Software: A multiuser GIS server software license; Data: A geocoded customer database). The descriptions of the project resource elements should be written on separate pieces of paper (sticky Post-it notes, or similar, are ideal for this for reasons that will become apparent in the next task). In the case of the Charles County E911 system discussed in the last two chapters, the following resource elements were required in order to create an implementation project:

- *Hardware:* A multiuser server and a high speed printer.

- *Software:* A multiuser server GIS, a multiuser DBMS, and a desktop word processing system. A maximum of four concurrent users are expected.

- *Data:* Some data will be obtained from the County E911 system and integrated with the County address database. An interface and a data reformatting task will need to be implemented.

- *Process:* The project will encapsulate the following workflow: (1) Interface to police department to obtain E911 false alarm data, (2) Standardize and geocode E911 data using the county address database, (3) Mail-merge addresses with a payment request letter, (4) Test and deploy, and (5) Operate.

- *Delivery standards:* The county's standard general IT and GIS project implementation standards will define the delivery standards for this project.

- *Applications:* Custom applications will be required to interface to the county E911 system, and for address geocoding, mail-merge, and printing.

- *People:* A project manager, application developer, two technical operators, and a database administrator (DBA) will be needed.

- *Sustainability:* There is an ongoing commitment for two technical operators and periodic maintenance by a DBA. Any major changes to the system will be covered by a change request and will form the basis of a new project.

- *Control:* The project will be governed by a project board as defined in the county's IT policy document. This is a relatively small project, so governance will fall under the purview of the existing GIS project board.

✔ 4.2 Rearrange as crosscutting, enterprise projects

Driving a major enterprise IT implementation from a series of individual, departmental projects is not always the most expeditious way to accomplish strategic business transformation in an organization. Typically when projects are defined directly from business opportunities, a program is nothing more than an aggregation of separate projects, and there is overlap and duplication in terms of the use of key resource elements. Additionally, it is possible for the executives that will make go/no-go funding decisions to pick and mix individual projects based on available funding, or their perceptions of value or importance to an organization. A better way to organize the projects, therefore, is to rearrange them not as a series of separate "stovepipe," or vertical projects, but as an integrated collection of crosscutting, or horizontal projects that deal with enterprise requirements for hardware, software, data, people, and so on. This has the added benefit that an organization's specialists can concentrate on projects that fall into their area of expertise and responsibility. For example, the IT department can take control of specifying, obtaining, and implementing hardware and software, and a data processing unit can clean, reformat, and validate data.

The process of rearranging vertically defined projects into horizontally defined ones is quite simple. All the pieces of paper with the resource element descriptions created in task 4.1 need to be sorted into categories based on the pyramid resource element type. For example, all the notes that concern hardware will be put in one pile, software in a second pile, and so on. These piles identify the common groups of activities that will be needed to implement all the business opportunity projects. Closer inspection of the piles of notes may reveal that a number of separate, discrete projects are required for successful implementation. For instance, if there are several notes related to hardware, it will probably be appropriate to create a discrete project that focuses on "hardware infrastructure acquisition and installation." This discrete project can then be scoped, managed, and costed separately from other projects. This helps to isolate like activities into a single project where they can be more effectively managed and delivered.

✔ 4.3 Define the enterprise projects

Once a series of crosscutting discrete projects has been identified, using the process described in the last two tasks, these new projects need to be defined and articulated more fully.

A project definition template is provided (figure 4.2) to assist with the development of standardized project descriptions. The template is used to define overall project objectives, key activities, key outcomes and expected deliverables, and the estimated duration. A document derived from the project definition template should be completed for each of the proposed projects.

Tools: Project definition template

The project definition template is provided to assist you with task 4.3. It is located on the accompanying Web site, http://gis.esri.com/ROI, under step 4. This template encourages you to create a one- or two-statement description of each GIS project, succinct bulleted items to identify the project objectives, a list of numbered key activities, and a description of outcomes and deliverables.

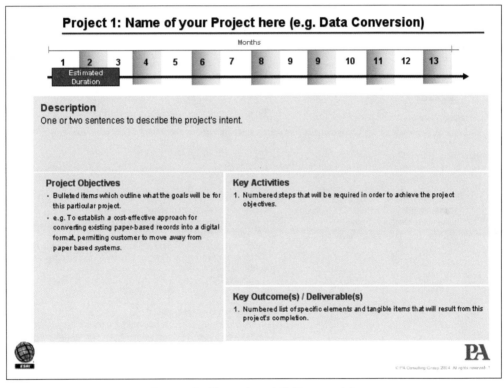

Figure 4.2   The project definition template.

The project definition template has five main areas: duration, description, project objectives, key activities, and key outcomes. The duration is the approximate number of months (or partial months) that it will take to complete the project, not the actual start and end date (this will be added in chapter 8). The description should be one sentence or a few sentences that summarize the project. The project objectives are obviously the main elements that the project seeks to resolve. The key activities are the primary work packages that will be required to implement the objectives. Finally, the key outcomes are the significant business benefits that will be obtained by implementing the project that tie back to the business opportunities from chapter 3. Figure 4.3 shows an example project definition document for the Charles County E911 system described in the last two chapters. This is derived from the descriptions of resource elements created in task 4.1.

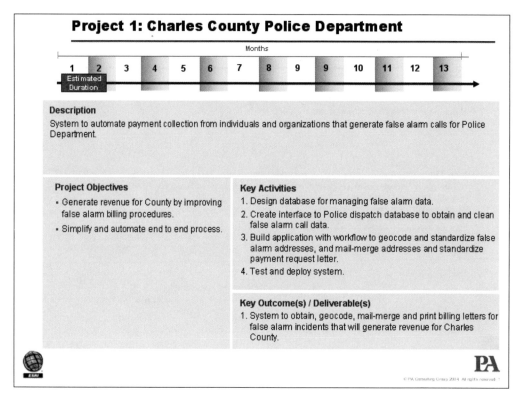

Figure 4.3   Example project definition document for the Charles County E911 system.

✔ 4.4 Arrange the GIS projects in order

Once program definition documents have been completed for each of the projects, the total program should be examined as a portfolio of solutions. When viewed as a whole, it is possible to identify project interdependencies. As such, it is possible to determine the program chronology and assess which project will need to be started and/or completed before another is initialized. For example, if three of the GIS projects presume that data has been collected to provide the materials for the projects, then it can safely be assumed that a fourth project will need to be added to the program that is specific to data mining, tuning, collecting, or sanitizing, for example. Further, this data project must be executed prior to any of the other three projects proposed, since they all depend on the results of this data-specific project.

It should not be assumed that a program will progress as a "waterfall" model, cascading from one project to the next as each is completed. For instance, it may be that two or more projects can proceed at the same time, or that more than one business opportunity can be satisfied by the same project or by the results of multiple projects implemented simultaneously, without disruption or adverse results.

Insight: Stay neutral

When building your portfolio of GIS projects, keep in mind that this program should not include your personal or professional biases or preferences. The program should comprise all projects that would benefit the business processes of the departments and groups as represented by the key stakeholders. It will probably be appropriate to return to your business opportunities spreadsheet (see step 3.2) and the communications you had with all of the members of your stakeholder audience, in order to be sure to include the input from all ROI team members, key executives, business representatives, and operations personnel.

OUTCOME

At the conclusion of this chapter, the completed tasks result in descriptive outlines for all of the projects identified as required to deliver the business opportunities identified in chapter 3. This will include a program of realistic, technology-neutral projects that are defined at a fairly high level in terms of the general duration, overall objectives, key activities that will need to be completed, expected outcomes, and use of project resource elements. This portfolio of business transformation projects will be the basis for the work of all future steps in this methodology, and so it is essential to ensure that they are well defined and that they represent the collective will of an organization. In the next chapter, a governance structure will be defined for this program of works.

CONSTRUCT THE GIS PROGRAM

In this part of the case study, Brian Sobers, GIS manager at the City of Springfield, and his team will turn the business opportunities identified and prioritized in the last chapter into a GIS program of works (a series of GIS projects).

C4.1 Define resource elements for each project

In defining a program of GIS projects, the ROI team looks for a mixture of projects that provide quick and early success to ensure momentum, as well as projects that solve the more challenging long-term issues defined by the executives. After analyzing the opportunities prioritized in the Springfield business opportunities document (figures C3.1 and C3.2), the team decides to focus on several of the high- and medium-priority projects, four in total: Tree Cover Assessment, Fire Hydrant Inspection and Maintenance, Brownfield Site Finder, and Inward Investment Application.

Using the project definition pyramid as a guide, the team first identifies and describes all the resource elements needed to implement each of the business opportunities. Each of the resource element descriptions is written on a Post-it note.

C4.2 Rearrange as crosscutting, enterprise projects

The Post-it notes for describing the resource elements are then grouped by element category to help spot areas where the city should implement crosscutting, enterprise projects. The team realizes that the projects they defined have a requirement for a citywide basemap and a standardized street address database. In both cases the data already exists within Springfield, but it needs to be cleaned, integrated, and reformatted for use in the GIS program. They, therefore, add two additional foundational projects that implement these capabilities. The team also contemplated aggregating all the hardware acquisition and installation activities into a single project, but in the end decided against this because of the highly devolved nature of the IT support function in the city. Thus, the final six projects defined by Brian and the ROI team are the following:

Citywide Basemap Web Service

Citywide Geocodable Address Database

Tree Cover Assessment

Fire Hydrant Inspection and Maintenance

Brownfield Site Finder

Inward Investment Application

C4.3 Define the enterprise projects

The next task is to define and articulate more fully the six enterprise projects identified previously using the project definition template (figure 4.2). Details of the six projects that Brian and the team defined are in the file "Springfield_Project_Definition.ppt," available on the accompanying Web site, http://gis.esri.com/roi. Information about one of the projects is included here by way of illustration (figure C4.1). More information about the technology and architecture is presented in section C6.1 in chapter 6.

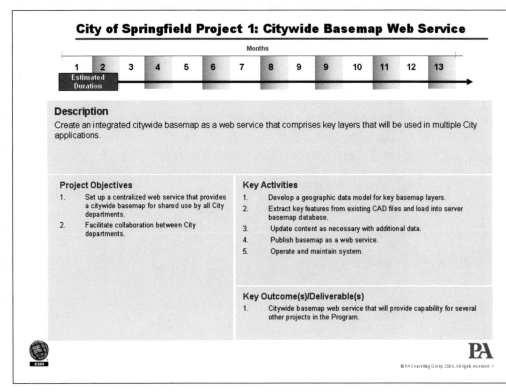

Figure C4.1 Citywide basemap Web service project for the City of Springfield.

Given the strong departmental organizational structure at the City of Springfield, only two of the projects that Brian and his team defined could be considered truly "enterprise" and crosscutting, the citywide basemap Web service and the citywide geocodable address database. Although this is not ideal, given the structure of the City of Springfield, this is probably the best that can be achieved.

C4.4   Arrange the GIS projects in order

As part of the process of arranging the projects into an overall program, the ROI team consults with Brian's boss about other projects and initiatives that are underway within the city to ensure that their plans mesh with any other high-priority activities currently underway. Brian then rearranges the order of the projects to reflect the sequence in which they will be undertaken. Even though almost all of the projects are in separate departments, they cannot be undertaken at the same time because the same resources will be needed on several of the projects (e.g., GIS manager and enterprise servers). The final order of projects is as follows:

P1. Citywide Basemap Web Service

P2. Citywide Geocodable Address Database

P3. Brownfield Site Finder

P4. Inward Investment Application

P5. Tree Cover Assessment

P6. Fire Hydrant Inspection and Maintenance

Figure C8.1 in chapter 8 provides a good view of the timelines for each of the projects in diagram form.

C4.5   Discussion of chapter 4 case study

In this chapter, Brian Sobers and his ROI team draw extensively on their technical GIS skills. The main task is to translate the business opportunities into real enterprise GIS projects that can be implemented. The final description of each of the projects outlines only the major steps to be followed and the expected outcomes. The projects do not need to be described in any greater detail—this is not an implementation plan–since at this juncture the purpose is only to establish the ROI case for GIS projects within the city. In addition to the four substantive projects identified in the previous business opportunities chapter, two new, crosscutting projects were added that provide foundation basemap and geocoding Web services for the other projects. Decisions such as this are organization-specific, but generally it makes sense to look for crosscutting projects that will act as enterprise GIS enablers.

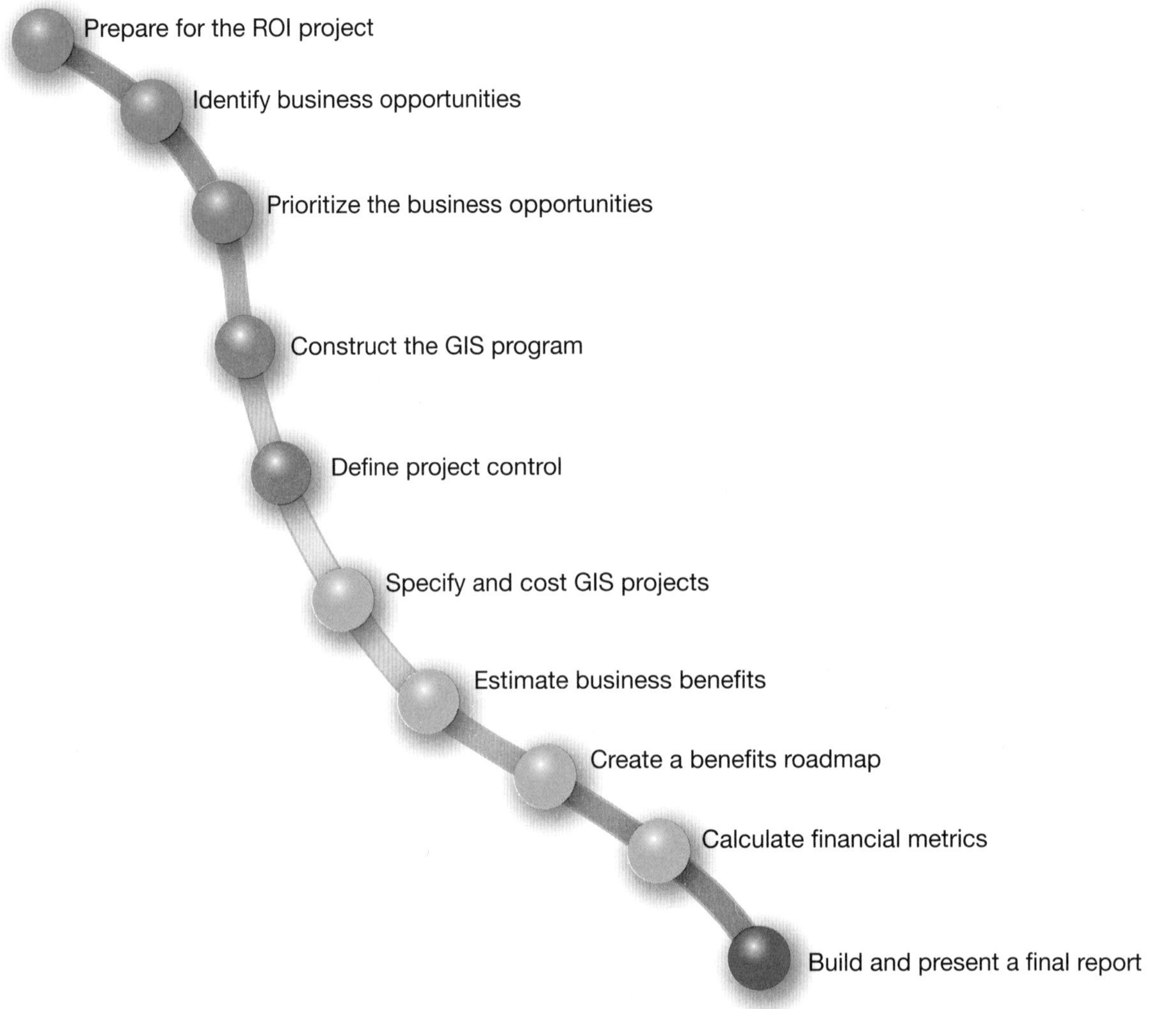

Prepare for the ROI project

Identify business opportunities

Prioritize the business opportunities

Construct the GIS program

Define project control

Specify and cost GIS projects

Estimate business benefits

Create a benefits roadmap

Calculate financial metrics

Build and present a final report

5

 Define project control

Clear lines of responsibility and accountability are vital aspects of successful IT projects. This chapter allows organizations to assess their ability to manage a GIS program to successful completion. It also looks at team design for a GIS program based upon structuring appropriate resources, both internal and external, to optimize the program team. The case study material in the final section shows how these can be used in a project.

OBJECTIVES

It is a well-accepted fact that many GIS programs fail to deliver the value that was expected as a consequence of the following:

- The programs are treated as technology projects, not change management initiatives.

- There is a lack of organizational support at all business levels.

- There is an absence of strong governance and project control.[1]

The material within this chapter will help ensure the right level of program governance is in place to improve the chances of success and to manage the inevitable changes that will occur throughout the life of a GIS program.

The first objective will be to assess the prospective delivery team's current level of program governance capability and maturity. Using a capability maturity model (CMM) template (figure 5.1), the ROI team will examine the prospective program team's current strengths to determine the required level of competency to successfully deliver the GIS program, defined in the previous chapter. Naturally, each GIS program has a different depth of complexity, so the right level of governance will be different for every program.

					1	2	3

Capability	Capability Description	Current Capability	Desired Capability	Rationale for Desired Capability Score	Entrant		
Change Management	The ability of GIS Team to effectively manage changes in scope will be essential for delivering the project on time and budget				No change control process is in place. When changes are accepted, work has to be re-prioritized with little consideration of the impact on project delivery schedule.		
Communication	The level of acceptance of users to change will be impacted by the quality, quantity and timeliness of communications they receive i.e. how well informed they are of changes and how it will impact them. It will also be impacted by the level to which users are listened to.				Limited and ad-hoc communication between stakeholders and project team.		

Figure 5.1   The "Change Management" and "Communication" categories
of the capability maturity model.

The secondary key objective, therefore, is to define a team structure that exhibits the characteristics of a well-structured and functioning GIS department or program team.

By completing the two tasks described below, the GIS program will be structured and managed in an effective way, from both the project lead and stakeholder perspectives. This provides everyone in an organization additional confidence that the GIS program will be successful.

TASKS

✔ 5.1 Rank competencies

There are several methods to assess the maturity level of an organization's program governance structure. The method developed as part of this ROI methodology involves assessing the relative maturity of established processes and procedures using a set of survey-type categories, based on a Likert scale of 1 to 10 (see figure 5.1). This approach is often referred to as a *capability maturity model* (CMM). Borne out of assessment work in the information technology industry, in this case it provides a process improvement tool, through which a project team can evaluate a project governance plan's strengths and weaknesses.

3 4 5	6 7	8 9
Developing	**Committed**	**Best Practice**
Change requests are documented and follow a process, which includes a suitably represented change control board. Some informal consideration of impact. Possible residual resistance to the process exists.	Change requests are recorded and follow a clearly defined process, which includes a change control board and a person assigned to coordinate the process. Impact Assessments are carried out for perceived major changes. Following change request acceptance, project plans are updated. Deliverables are under change control.	Change control is embedded in the delivery lifecycle and accepted as part of the process by the stakeholder and project community. Impact assessments are carried out for all change requests. A change control board is in place to evaluate changes. Changes requests are formally recorded. Project deliverables are under change control. Project plans are updated following changes. Process linked to configuration and release management.
Regular, clear communications are distributed	Communication plan exists and is adhered to, which outlines reporting and communication frequency, audience (including project team) and format. Communications are regular, clear and timely.	Published communication plan exists and is adhered to. Communications are timely, clear and honest. Stakeholders have opportunity to provide feedback.

The key process areas assessed in the ROI methodology competency evaluation are generally considered part of the traditional IT program management best practices: change management, communication, document management, delivery standards, financial management, planning and estimating, project management, requirements management, risk and issue management, testing and quality assurance, vision and strategy, vendor management, and version control and configuration management. Each of these categories is assessed on a 10-point (low to high) scale. To assist with ranking under each category, four maturity levels are used: entrant, developing, committed, and best practice. Full definitions of the maturity levels are provided in the CMM template.

Tools: Capability maturity model

The capability maturity model (figure 5.1) provides a model from which you measure your organization's program management competencies. The digital file can be found on the supporting Web site, http://gis.esri.com/roi, under step 5.

In order to make the most out of the CMM tool, assemble the ROI team and then collectively review, discuss (sometimes constructively argue), and agree on both the current rankings and the desired rankings. This approach has been applied successfully in the past by having one person facilitate the discussion, often using a projector for display, presenting the CMM categories one at a time for discussion and debate.

Using the CMM template, for each of the key process areas, the team collectively ranks its view of the *current maturity*—that is, where the prospective program team is today—and the *desired maturity*—that is, where the team needs to be in order to provide confidence to all stakeholders that the program has the appropriate governance structure and therefore a higher probability of success. It is important to undertake an honest analysis of how the organization is currently ordered for success, including managing risk, handling change, and encouraging open communication. Once all the assessments have been entered into the document derived from the CMM template, a spider diagram will automatically be generated by the embedded macros. This diagram will serve to visually punctuate the gaps between existing and desired organizational maturities (figure 5.2 shows an example spider diagram). The spider diagram demonstrates that, in this example, there are some significant gaps between the current level of maturity, shown in blue, and the desired level of maturity, shown in orange.

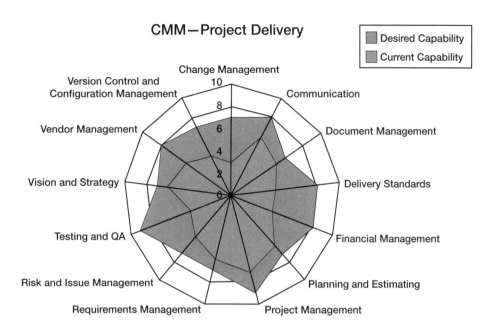

CMM—Project Delivery

Legend:
- Desired Capability
- Current Capability

Axes (clockwise from top): Change Management, Communication, Document Management, Delivery Standards, Financial Management, Planning and Estimating, Project Management, Requirements Management, Risk and Issue Management, Testing and QA, Vision and Strategy, Vendor Management, Version Control and Configuration Management

Scale: 0, 2, 4, 6, 8, 10

Figure 5.2 Example capability maturity model spider diagram.

In the case of the example shown in figure 5.2, it can easily be seen that the area of "Testing and QA" has the largest gap between the current and desired competency capabilities, with a current maturity level of "4," but a desired level of "9." The spider diagram provides a means to plan specific actions to shrink the gaps. For instance, to bridge this gap, some of the GIS implementation team could take a training course to acquire the latest certification in QA/QC methods; or perhaps set up a more formalized process for software unit testing; or establish a new QA testing lab dedicated to usability and quality control. Once the competency gaps have been identified, and procedures are in place to eliminate or reconcile the differences, the organization is ensuring a more robust design of program management in preparation for successful project delivery.

Of course, not every desired capability needs to have a rank of 9 or 10. It will be necessary to weight and prioritize the key capability areas according to the specific requirements of an organization and GIS program. For instance, the team may collectively assess that if "Document Management" scored a maturity level of "6," this would be adequate, since regular backups and recovery testing are not deemed necessary. The justification for scoring each capability on the CMM template should be recorded in the CMM document in the column provided ("Rationale for Desired Capability Score").

The CMM and resulting spider diagram is a simple yet powerful way to determine if an organization has the appropriate and acceptable level of governance to ensure delivery success. It can also be used as a device to initiate training activities to improve an organization's program management skills and practices.

✔ 5.2 Determine optimal team design

After task 5.1, the ROI team should have a strong understanding of the capabilities required for success. The CMM visually communicates the skills that will be needed in the implementation process of a GIS. Not surprisingly, it may often be concluded that in order to establish a more comprehensive program governance structure, some additional resources need to be added or the implementation team augmented with new skills. For example, it may be necessary to reconfigure the existing team's responsibilities and reporting structure, or add additional capabilities from other parts of an organization, or perhaps from an outside vendor/contractor.

With respect to these potential changes, it is also recommended that the characteristics of the existing team be assessed in relation to those that represent an ideally structured and organized GIS program implementation team. A well-designed GIS program team needs to exhibit several important organizational characteristics in order to be successful:

1. **Agile:** This refers to the team's ability to respond to shifting technology and business needs by changing the required mix of competencies quickly.

2. **Innovative:** The team should be able to take advantage of new technologies and best practices as they develop in the marketplace, and not simply continue doing things as they always have in the past.

3. **Able to manage risk:** It is important to identify and manage the inevitable program risks by sharing them with vendors and internal business partners in a balanced way.

4. **Collaborative:** The GIS program team cannot own and undertake everything, and instead should try to leverage the expertise that exists in the marketplace and within other internal business units, such as the IT department.

5. **Commercially-driven:** In the modern world, all organizations need to look for ways to reduce costs and improve operating efficiencies, for example, by putting metrics and controls into commercial contracts with vendors to effectively manage accountability and quality of service.

6. **Service-based:** One of the best ways to improve operating effectiveness is to maintain a consistent focus on service quality to both internal and external customers.

7. **Business-focused:** This helps to ensure that a GIS program retains and fosters domain expertise relating to the strategy and business goals of an organization. Unfortunately, GIS teams can become technology-driven and, often unknowingly, lose their focus on delivering what the organization *really* needs.

To be certain that an organization has an appropriate and complete governance team for controlling a GIS program, it is useful to diagram the proposed team structure. A program organizational design template (figure 5.3) is provided on the accompanying Web site for this purpose (http://gis.esri.com/roi). The diagram groups the organizational roles into three groups: the program team, internal vendors, and external vendors. Distinction between these groups is important because of the way they are typically funded and organized, and how they contribute to the management process.

The program team comprises all the people directly participating in the GIS program. There are three subgroups. The executive oversight committee is usually staffed by a small number of senior executives drawn from the main stakeholder units, and chaired by an independent, experienced senior staff member (a vice-president or director). The GIS program manager will typically represent the project members of the business primes (the representatives of business units participating in the projects). The core program team is made up of senior leads from the projects within the GIS program. Each of these major business units will usually be asked to nominate a lead or prime to represent the unit's interests in the governance process.

The internal vendors group is made up of all the teams within the organization that will be providing services to the GIS program. Typically, this will be teams from the IT, Finance, Data Processing, and Office Services departments, but there may be many others, depending on the nature of the project.

The external vendors group comprises all the hardware, software, data, and other consulting groups engaged to support the GIS program. Some of these may be long-term full-time participants that work under contract within the organization, whereas others may operate offshore.

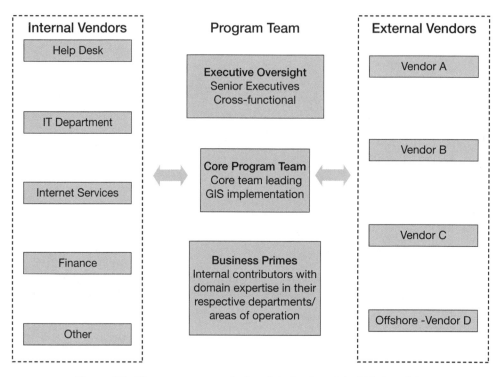

Figure 5.3 The program organizational design template. This template can be modified to show the high-level delivery management or governance structure for a program.

Insight: Determining the optimal team composition

It is very important to determine the best balance between an outsourced and in-house team composition that is most appropriate and effective for an organization (see figure 5.3). Attention should be focused on the key characteristics of good organizational design: agility, innovation, risk management, collaboration, commercially-driven, service-based, and business-focused.

When designing a team to support and deliver the benefits of a series of GIS projects, the immediate reaction may be to hire resources to build in-house teams that can perform software development, technical support, customer service, and so on. But of course, these are just a few of the many skill sets that will be required to support the various life cycles of one or more GIS projects. If all of the resources are recruited as full-time, in-house employees, be aware that there will probably need to be a budgetary figure for this support team, since they will need continuous training and development, in addition to the standard operating expenses for maintaining full-time employees (FTEs). Further, when using in-house resources, ensure that there is a plan to use them beyond the current project(s), as well as the time required for any necessary training or introductory experience.

Clearly, it is not mandatory to build a GIS program implementation team solely using in-house FTEs. External service providers can be used as well, particularly when special skills are required, or for one-time-only specialist consultations. In this way, as organizational changes occur, a more suitable external vendor can quickly be retained to provide consulting services. In addition, an organization will be selecting the specific domain experts required who can collaborate with in-house teams to better strategize and meet the business goals of an organization. No matter how the team is designed, the goal is to craft a GIS program support structure that is fully prepared for changes and able to overcome obstacles. This means that the contributing members of the team will need to know how to adapt quickly when technologies change, treating them as opportunities for new enhancements or project improvements.

If engaging with outsourced providers, it is important that an organization ensures that enforceable service level agreements (SLAs) are in place to guarantee the level of quality and performance that is expected from these external entities. Proper contracts guarantee the ability to correct or terminate any vendors and providers that do not meet the requirements of the agreements, which ensures expectations are met and the quality of service to customers or citizens is upheld. By staying in control of contracts with vendors or service providers, the program team can continue to support the premise that it is commercially-driven and focused on the business goals of an organization.

This task has attempted to provide some guidance on how to build a core GIS program team that will embody the optimal organizational characteristics. It is of course more complicated than simply looking at which groups might perform what tasks on a GIS project. It concerns building the right long-term relationships and partnerships with both internal and third-party service providers (e.g., vendors, contractors, and consultants—both onshore and offshore). There is no single right answer for an optimized GIS organizational design, but the guidelines presented here should help to ensure that the widest possibilities have been considered for a GIS program governance structure.

OUTCOME

This chapter has identified the capability level of the core GIS program team, and highlighted any areas of potential weakness in program governance that need to be addressed. The purpose of this is to allow appropriate action to be taken to shore up areas of deficiency so that a GIS program is given the best chance for success. Determining that a GIS program has the right level of governance will give both the program manager and the executives confidence that the program is set up to succeed.

The tasks in this chapter are also designed to structure the team of internal staff and external vendors in the most effective way possible so that it can deliver consistent and reliable results throughout the execution phase of a GIS program, both in terms of quality and cost.

Case Study

DEFINE PROJECT CONTROL

Between defining the GIS projects in the last chapter and specifying and costing them in the next, Brian Sobers and his team, who are undertaking the GIS ROI study at the City of Springfield, take a diversion following the course set by the methodology to consider how the GIS program will best be managed.

C5.1 Rank of competencies

The first task for the ROI team is to consider the ability of the eventual GIS implementation team to successfully deliver the expected business benefits in the ROI methodology; this is achieved by determining the GIS program team's current and desired capabilities with respect to the program requirements. The first part of the results of using the capability maturity model (CMM) is shown in figure C5.1. A digital version of the full document is on the accompanying Web site, http://gis.esri.com/roi, in the file "Springfield CMM.xls."

Figure C5.1 (following pages)   First part of completed capability maturity model for the City of Springfield.

Capability	Capability Description	Current Capability	Desired Capability	Rationale for Desired Capability Score	Entrant
Change Management	The ability of GIS Team to effectively manage changes in scope will be essential for delivering the project on time and budget	2	5	The GIS projects are relatively small and self-contained and do not need an overly complex bureaucracy.	No change control process is in place. When changes are accepted, work has to be re-prioritized with little consideration of the impact on project delivery schedule.
Communication	The level of acceptance of users to change will be impacted by the quality, quantity and timeliness of communications they receive i.e. how well informed they are of changes and how it will impact them. It will also be impacted by the level to which users are listened to.	2	8	Communication is essential in City government and this is one of the big areas on which the City is trying to improve.	Limited and ad-hoc communication between stakeholders and project team.
Document Management	The ability of GIS Team to effectively manage documentation associated with the project will improve all stages of project delivery from requirements management through to user adoption	3	6	This is essential to multiple participation in a distributed, multi-department implementation.	Documents contain a version history page but are not formally version controlled. They are not stored in a structured manner and it is unknown what document versions exist.
Delivery Standards	The level to which standards are documented as well as their completeness, quality and level of adoption will impact the ability of the GIS Team to deliver the project	2	7	The City needs strong standards for sharing information internally and externally. Transparency is an essential requirement of local government.	Individual and ad-hoc standards employed by project team members. No consistency.
Financial Management	The level of rigor applied to fiscal matters will determine whether budget is secured and quantifiable value derived	2	7	City is not strong on automated financial analysis. One of the goals of the current initiative is to tighten up the way the City justifies projects.	Substantial manual assimilation required to determine financial picture of project (e.g. cost to complete, spend vs. budget). No documented business case and indefensible budget.
Planning and Estimating	The ability of GIS Team to understand project status, the level of resources consumed to date, the level of resources required to complete the project and ongoing progress will determine whether stakeholders remain committed and delivery credibility is established	3	6	Frequent reports on project status require a formal planning and estimating mechanism.	No overall project plan exists.
Project Management	The ability of the GIS Team to effectively manage the project to deadlines, manage the stakeholders, and the project resources to consistently deliver the GIS on time and to budget.	3	7	IT projects such as GIS are new at the City and so a full-time PM will be required to keep things on track and to communicate status.	There is not a full-time, dedicated project manager. Progress is not measured but probably behind where is should be. Project conflicts remain unresolved. Stakeholder management is ad-hoc at best.
Requirements Management	The ability of GIS Team to deliver a solution that meets the needs of the users is reliant upon requirements being clearly defined, documented and managed.	4	7	User involvement is essential to the success of this project, so well established requirements analysis is key.	No requirements management process exists. No business requirements exist.
Risk and Issue Management	The ability of GIS Team to identify, document, escalate and mitigate risks and issues will determine whether the project is successfully delivered or derailed.	3	5	The size and scope of the GIS projects does not require detailed risk management.	No management of risk or issues.
Testing and QA	The ability of the GIS Team to ensure the quality and reliability of the project delivered is reliant on effective testing and QA.	3	7	The technical capabilities of end users are limited and so it is important that robust and reliable applications are delivered.	Ad-hoc testing and unstructured QA.
Vision and Strategy	A clearly articulated vision may mean the difference between all stakeholders pulling in the same direction or in many directions, which is likely to lead to project delivery failure	4	8	A clearly articulated vision and strategy is critical to the success of this project. As much as anything else this project will set the future agenda for how the City delivers change.	Some ideas but no communicated vision or strategy
Vendor Management	The level to which Vendors are managed including at the time of proposal and sourcing, contractual matters, performance management and ultimately whether the GIS Team gets what it paid for	5	9	Strong vendor management is important to the ongoing success of this project. The City must ensure sound practices and even-handedness.	No vendor management
Version Control and Configuration Management.	The level to which the GIS Team manages versions of the system, associated source code and images	2	5	Given the limited IT capabilities of user departments a centralized version control system will be implemented.	Source code and versions are not managed. Multiple versions of each probably exist.

Developing	Committed	Best Practice
Change requests are documented and follow a process, which includes a suitably represented change control board. Some informal consideration of impact. Possible residual resistance to the process exists.	Change requests are recorded and follow a clearly defined process, which includes a change control board and a person assigned to coordinate the process. Impact Assessments are carried out for perceived major changes. Following change request acceptance, project plans are updated. Deliverables are under change control.	Change control is embedded in the delivery lifecycle and accepted as part of the process by the stakeholder and project community. Impact assessments are carried out for all change requests. A change control board is in place to evaluate changes. Changes requests are formally recorded. Project deliverables are under change control. Project plans are updated following changes. Process linked to configuration and release management.
Regular, clear communications are distributed	Communication plan exists and is adhered to, which outlines reporting and communication frequency, audience (including project team) and format. Communications are regular, clear and timely.	Published communication plan exists and is adhered to. Communications are timely, clear and honest. Stakeholders have opportunity to provide feedback.
A project folder is established e.g. network drive ,which contains what are likely to be most documents and latest versions (e.g.. possibly including a document inventory) although there is no assurance of this.	A version controlled project library is established. It contains the latest versions of documentation in a single, accessible location. All versions of a document are present and a process is in place to make documentation updates.	A project library is established and version controlled. It contains the latest versions of documentation in a single, accessible location. All versions of a document are present and a process is in place to make documentation updates. The project library is backed-up regularly and recovery tested periodically.
Delivery standards documented and informal methodology adopted and adhered to consistently within project team	Consistent, end-to-end formal delivery method adopted and used within the project. Delivery standards documented	Sophisticated end-to-end delivery methodology adopted consistently and standards fully documented and embedded within the project
Defensible budget created and supported by business case. Substantial manual assimilation required to determine financial picture of project.	Defensible budget supported by business case. Project value appreciated but communicated infrequently. Manual assimilation of financial picture required.	Defensible and comprehensive budget created, supported by business case. Project value clearly understood and used a delivery and reporting metric. Complete project financial picture available with minimal assimilation
High level project plan exists and is used by project team to understand delivery schedule and key work areas.	Detailed project plan exists and includes resources. Project plan is used by the project team to understand progress, activities, milestones and dependencies. An agreed work breakdown structure exists and has complete scope coverage.	Detailed project plan exists and is used by the team as the primary means of understand work, progress, milestones and dependencies. All resources and activities are reflected in the plan. An agreed work breakdown structure exists and has complete scope coverage. Estimates exists for levels of rework, risks and contingency. The level of unscheduled work is measured.
A full-time, dedicated project manager is in place. Progress is measured occasionally against a baseline. Project is broadly on track.	A suitably qualified project manager is dedicated fulltime to manage the project. Progress is measured occasionally against a baseline. Project is on track. Stakeholders are motivated and committed.	A suitably qualified project manager is dedicated, fulltime to manage the project. Progress is measured frequently and in detail against the baseline. Project conflicts are resolved swiftly and fairly. Stakeholders, including the project team are managed in a structured way to ensure all parties remain motivated and committed. Morale is high and project is on track or ahead of schedule.
High level requirements documented. No formal process for sign-off or management of requirements.	Detailed requirements documented. Requirements signed-off by users.	Detailed requirements fully documented including source of requirement. Requirements stored in suitable repository under change management and link to test case development. Requirement gathering process includes user sign-off.
Some risks and issues documented but not frequently reviewed and no mitigating actions in place.	Detailed risk register and issue log in place. Updated and reviewed occasionally. Most risks and issues have owners identified.	Comprehensive risk register and issue log available. Frequently reviewed and proactively managed. All risks and issues have identified owners and mitigating actions. Contingency plans in place for high probability, high impact risks.
Test and QA process documented and adhered to.	Test and QA process documented, appropriate for the project and adhered to. Established strategy detailed and roles and responsibilities clearly defined. Stable test environment exists and is baselined. Formal plans and scripts available. QA conducted to high quality but low coverage.	Test process defined, documented, appropriate for the project and adhered to. Test strategy detailed and roles and responsibilities clearly defined. Stable test environment exists and is baselined. Formal plans and scripts are available and include entry and exit criteria. Test tools used to facilitate process e.g. fault tracking, load testers etc. QA conducted to high level (both quality and coverage).
Clearly defined and communicated vision, helping to pull stakeholders in the same direction. Unimplementable strategy.	Clearly defined and communicated vision, helping to pull stakeholders in the same direction. Implementable short-term strategy	Clearly articulated vision communicated to all relevant stakeholders. Implementable strategy for the short, medium and long term tied to benefits and value delivery.
Preferred suppliers established and some understanding of market rates. Vendors perceived to deliver.	Preferred suppliers established but reviewed periodically. Good understanding of value of money and market rates. GIS Team ensures that contractual obligations are satisfied.	Strong understanding of vendor rates and value for money concepts. Framework contracts in place with key vendors to benefit from bulk sourcing. Vendors consistently deliver high proven quality and vendors are performance measured. GIS Team checks that contractual obligations are satisfied.
Source code is managed using a configuration management tool but GIS versions are not. Multiple GIS versions are in use.	Source code and versions are managed using configuration management tools. A single GIS version is in use. Releases are deployed ad-hoc.	Source code and versions are managed. Releases are bundled prior to deployment.

Brian Sobers and the ROI team complete the template by organizing a working session with a digital projector. They display the capability maturity model and step through each capability category one by one, discussing, debating, and gaining consensus on what the current and required (desired) level of maturity would need to be for success.

The spreadsheet template automatically creates a spider diagram that allows the team to compare current (actual) and desired capabilities for Springfield (figure C5.2). This diagram clearly shows that in all cases the desired capability (orange) exceeds the current capability (blue). The biggest gaps are in the areas of communication, delivery standards (definition of what will be provided at the conclusion of a project), and financial management. This can easily be observed using the spreadsheet summary (figure C5.3).

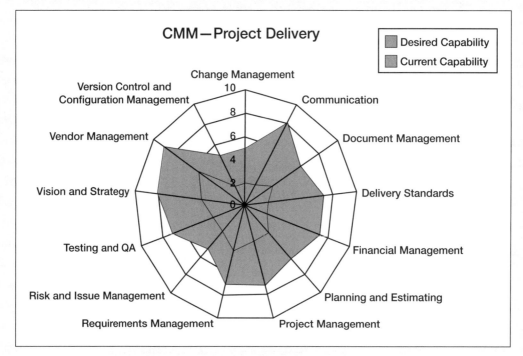

Figure C5.2   City of Springfield CMM spider diagram.

Category	Capability Measure	Current Rank	Desired Rank	Magnitude of Change
Project Delivery	Change Management	2	5	3
	Communication	2	8	6
	Document Management	3	6	3
	Delivery Standards	2	7	5
	Financial Management	2	7	5
	Planning and Estimating	3	6	3
	Project Management	3	7	4
	Requirements Management	4	7	3
	Risk and Issue Management	3	5	2
	Testing and QA	3	7	4
	Vision and Strategy	4	8	4
	Vendor Management	5	9	4
	Version Control and Configuration Management.	2	5	3

Figure C5.3   City of Springfield CMM summary.

These are areas that Springfield's implementation teams must improve. For example, the teams could take some training, work internally to improve processes, or add other resources that have competence in the deficient areas. Although the gap for vendor management is slightly less, it has the highest score on desirability, and it should also be added to the action list.

C5.2   Completed program organizational design chart

To demonstrate that a GIS program will be effectively managed, the ROI methodology advocates creating an organizational design diagram (figure C5.4) to highlight the people responsible and accountable for successfully completing the GIS program of work. Given that the projects in the program at this stage are only hypothetical, the exact composition of the governance team is only anticipated. The people in the proposed governance team are drawn from several departments in the City of Springfield and represent the key groups that will be affected by GIS. In formulating the governance team, the executives at the City of Springfield were keen to give all major players a voice and to include people with the appropriate range of talents. Like all major projects at the City of Springfield, three senior executives will be nominated by the city manager to provide executive oversight. The business primes are representative experts from the participating departments. Two of the external vendors with which the city has long-term contracts are defined—Dell (hardware supplier) and ESRI (GIS software provider)—but a third external vendor that will assist with application development will be determined during the course of the program through open procurement. Finally, the IS Department will be providing some support services to set up hardware and associated systems, and the Finance Department will control the program budget.

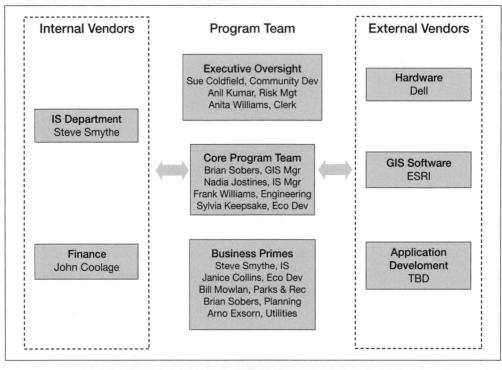

Figure C5.4 Program organizational design diagram for the City of Springfield GIS program.

C5.3 Discussion of chapter 5 case study

It is a well-accepted tenet that the main reason why IT projects fail is because of poor management. Thus, governance and accountability are critical to the success of any major program; and of equal importance is the fact that it is critical to convince an executive management group that the right team, with the right controls and structure, will be able to deliver on the expected benefits. Assessing any team's capability, especially on subjective topics such as planning and estimating, and vision and leadership, is difficult, and there are frequently divergent views. Nonetheless, active discussion and convergence of views in the long run is a good way to create shared understanding and responsibility, as well as to build a team. Looking at the organization design diagram (figure C5.4), the City of Springfield appears relatively light on internal and external vendors, mainly due to the domain-specific nature of the proposed projects and the city's wish to use in-house resources wherever possible. On the other hand, the program team is quite complete in its specification and well-supplied with talent.

Endnote

1. Sugarbaker, L., "Managing an operational GIS," in *Geographical information systems,* ed. P. A. Longley, M. F. Goodchild, D. J. Maguire, and D. W. Rhind (London: John Wiley & Sons, Inc., 1999), 611–20; Douglas, B., *Achieving business success with GIS* (Chichester: John Wiley & Sons, Inc., 2008).

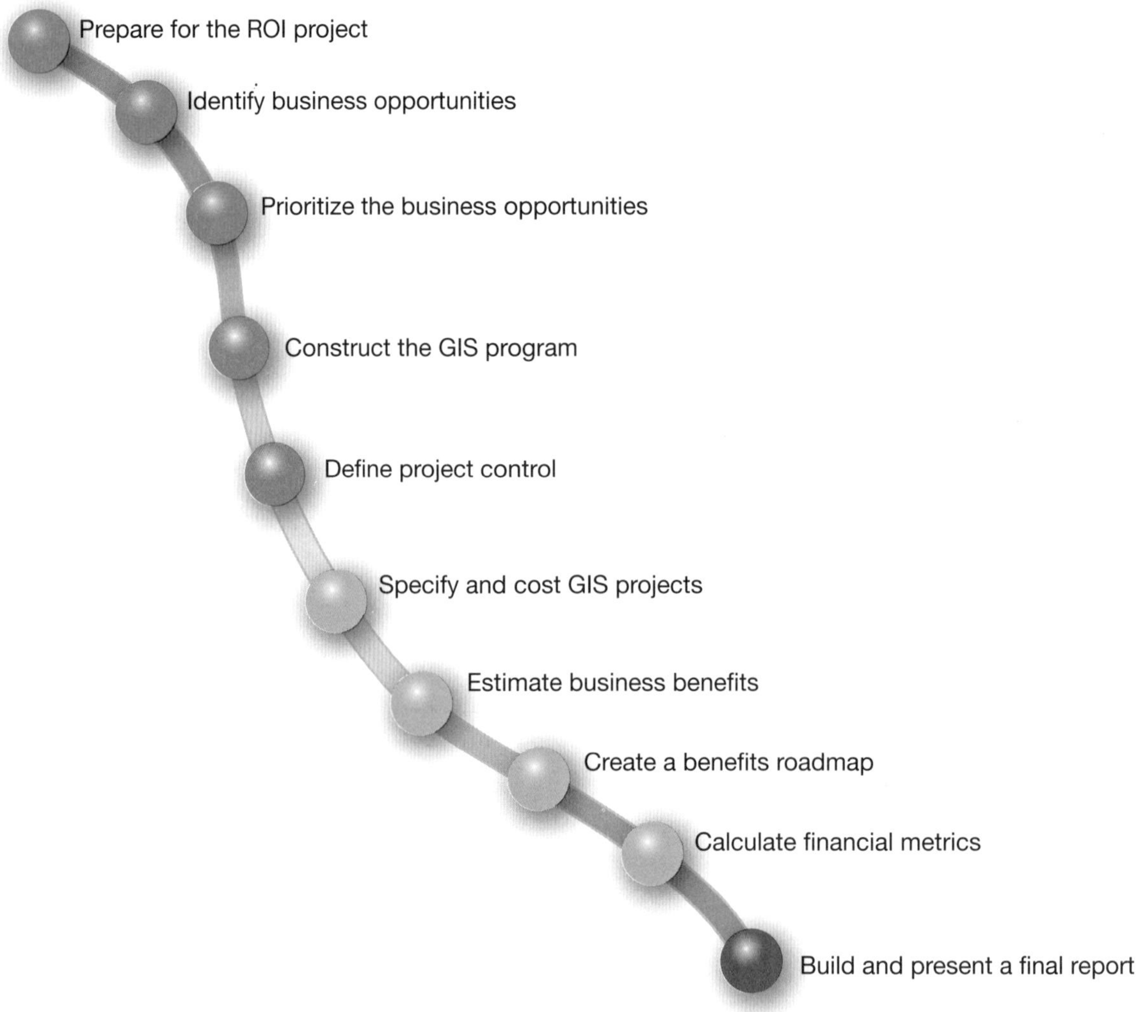

Prepare for the ROI project

Identify business opportunities

Prioritize the business opportunities

Construct the GIS program

Define project control

Specify and cost GIS projects

Estimate business benefits

Create a benefits roadmap

Calculate financial metrics

Build and present a final report

6

Specify and cost GIS projects

No return on investment study can be complete without specifying the costs associated with a program of projects. This task is achieved by creating a budget that defines all the program resource types, quantities, and associated costs. This chapter steps through the process of specifying and costing the projects for a three-year period using a budget template. Once complete, the budget will be used to drive later timeline and financial calculations. The case study for the City of Springfield includes all of these ideas in the final section.

Creating a budget is essential for estimating the cost side of equations that calculate financial measures of business success. This chapter will detail the construction of a three-year GIS program budget. During this process each of the GIS projects, established in previous chapters, will be broken down into constituent parts, and quantities and costs will be specified in a structured and logical manner. The costs will be assembled into a budget worksheet that summarizes the expenditures and provides a series of useful financial budgetary indicators and charts.

OBJECTIVES

The objective of this chapter is to build a well-thought-out budget that will stand up to scrutiny and dissection by key executives or members of an organization's finance department. The team undertaking the ROI study must be confident that it will be able to deliver the benefits expected, as defined later in chapter 7, using the financial budget that will be created within this chapter. This budget must be a true reflection of the total cost of the GIS program.

Several concepts and terms are introduced in this chapter: budget forecasting, capitalization, operational versus capital expenditure, internal labor, and ongoing costs. Operational expenditures (OpEx) are the ongoing costs for running a product, business, or system, consisting of salaries, research and development costs, and other miscellaneous charges that must be subtracted from the organization's income. Capital expenditures (CapEx) are funds used to acquire or upgrade physical assets such as equipment, property, buildings, and so on. Not surprisingly, successful budget approval often can come from ensuring that program elements are correctly assigned and that OpEx is minimized.

Many GIS professionals tend to be technology-focused and may not deal with financial issues regularly, but there is no need to be intimidated by the terms, tools, and processes used here. Each of the concepts are defined and discussed as they become relevant during the budget-building process.

TASKS

Using the structured template ("GIS Budget Template.xls") available for download from the supporting Web site, the task here is to build a capital and operational budget for three years—with projections into future years if appropriate. This budget will capture the complete investment that makes up the GIS program defined in chapter 4. A three-year time frame is used for the budget because this is all that is usually needed to account for all the basic project costs. Any ongoing costs beyond three years will most likely be operation and maintenance costs, which will be more or less the same each year. For ROI studies that need to extend a budget beyond three years, this can easily be done manually by simply using the same operational expenditure (OpEx) costs as year 3, adjusted for inflation as appropriate.

Tools: GIS budget template

The budget template (figure 6.1) provides the model for you to input budget variables, key resource information, specific project data and other values addressed in the tasks in chapter six. The digital template can be found under step 6 on the supporting Web site at http://gis.esri.com/roi.

Figure 6.1 shows the opening screen main menu from the budget template. The name of the project should be entered at the top by clicking <Enter Project Name>. The budget should then be saved under a new document name to avoid overwriting the budget template.

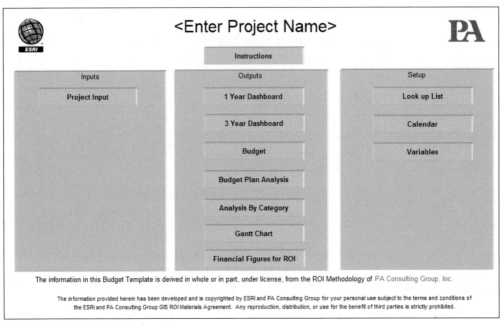

Figure 6.1 The budget template, main menu.

✔ 6.1 Get approval

The first task is to show the budget template to a representative of a finance department or an appropriate person who supports the budgeting process within the organization. It may be necessary to obtain approval from this person on the structure and contents of the budget. Further, it is often the case that there will be specific forms that a financial department requires to be completed for major projects within an organization, so it is recommended to validate the budget template with them prior to moving forward. This person will also be able to explain some of the terms and conventions used in the budgeting process, and also how they are interpreted and used within the organization.

✔ 6.2 Define budget variables

The first stage of building a budget is to collect and validate the lowest-level resource components, called *budget variables.*

Insight: Determining resources required

When determining the resources required, you will probably find it useful to consult the project definition template completed in task 4.3 and the program organizational design diagram completed in task 5.2.

Using the spreadsheet document created from the budget template, individuals can be added to each of the *resource* classes that will be included in a budget. A unit *cost* is then associated with each type of resource. To populate a budget resource value in the spreadsheet document, click the "Variables" button on the main menu (under "Setup"). This will display a screen where resource types and costs can be entered for each of the resource classes (figure 6.2). Note that in the budget template, as with all other templates, yellow cells can be edited.

Resource	Cost
GIS Manager	340
IS Application Developer	320
IS Support	300
Economic Development Tech	280
Planning Tech	285
DBA	375
Parks and Recreation Tech	280
Utilities Surveyor	300
IS Trainer	320
Executive	600
Planning Officer	310
Parks and Recreation Officer	310

Inside Labor

Figure 6.2 Example of inside labor resource types and costs.

The budget template defines six expenditure groups: inside labor, outside labor, hardware, software/licenses, dataset, and maintenance. These categories are derived from the expenditure groups in the look-up lists. Most likely, you will not need to change the expenditure type, expenditure group, and cost type entries, but they are editable if you need to modify or supplement them, as indicated by shaded yellow cells in the template (figure 6.3).

Expenditure Group	#
Inside Labor	1
Outside Labor	2
Hardware	3
Software/ licenses	4
Dataset	5
Maintenance	6
Misc	7
[blank]	8
[blank]	9

Figure 6.3 The default expenditure groups from the look-up list that are propagated to the variables to be associated with a unit cost.

More detail is provided about each of the resource classes that follow.

Inside labor

There are generally two reasons to capture the internal labor costs for GIS projects:

- To capture when one department or cost center charges another for internal resources. For instance, if a QA/QC specialist in another department and cost center is used temporarily to test a GIS application, then this cost center would expect to be reimbursed.

- To determine the amount of internal labor that can be capitalized. This means that a portion of an internal staff member's time can be accounted for as capital expense, thus reducing the amount of operational expense incurred. For an explanation of capital and operation expenditure and why capital is usually preferred, see section 6.5.3.

It is important to ensure that the internal labor cost is adequately captured for each of the projects by considering all the people who might be involved in a project from all departments within an organization.

Of course, not all the internal labor resources will bear the same cost (e.g., a software analyst may carry a different cost than an IT specialist). All labor costs should be fully loaded; that is, the appropriate overhead cost should be added to the base salary cost, using guidance from a person within a finance department. For example, in figure 6.2 the total daily rate cost of $320 for an IS application developer is based on the following:

- The hourly cost of the employee based on their job role—which can usually be obtained from a finance department

- The number of working hours in a day (usually 8 hours, although some organizations use 7.5 hours, per day)

- The percentage of overhead cost added to the base hourly cost of the employee

In the example given, the math is simply as follows:

$$\text{Total daily cost} = \left((\$28.78 \text{ per hr} \times 8 \text{hrs per day}) + 39\% \text{ overhead} \right) = \$320$$

Outside labor

Many organizations use vendors or contractors to supplement their workforce for projects. This is especially common when the projects have a fixed duration. Identifying the expected amount for external resources can generally be done by looking at past work completed for an organization, or by asking some typical vendors that may be engaged about their normal daily rates.

It is likely that an array of skill sets will need to be considered and hence several types of resources may need to be defined, for example, business analysts, project managers, data collectors, developers, architects, and instructors. Again daily rates should be captured for these resources. Figure 6.4 shows a selection of outside labor resources entered into a budget. There is sufficient space in the template provided for 16 external resource types and their daily costs to be added.

	Consultant	1,800
	Contractor	1,600
	Software Developer	1,200
Outside Labor	External Project Manager	1,110
	Data Technician	300

Figure 6.4   Example of outside labor resources.

Hardware

Hardware is often driven by scalability concerns—the more users and the more complex the applications, the more hardware that will be needed. As a consequence, each hardware component in the projects should be broken down into all possible parts. Some typical hardware items include servers, desktops, printers, plotters, hard drives, laptops, field devices, and so on. Typical hardware costs can normally be obtained through an IT department representative or, as with the software licenses, assistance can be sought from hardware vendors.

Software and licenses

There are many factors that contribute to the software cost of supporting GIS projects. These include the types of modules or products and plug-ins, the number of users, and the use of the software post-project.

It is necessary to do some general estimating of the volume and type of licenses that are expected to be used. The most effective way to do this—and the most defensible if challenged on the costs—is to involve sales representatives from software vendors. By working collaboratively with vendors to understand their software licensing structure, the most informed and logical license cost breakdown can be determined. It is also possible to arrive at an appropriate purchasing schedule so that the costs for licenses purchased are only incurred when the program needs them rather than at the start of a program. Spreading out the purchase of licenses helps to smooth the forecasted monthly expenditures and reduce the size and number of spending peaks.

Once the software license costs have been determined for the estimated types and numbers of licenses, the figures can be entered directly into the "Variables" list, accessible from the main menu of the budget document (see figure 6.1). Should anyone ask for justification of the license costs, it is useful to keep a copy of all quotes from vendors. Being able to justify and defend a budget is a critical component of gaining credibility and acceptance, and so all supporting documentation should be kept as a matter of course.

Sometimes it is difficult to predict software license needs because detailed requirements analysis or architecture definition has not yet be completed. If this is the case, it is recommended the "most likely scenario" should be estimated based on the expertise available and, based on the confidence level, a contingency factor is added that provides some room for change. If this rationale is explained to members of a finance department and they buy in to this logical and sound process, then typically there will not be any push-back with estimates of this nature.

Insight: Budgeting for your software

It is likely that software vendors will provide you with a "list price" quote, or a discounted quote if the volumes you expect to buy are sufficiently large. It is prudent to budget for the list price amounts rather than the discounted amounts. Given that your budget cycle is likely to be several months ahead of the purchase time, list price budgeting guarantees that you will have sufficient funds in the event that the final quote you receive at purchase time is greater than the discounted estimated quote.

Dataset

Most large GIS programs will need to source data from external organizations or specific-purpose data vendors. Landbase (background maps) or business data are two of the more typical types of datasets that organizations will need to purchase. Again, it is recommended that vendor costs are obtained for these resources. It may also be necessary to create, integrate, or update data internally, which also should be added to the budget.

Insight: Creating, integrating, or updating internal datasets

We recommend that you consider the full costs related to the creation, integration, or update (consolidation) of disparate data, not only the technical work involved. If you are modifying data that currently supports your existing organization's business activities, you may, for example, have associated training costs that will need to be budgeted. Further, even small-scale data migration, consolidation, or integration will require program overhead to make sure business-as-usual activities are not impacted, and data integrity and quality are improved, not degraded.

Maintenance

Maintenance and support are often included in the software, dataset, and hardware vendor's quotes based on a percentage of the purchase price, for example, 15 to 22 percent. It is imperative that yearly costs for maintenance and support are considered in a budget so that the ongoing costs can be captured for subsequent year budgets. The operational cost, or OpEx, of maintenance and support can sometimes influence the ROI calculation year on year. Figure 6.5 shows the maintenance and support costs for some example resources.

Maintenance	ArcGIS Server Maintenance	10,000
	U.S. & Canada Dataset	30,000

Figure 6.5 Example of maintenance resources.

✔ **6.3 Complete the calendar section of the budget**

The next task is to enter information about the calendar for the budget period. The "Calendar" section, accessed off the main menu, contains input fields to capture this information (figure 6.6). The "Budget Start Date" should be set to the start of the calendar year, or perhaps the fiscal year if this is more appropriate. In order to be certain that an accurate number of working days is calculated, the "Calendar" section also has space to enter holiday dates observed by different organizations. When using the template provided, calculations used to define the timeline or duration of individual projects will intentionally omit the nonwork days, making the budget forecast more accurate.

Holidays	
Date	Holiday
1/1/2008	New Years Day
1/21/2008	Martin Luther King Day
2/18/2008	Presidents Day
5/26/2008	Memorial Day
7/4/2008	Independence Day
9/1/2008	Labor Day
10/13/2008	Columbus Day
11/11/2008	Veterans' Day
11/27/2008	Thanksgiving
12/25/2008	Christmas Day
1/1/2009	New Years Day
1/19/2009	Martin Luther King Day
2/16/2009	Presidents Day
5/25/2009	Memorial Day
7/4/2009	Independence Day
9/7/2009	Labor Day
10/12/2009	Columbus Day
11/11/2009	Veterans' Day
11/26/2009	Thanksgiving
12/25/2009	Christmas Day
1/1/2010	New Years Day
1/18/2010	Martin Luther King Day
2/15/2010	Presidents Day
5/31/2010	Memorial Day
7/4/2010	Independence Day
9/6/2010	Labor Day
10/11/2010	Columbus Day
11/11/2010	Veterans' Day
11/25/2010	Thanksgiving
12/25/2010	Christmas Day

Dates	
Budget Start Date	1-Jan-08
Budget End Date	31-Dec-10
Budget Year 1	2008
Budget Year 2	2009
Budget Year 3	2010

Figure 6.6 The "Calendar" section input screen from an example
budget template document.

✔ 6.4 Populate the look-up lists

The final information needed to set up the budget for project data entry is the names of the projects. The "Look-up List" screen is accessed from the main menu of a budget document (see figure 6.7). The names of the projects should have been specified in chapter 4, when the GIS projects were defined.

#	Project
1	E911 System
2	Fire Station Siting Application
3	Crime Analysis System
4	Project 4
5	Project 5
6	Project 6
7	Project 7
8	Project 8
9	Project 9
10	Project 10
11	Project 11
12	Project 12
13	Project 13
14	Project 14
15	Project 15
16	Project 16
17	Project 17
18	Project 18
19	Project 19
20	Project 20
21	Project 21
22	Project 22
23	Project 23
24	Project 24
25	Project 25

Expenditure Type
Opex
Capex
[blank]
[blank]

Expenditure Group	#
Inside Labor	1
Outside Labor	2
Hardware	3
Software/ licenses	4
Dataset	5
Maintenance	6
[blank]	7
[blank]	8
[blank]	9

Cost Type
Fixed Price
Point Purchase
Resource driven

Figure 6.7 The look-up lists containing the names of projects.

✔ 6.5 Project data input

When all the information has been entered to establish the structure of the budget, as described in the previous sections, it is time to enter the budget data regarding each of the projects in the GIS program. Project data entry involves assembling and entering several types of information for each resource used on every project. For example, each of the projects will require information about the resource type used, the quantity of resource required, the cost type, and the timeline for resource usage. These are all considered in the next subsections.

The input screen for project data entry is accessed from the main menu by clicking the "Project Input" button. The empty project data input screen is quite daunting at first, but the whole process will be explained one step at a time in the following sections. Notice, however, that the names of the projects entered into the look-up list in the previous section are already numbered and included in the budget. Much of the other structural information will also become accessible when data entry begins. Project data entry is typically an iterative process, and adjustments normally need to be made to information such as the start date and project duration, because as the project timeline becomes increasingly complete, resource conflicts are often detected.

6.5.1 Resources used to deliver a project

Some projects will be entirely labor-related, while others will be a mixture of several resource types. It is a good idea to start by making a list of the resources that will be needed for each project.

In the example shown in figure 6.8, the project requires the following resource types: a business analyst from within the organization (inside labor), a consultant and a software developer external to the organization (outside labor), and a laptop (hardware). These cost elements and descriptions were entered by clicking the cell and selecting a choice from the drop-down list that appears. The unit cost will be filled in automatically based on the data entered in the "Budget variables" section described in task 6.2.

	Cost element	Description	Unit cost	Fixed cost	Qty per week	Opex / Capex	Cost Type
1	Inside Labor	Business Analyst	400		5.00	Opex	Resource driven
2	Outside Labor	Consultant	-	50,000		Capex	Fixed Price
3	Outside Labor	Software Developer	1,200		5.00	Capex	Resource driven
4	Hardware	Laptop	2,000		1.00	Capex	Point Purchase

Figure 6.8   The first part of a set of resource definitions for an example project.

6.5.2 Resource quantity and cost type

Continuing with the example shown in figure 6.8, it has been determined that the business analyst is required for five days per week and the software developer for five days per week. All resources have one of three types of cost: resource driven, fixed price, or point purchase. These are defined in the accompanying "Insight" box. Both the business analyst and software developer are considered resource-driven cost types. This means that the cost is dictated by how much and how long they will be used on the project. It has also been determined that the consultant can be hired on a fixed price contract to do the necessary work. This means that the activity being planned for the consultant will be purchased for a fixed amount, rather than estimating the total cost based on the unit cost and duration of activity. Finally, as far as figure 6.8 is concerned, the laptop cost type has been set to "point purchase," since the purchase occurs at a given point in time with only one invoice issued.

Insight: Capturing cost type

Resource driven means that the cost is determined by how much and how long a resource is used on a project. All internal labor, and any labor where the exact quantity is difficult to obtain from a vendor, is usually included in this category. *Fixed price* means that a firm amount has been agreed for payment: the contractor specifies only the task to be completed, not the level of resource to be consumed. External labor is often contracted on a fixed price basis in order to control budgeting. *Point purchase* is a type of one-off, nonrecurrent cost. Hardware, software, and data purchases are usually of this type. The key difference between point purchase and fixed price is that the former is normally associated with multiple invoices being issued over a period of time, for example, monthly or quarterly. This is relevant to the budget forecast, as finance departments will usually want to know how much of your overall budget will be spent in any given month.

6.5.3 Capital or operational expenditure

Each of the resource costs will also need to be classified as either capital expenditure (CapEx) or operational expenditure (OpEx). The distinction is important from an accounting and finance perspective because capital expenditures can be written off over a long period of time and, therefore, the costs can be spread over multiple financial years. As a consequence, successful budget approval is more likely if as many program elements as possible are correctly assigned as CapEx, and if OpEx is minimized wherever possible, as mentioned earlier. Certain areas of a program will clearly be CapEx, for example hardware and software purchases. However, GIS programs often require significant expenditure on tasks that may not be viewed as CapEx by the finance team, for example, undertaking data migration from one or more legacy platforms or data formats.

Carefully applying some basic rules to CapEx assignment can result in a more justifiable and defensible budget split. The correct classification can usually be obtained by answering a few basic questions. If the answer to any of the following questions is yes, then almost certainly a project should be classified as "CapEx." For instance, is the project

- a one-time effort (i.e., not operational)?

- going to have a transformational impact on the business (e.g., provides new capability not possible with existing data in its current form)?

- going to result in a new consolidated dataset (e.g., built from a collection of disparate legacy data platforms or sources)?

- likely to add value to some existing data assets (e.g., through cleansing, alignment, standardization, or through improving the resolution of existing data)?

The ultimate decision lies with the finance team, however, and the case will need to be made to them for assigning components of a budget to CapEx rather than OpEx.

The resources already entered into the example shown in figure 6.8 have been classified as OpEx (the business analyst) or CapEx (all the others).

6.5.4 Resource start date and duration

The next information to enter for each resource, start date and duration, is dependent upon the amount of resources available and the number of concurrently running projects that can be managed. For resource-driven and fixed-price resources, there will be a start date and duration, but for point purchases, such as hardware resources, the planned date of purchase should be entered.

Figure 6.9 shows additional data for the resources already discussed in figure 6.8. The business analyst will start work on 2-Feb-08 for five weeks. These dates relate to the forecast of expenditure. In other words, the finance department can discern when the planned budget expenditure will occur, that is, in what month(s) there will be an expense against the budget.

Start date	End date	Dur'n weeks	Dur'n months	Average cost per month	Notes	Prior to Jan-08	Jan-08	Feb-08	Mar-08	Apr-08
2-Feb-08	7-Mar-08	5	1.25	8,000	Business process re-design			7,941	2,059	
2-Feb-08	25-Apr-08	12	2.75	-	Provide a Requirements doc			16,265	18,675	15,060
2-Feb-08	14-Mar-08	6	1.50	24,000	Build prototype			23,707	12,293	
1-Jan-08	1-Jan-08			-	Laptop for Contractor		2,000			

Figure 6.9 Example of completed start, end, and duration data for four resources.

The embedded spreadsheet macros will automatically calculate the monthly spend, as is partially shown on the right of figure 6.9. As can be seen, the business analyst cost (first resource) is incurred only in the months of February and March, whereas the consultant (second resource) costs are spread over multiple months.

Insight: Managing cash flow

In order to manage cash flow, organizations, especially those that are publicly traded, seek to spread spending equally throughout a fiscal year. Budget forecasts should therefore try to avoid all of a budget being spent in one particular month in a fiscal year and very little in the other eleven months. A finance department is interested in understanding when costs will be incurred so that it can manage cash flow within the organization, and track whether monies allocated are being spent at the forecast pace. This is particularly important for publicly traded companies, where there is increased outside scrutiny on how capital within the business is allocated and leveraged for shareholder advantage.

✔ 6.6 Budget output

A considerable amount of output is generated automatically by the macros embedded within the budget template. This can be accessed from various options on the main menu.

One-year dashboard

The one-year dashboard provides a view of the distribution of expenditures across all the projects in a program. Figure 6.10 illustrates that in this GIS program example, there is a relatively unequal distribution of expenditures over the 12-month period, showing a peak in March Q1 08.

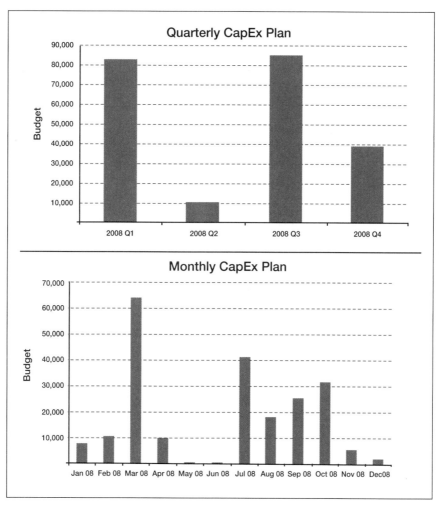

Figure 6.10 An example of quarterly and monthly output from a one-year dashboard.

Three-year dashboard

The three-year dashboard, also accessible from main menu, shows the distribution of expenditures over a three-year time frame. It includes charts on CapEx budget plan, CapEx monthly plan, CapEx quarterly plan, and, for each year, budget by category, cost type, and OpEx/CapEx budget. This is most useful for analyzing spending patterns.

Budget plan analysis

In this series of charts, the same CapEx budget plan, CapEx monthly plan, CapEx quarterly plan presented in the three-year dashboard are shown separately.

Analysis by category

This shows charts and tables on budget by category, cost type, OpEx/CapEx budget, and, for each year, budget by category, cost type, and OpEx/CapEx budget. This information will be used in chapter 9 for calculating depreciation.

Insight: Depreciation and amortization

Depreciation and amortization refer to the process of splitting the acquisition costs of tangible and nontangible assets systematically over their estimated useful life (see also section 9.3 for further discussion). A number of the tangible assets specified in a budget, such as hardware and datasets, will need to be appropriately depreciated and represented in later financial ROI calculations. Also, the internal labor costs specified in a budget, applied to capital rather than operational costs, might need to be amortized. The information necessary for this is provided in the "Analysis by Category" section accessible off the main menu of a budget document. Since depreciation and amortization are quite advanced topics and are handled differently by organizations, it is recommended that a finance department representative be consulted about how to account for these expenses correctly during financial analysis.

Gantt chart

The added benefit of planning the budget spending is that it makes obvious the delivery of benefits by the program, the volume of work planned for any given month, and the complexity of program dependencies. The indicative Gantt chart within the template gives a visual picture of the activities planned based on the budget—thus helping to structure project start and end dates appropriately.

Financial figures for ROI

The last output type on the budget main menu presents the key financial figures that will be needed for financial analysis in chapter 9. Figure 6.11 shows example financial figures for ROI output. Although much of the budget information is used elsewhere in the methodology, after all the work that goes into creating a budget, the final financial output is quite modest.

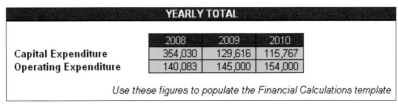

YEARLY TOTAL			
	2008	2009	2010
Capital Expenditure	354,030	129,616	115,767
Operating Expenditure	140,083	145,000	154,000

Use these figures to populate the Financial Calculations template

Figure 6.11 Financial figures for ROI.

OUTCOME

In this chapter, several vital steps have been completed in order to build a budget. Working with a member of a finance department to gain approval and/or assistance, the unit costs for the various resources required to complete a GIS program have been populated. These resources include people (inside and outside labor), hardware, software, and datasets. By completing the "Calendar" section of the template, a time frame for projects and the budget have been determined. The types of resources for each project have been identified and the costs assigned to each of them. Finally, all the information has been assembled to view the spread of spending for each of the projects, their resources, duration, and requirements. As such, many of the tasks may have been revisited multiple times, to tune, refine, reallocate resources, and adjust the start date and duration of projects over the course of the project timeline.

Case Study

SPECIFY AND COST GIS PROJECTS

This part of the Springfield case study involves creating a budget for the GIS program of work by completing a document derived from the budget template spreadsheet provided on the accompanying Web site (http://gis.esri.com/roi). Although this involves several tasks, the discussion is structured for convenience into just two sections.

In undertaking this task, Brian Sobers, GIS manager at the City of Springfield, and the ROI project team make some assumptions, as follows:

- The city will purchase a single enterprise server (and a duplicate, failover server) for all centralized server-based applications. This will be managed by the Information Systems (IS) Department server team.

- In most cases, there will be no need to include the cost of internal application staff that will run the GIS applications, since they will essentially be doing the same work as before (but in the future they will be doing it using GIS).

- Wherever possible, internal city resources will be used and external resources will be purchased only where absolutely necessary, mainly for financial reasons but also because there is a wish to develop the skills of in-house staff.

- The city's preferred hardware vendor is Dell.

- The city's preferred GIS software vendor is ESRI.

- Standard city infrastructure, such as network and telephones, and overhead, such as corporate administration, space, and travel, do not need to be included in the budget, following general city policy.

C6.1 Springfield budget

After obtaining approval from the Springfield Finance Department, Brian and team enter all the details about the budget into the spreadsheet template provided. The results are in the file "Springfield GIS Budget.xls," which is available on the supporting Web site.

Brian begins by entering information to populate the look-up lists, calendar, and variables he obtains from the Finance Department and city Web site. Given that the purpose of the budget is to provide a high-level view of costs for the purposes of determining the ROI, Brian enters the core budget information relatively quickly, focusing on the macro activities, resources, and expenditures. Details about the cost of various hardware and software systems were obtained from local vendor reps.

The following sections describe Brian's thoughts in compiling the cost elements for each of the projects. A description of the GIS projects and the process used to create them can be found in section C4.1.

Citywide basemap

The budget for this project includes all the hardware and software for the citywide enterprise servers (including maintenance payments in years two and three) that will be used for the basemap, geocodable address database, and inward investment projects. Two servers will be procured (a main system and a backup/failover system) and set up by an IS support person. The GIS manager (Brian Sobers) will act as project manager, and, together with a DBA from the IS Department, he will be responsible for data model and database design. This project management and design pattern is repeated for all the projects, and so will not be discussed in the following sections. Application development and data integration will be undertaken by a combination of an internal IS Department developer and an outside consultant (working on a fixed-price contract). Ongoing IT support for the hardware and software will be provided by an IT support person from the IS Department. Geodemographics data (geographic and attribute data about the socioeconomic and financial characteristics of the city and surrounding region) is budgeted here as it is considered an enterprise expenditure, even though the main user will be the inward investment project.

Geocodable address database

Since the address database will be hosted on the citywide enterprise servers, most of the expenditure for this project is already covered in the basemap project. The only additional expenditure is to develop the address database itself. A resource from the IS Department will perform data cleansing and preparation prior to loading onto the server; a resource from this department will undertake a similar task for data updates in the second year of operation. The same person will also be used for long-term, periodic maintenance over the three years of the budget. An internal programmer and an external consultant will develop the address database application. Finally, the IS Department will be responsible for ongoing support of the data and application (base hardware and software is covered under the basemap project above).

Tree cover assessment

The tree cover assessment project (for the purpose of obtaining a federal highway clean air attainment grant) will run inside a desktop GIS software package on a dedicated PC that will be set up by a Parks and Recreation Department technician. The assessment methodology will be developed and implemented by expert staff in the Parks and Recreation Department. This will involve development and testing of an initial prototype in fall 2008, and then rollout of the full methodology in spring 2009. After completion of the tree cover assessment, a Parks and Recreation Department officer will complete a submission to the Federal Highway Funding Agency for a clean air attainment grant.

Fire hydrant inspection and maintenance

This project involves essentially out-of-the-box desktop GIS software running on a dedicated PC, and handheld field units equipped with GPS and mobile GIS software. The systems will be installed and managed by resources from the IS Department. Field inspections will be undertaken by two inspectors; the cost of their systems, transport, and labor is all included in the budget.

Brownfield site finder

The brownfield site finder will run on standard desktop GIS software on a dedicated PC. This will be set up and maintained by a Planning Department technician. An easy-to-use application will need to be developed, along with land-use and cadastral data layers; these tasks will be performed by an external GIS programmer/consultant. After the brownfield site finder application has been in successful operation for several months, a planning officer will be responsible for preparing a grant designed to encourage municipalities to redevelop brownfield sites, for submission to the Environmental Protection Agency.

Inward investment

The base infrastructure to run the inward investment application has already been included in the budget under the basemap project (see "Citywide basemap"). This part of the budget, therefore, includes only a few additional resources such as an external GIS programmer to build the applications, an IS Department support person to set up the system in the Economic Development Department, and an Economic Development Department technician to support the Economic Development staff while they operate the system.

Other projects

Two other nonapplication projects are also included in the budget: one addresses training and the other addresses overall project governance. Two instructors, one internal and one external to the city, will provide base training for all the city staff. The governance project is designed to provide top-level oversight of the GIS projects once they are underway (see chapter 5 for more details about the governance process). The governance team will meet on a periodic basis throughout the lifetime of the program to review progress and support the project teams.

C6.2 Springfield budget output

Figures C6.1 and C6.2 show two types of output from the budget created by the ROI team. Figure C6.1 shows the multiyear (three-year dashboard) output screen from the Springfield budget. The team was confident that the budget would receive executive support because of the following:

- Most of the capital expenditure (CapEx) occurs in the early part of the project and is reasonably evenly spread (no need for massive cash injections).

- Operating expenditure (OpEx) is proportionally much smaller than CapEx. As determined, it is advantageous from an accounting perspective to capitalize expenditure wherever possible.

- There is a good spread throughout the main expenditure categories, suggesting that there is no major risk or single point of failure for the project.

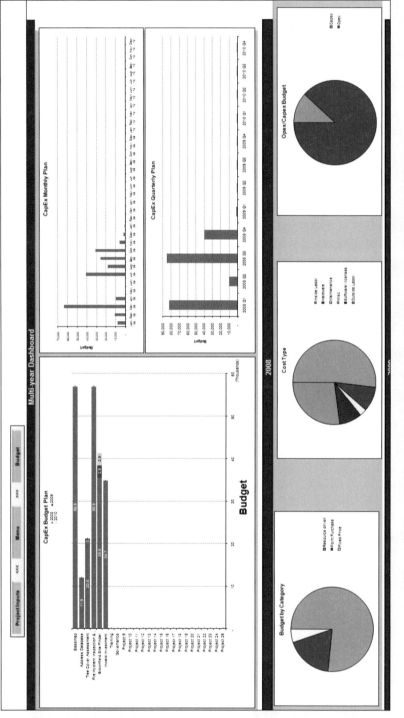

Figure C6.1 Part of the multiyear dashboard output screen from the Springfield budget.

Figure C6.2 shows the bottom line for the Springfield budget. These are the CapEx and OpEx figures that will be used in the case study financial analysis in chapter 9. Over a three-year period, the Springfield GIS program will require a budget of $355k.

YEARLY TOTAL			
	2008	2009	2010
Capital Expenditure	243,460	5,199	4,889
Operating Expenditure	34,245	35,274	32,851

Use these figures to populate the Financial Calculations template

Figure C6.2   Yearly totals for the Springfield budget.

C6.3   Discussion of chapter 6 case study

Although it is fairly straightforward to enter the basic requisite information into a budget document, it is time-consuming to determine the resource requirements and quantities for each of the projects. There is often a need for discussion about a number of the budget topics, and Springfield's budget was no exception; it went through many revision cycles before consensus was reached among the members of the ROI team. The budgeting process helped refine and focus the project specifications from chapter 4, and it may be necessary to revisit them again before the whole methodology is complete. The number of entries that can be made for each project is purposefully limited to 15 to ensure that the budget does not get too detailed; its goal is solely to provide the cost elements for ROI calculations. Even for a relatively small budget like Springfield's, it proved to be a bit of a challenge.

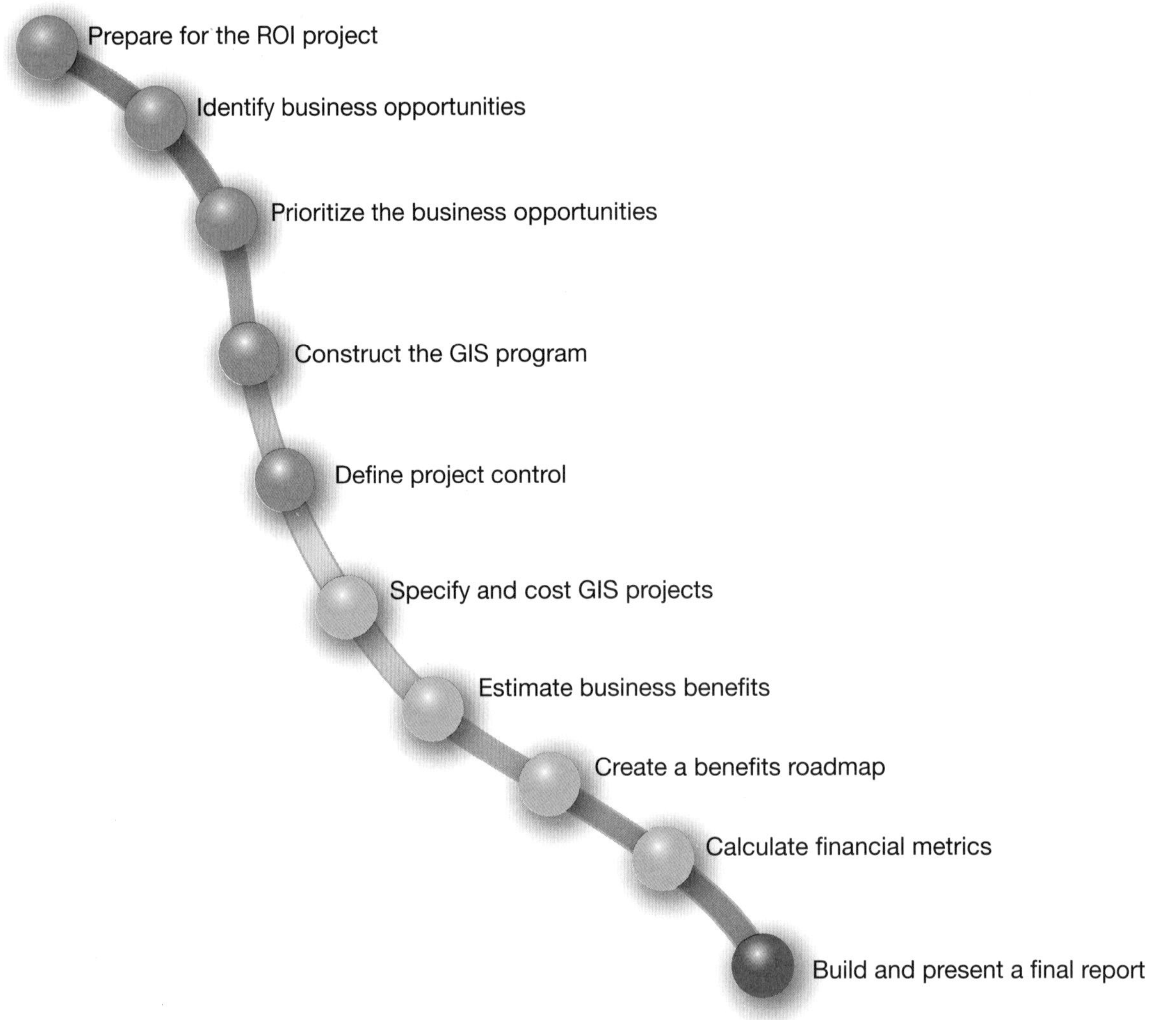

Prepare for the ROI project

Identify business opportunities

Prioritize the business opportunities

Construct the GIS program

Define project control

Specify and cost GIS projects

Estimate business benefits

Create a benefits roadmap

Calculate financial metrics

Build and present a final report

7

Estimate business benefits

Using the template provided, this chapter takes a logical and structured approach to identifying and quantifying the business benefits that will arise from implementing a GIS program of work. By decomposing the business processes and workflows at an organization into manageable input variables and key parameter values, it is possible to build a strong business benefits model that can withstand detailed scrutiny. This chapter breaks the process down into a series of tasks and provides a case study example.

The approaches to quantifying benefits can be as varied as the number of benefits that can be measured, as is shown in two recent reviews of the literature on GIS return on investment.[1] Many commentators have provided their own classification of benefits,[2] but the authors have found each of these to be too high level and lacking in some areas of scope.

Chapter 2 provided an introduction to identifying GIS benefits and extracting the business opportunities at an organization through discussions with key stakeholders. It will be apparent that some of these describe future "planned" benefits, and that the textual description is not always precise and sometimes leaves the reader wishing that the benefit had been expressed in monetary terms rather than, for example, in time saved or processes improved. In some cases, it is possible to undertake further analysis that will allow an increase in the usefulness of weakly tangible or intangible benefits, so that they can be turned into highly tangible benefits. The general point to make here is that the value of a benefit is proportional to the amount of work that has been done to extract that value. In choosing benefits, it is important to avoid generalized statements such as "GIS will reduce costs" or "With GIS we can improve operational performance." The best benefits are specific, measurable, and relevant to an organization.

OBJECTIVES

As stated, benefits that are precisely measurable and achievable are the most useful. Identifying the benefits that arise from a program of GIS projects is generally the most challenging of all the steps that need to be completed in order to define an ROI business case for GIS. This is because, unlike costs, which can be precisely defined and directly measured, benefits, at least at first inspection, are often vague and more difficult to measure. However, with guidance and a little experience, it is possible to identify and quantify the business value of the benefits of a GIS program. This methodology uses a generalized approach and provides an associated template to define and then model the value of key benefits.

TASKS

The tasks in this chapter revolve around understanding an organization's workflow and business processes, in order to identify, define, and measure a series of benefits that will then be entered into a model spreadsheet. The process begins by reviewing the list of possible benefits created in chapter 3 ("Prioritize business opportunities"), then focusing on the tangible, measurable benefits. Through a series of steps, the benefit will be expressed in numeric terms that will be entered into a document derived from the spreadsheet template provided (the benefits model template). The term model is used to describe this process because, in essence, the numerical aspects of a benefit are being formulated in a spreadsheet.

✔ 7.1 Reference the list of possible benefits

The first task to be undertaken is to create a list of possible benefits that will be used to make the case for a GIS program. These should have been borne out of the interviews from chapter 2 when the business opportunities were identified in an organization. Recall that there are a number of resources to help formulate a list of benefits: the supporting digital files and the accompanying discussion in chapter 2; the portfolio of work defined in chapter 4, as derived from the stakeholder interviews in chapter 2; and case studies developed from the work of similar organizations. To reiterate, a good benefit is one that is specific, measurable, attainable, relevant, and timely. Remember that the purpose of the benefits defined here is to build a return on investment case to persuade senior executives to fund a GIS program. The benefits must therefore be based as much as is possible on verifiable facts. It is important not to exaggerate the aspects of any benefit; otherwise this may return as an issue of contention during the evaluation stage of the business case report. One approach is to quantify benefits by focusing on "before and after" scenarios—that is, comparing the value of the changes to an organization after a GIS has been implemented to situations without a GIS at all.

Each benefit should be defined clearly and succinctly in a few sentences. For example, the benefit of improving the efficiency of truck deliveries might be described in the following way:

Benefit: Reduce total delivery fleet operating cost per year by improving the efficiency of the delivery schedules to effect a reduction in fleet mileage and fuel expenditure.

The benefit of generating revenue from selling data could be expressed as follows:

Benefit: Generate new revenue by selling basemap and coverage data collected as part of normal work practices to government and private organizations in the same region.

Ten to twelve good benefits will normally be sufficient to make a strong case for a GIS program, and so there is no need to spend exhaustive amounts of time creating benefit examples. Remember that some benefits are tangible and others are intangible, and at least half of the list should consist of the more compelling tangible benefits. Of these, some will add value (i.e., make money), while others will reduce/avoid costs. After creating a general list, split the benefits into tangible and intangible categories. Set aside the intangible benefits for now—they will not be used in this chapter, but will instead be included in the final report (chapter 10) as supplementary or supporting information to buttress the business case that will be built primarily on tangible benefits.

✔ 7.2 Benefits model spreadsheet

To arrive at quantifiable values that allow the benefits to be measured for each project, a benefits model template is provided (figure 7.1). This spreadsheet uses a step-by-step approach to estimate the value generated by the benefits delivered by a GIS program. It will also help to follow the value of benefits delivered as a GIS program progresses, since it highlights some key metrics that can be tracked going forward. Additionally, the spreadsheet is a tool that can be used to assess the impact of changes to the project direction over time.

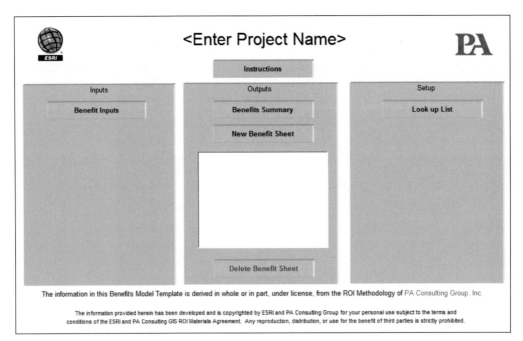

Figure 7.1   The main menu of the benefits model template.

Tools: Benefits model template

The benefits model template allows you to break out each of the elements associated with the specific projects in your portfolio to allow comparison between the benefit value of a calculated base case without GIS and a calculated case with GIS. The template is available on the accompanying Web site, http://gis.esri.com/roi, under step 7.

First, review the instructions on how the template works by clicking the "Instructions" button (see figure 7.1). Next, create a name for the project and enter it into the <Enter Project Name> field at the top of the main menu. At this point, create a new document from the template that will store the benefits under this new file name. Finally, the starting year of the project should be entered by clicking the "Look up List" button on the main menu. This should be the same year used in the budget template spreadsheet in chapter 6.

✔ 7.3 Complete the benefit input sheet

Each of the tangible benefits in the list created in step 7.1 should now be entered into the document created using the benefits model spreadsheet in step 7.2. Each individual benefit will have its own benefit sheet. A benefit sheet can be created by clicking the "New Benefit Sheet" button on the main menu and entering a name for the benefit sheet in the dialog box that appears. Once a name has been entered, it will display in the white box at the center of the screen. In the example provided, a new "Truck Delivery" benefit sheet is created. (figure 7.2).

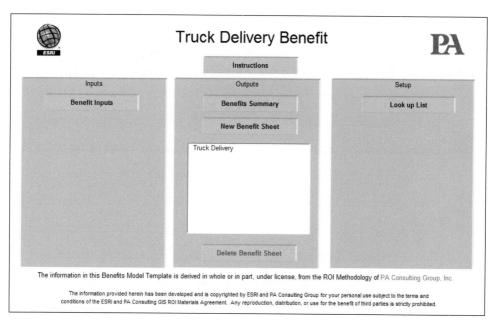

Figure 7.2 New "Truck Delivery" benefit sheet created in the benefits model document.

Double-clicking the "Truck Delivery" name will open up its associated benefit sheet (figure 7.3). Multiple benefit sheets can be stored in one project model.

Benefit Overview

<Enter Overview of Benefit here>

Confidence 100%

Inputs

Input Type	Input	Unit	Base Case	Change

Benefits

		Unit	Base Case
Base Case			
GIS Case			

Figure 7.3 Empty benefit sheet of the "Truck Delivery" example in the benefits model spreadsheet document.

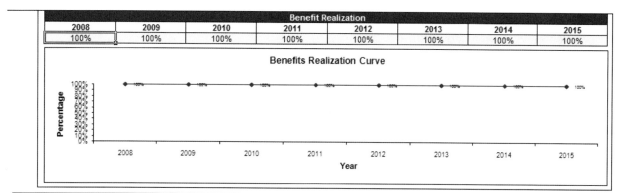

Benefit Realization							
2008	2009	2010	2011	2012	2013	2014	2015
100%	100%	100%	100%	100%	100%	100%	100%

Yearly Values								
	2008	2009	2010	2011	2012	2013	2014	2015
Base:								
Base:								
Base:								
Base:								
Base:								
Base:								
Base:								
Base:								
Base:								
Base:								
Base:								
Base:								

Yearly Values								
2008	2009	2010	2011	2012	2013	2014	2015

Several areas need to be completed for each benefit sheet: Benefit Overview (top left), Inputs (middle left), Benefits Summary (bottom), Benefits Realization Curve (top right), and Confidence Level (middle left).

To illustrate how to define and measure a benefit, an organization that uses trucks to make deliveries will be modeled. Many organizations have fleets of trucks that they use to deliver goods. Any reduction in mileage that can be created by GIS will be of great benefit in terms of reduced fuel usage, lower servicing costs, lower staff costs, and less pollution and road congestion. The best way to model this benefit is to compare the before and after GIS cases, that is, estimate the base cost of delivery and then determine the impact (reduced cost) of using GIS to route the trucks more efficiently.

7.3.1 Benefit overview

It is important to begin with a clear definition of a benefit. The "Benefit Overview" area provides space for a short title and a description of no more than 50 words. It will be much easier to understand what metrics need to be collected if articulation of the modeled benefit is very specific. Benefits that are not concisely defined will also be difficult to track when the GIS program enters the implementation stage. Tie these statements directly back to the benefits that were important and relevant to the executive stakeholders (as discussed in chapter 2).

Figure 7.4 shows the benefit overview statement for the truck delivery example introduced earlier. For the sake of simplicity and brevity, this example focuses on reducing fleet mileage and fuel expenditure, although in a more complete example, fleet servicing costs and staff costs should certainly be considered. The short title and description define the benefit and show how it can be realized, which is a guide to measure its impact.

Benefit Overview

Reduce Total Delivery Fleet Operating Cost per Year

By improving the efficiency of the delivery schedules to drive a reduction in fleet mileage, and fuel expenditure.

Figure 7.4 A clearly articulated benefit overview title and accompanying statement for truck delivery benefits model example.

7.3.2 Collect input metrics

In order to define the "Input Types" (middle left of benefit sheet) that quantify the impact of a benefit, some tangible metrics will need to be defined and entered. These metrics can be obtained from a variety of sources, such as a finance department representative, organization or department performance reports, interviews with expert workers, or even through searches of internal or external Web sites.

In the case of the truck delivery company example, the benefit of using GIS to reduce the cost of deliveries can be measured by calculating the cost of deliveries before and after GIS. The cost of operating a fleet delivery service is calculated as follows:

(((Average number of truck miles per day × Number of trucks required per day) / (Average truck miles per gallon)) × Average fuel price per gallon) × Average number of delivery days per year

Defining the inputs for a benefit is a two-part process. First, the basic building block elements that define a benefit are entered into a "Benefits Inputs" worksheet, and then these are used to model a benefit in the "Inputs" area of the benefit overview sheet.

Insight: Document your input sources

For each metric you collect, it is recommended that you keep a record of the source of each input metric. In this way, you can keep track of the origin of your information, and any future audit or inquiry can be provided full documentation on the source of your information.

The input screen for a given benefit can be accessed by clicking the "Benefit Inputs" button on the main menu of the benefit model document. This is where information is entered regarding the components that will be used to quantify a benefit. These elements may be measured using variables that represent monetary amounts ($), numeric quantities (#), or units of percentage (%). Although not editable, these Unit items are declared in the "Look up List" worksheet of the benefit model document (accessible from the main menu).

Populate this "Inputs" worksheet with all of the components of the project that can be measured using one of these variable input types. For instance, given the desired benefit overview defined above, there is a need to reduce the total operating cost per year of a fleet delivery service. The inputs for such an assessment include the average truck mileage per day, the number of trucks required per day, the number of truck miles per gallon, the average price of fuel, and the average number of delivery days (figure 7.5). All these input metrics need to be identified in order to model the reduction in delivery fleet cost benefit. Metrics that change year on year—such as average fuel price (per gallon), or average truck mileage—will require entries for multiple years (the benefits model uses eight years by default). Enter standard Microsoft Excel formulas into any field to calculate composite values. For example, the price of fuel is calculated using an annual estimated inflation rate of 4 percent. Any metrics that remain static—such as the average truck miles per gallon, or the average number of delivery days per year—can be expressed as fixed costs and only require one value for the first (base) year.

Input Name	Unit	Base Case	2008	2009	2010	2011	2012
Average number of truck miles per day	#	200.00	$ 200.00	$ 203.00	$ 206.05	$ 209.14	$ 212.27
Number of trucks required per day	#	10.00					
Average truck miles per gallon	#	16.00					
Average fuel price per gallon	$	$ 3.10	$ 3.10	$ 3.22	$ 3.35	$ 3.49	$ 3.63
Average number of delivery days per	#	240.00					
Estimated business growth per year	%	1.50%					
Annual rate of gas price inflation	%	4.00%					

Figure 7.5 Populated input metrics used in the truck delivery benefits model example.

7.3.3 Enter benefit sheet inputs

Once the worksheet that defines the input metrics has been completed, return to the benefits sheet to enter further information about a benefit, beginning with the "Input Types" area (middle left part of Benefits Sheet). This worksheet allows each individual metric to be assembled into one comprehensive table. Start with filling in the "Input Type" and "Input" columns in the benefit model (figure 7.6 shows the inputs for the truck delivery example). For each of the input metrics that are to be added, first determine if the input is fixed or variable and set the input type accordingly. As a reminder, "fixed" metrics are those that don't change or that a GIS will not influence in any way, and "variable" metrics are those that the GIS can influence.

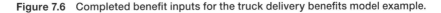

Inputs

Input Type	Input	Unit	Base Case	Change
Variable	Average number of truck miles per day	#	200.00	175.00
Fixed	Number of trucks required per day	#	10.00	
Fixed	Average truck miles per gallon	#	16.00	
Fixed	Average fuel price per gallon	$	$ 3.10	
Fixed	Average number of delivery days per year	#	240.00	
Derived	Total Fleet Mileage per day	#	2,000.00	

Figure 7.6 Completed benefit inputs for the truck delivery benefits model example.

Given the various input metrics entered, it is also possible to express input types that are "derived," that is, calculated based on other input metrics. In the case of the cost reduction example for this fictitious delivery truck fleet, given that 10 delivery trucks are required per day, and each truck averages 200 miles per delivery day, then the resulting input of "Total Fleet Mileage per Day" would equal 2,000 miles. Unlike fixed or variable input types, the basic formula must be defined to calculate the derived base case value. Calculate the derived values for future years, if these are necessary.

As the input types and input metrics are identified, isolate which input(s) the GIS will affect and set these as predefined inputs. In the example provided in figure 7.6, it was determined that a GIS would impact the average number of truck miles per day, reducing this from 200 to 175 miles (see the "Change" column). It is assumed, then, that the GIS will reduce the truck mileage because of better routing. This number was provided as a best-estimate from the manager of the truck fleet, after analysis of the way in which GIS would impact truck delivery routing.

Populating the various input columns also automatically completes a number of other columns by pulling data from the input sheet and initializing the formulas embedded in the benefit sheet. For example, figure 7.7 shows the "Yearly Values," to the right of the "Input" area, that have been automatically calculated. Any derived values, such as the "Total Fleet Mileage per Day," will need to have the formulas manually copied across into the appropriate fields in the "Yearly Values" section, since these will not update automatically.

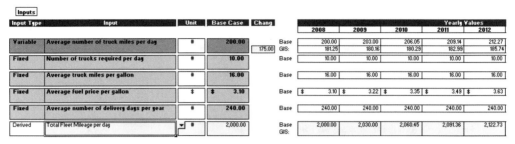

Figure 7.7 Completed inputs and yearly values for the truck delivery benefits model example.

7.3.4 Model the sensitivity of GIS impacts

In the upper right corner next to the "Benefits Overview" of the benefits model, is the benefits realization table and associated chart (figure 7.8). Linked to the benefit strategy worksheet from task 7.3.3, this table allows a sensitivity analysis to be incorporated into benefits modeling. The benefits realization table is used to account for the fact that all the benefits of a new GIS implementation may not be realized the day it is deployed. For example, if it is known there will be other corporate initiatives that will also influence the same metrics being modeled here, then only perhaps 75 percent of the benefit can be claimed. It may also be the case that it will only be possible to start a GIS project in, say, Q3, and hence a full year's benefit cannot be claimed for something that wasn't up and running in Q1 and Q2, in which case a value of 50 percent might be entered.

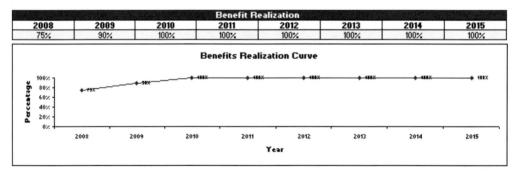

Figure 7.8 A benefits realization table and associated chart for the truck delivery benefits model example.

The percentages entered in the benefits realization table directly influence the return values reflected in the forecasted yearly values table in the spreadsheet, so the model will automatically update as the yield curve is adjusted. Usually, more and more of a benefit can be realized as a GIS matures and projects deliver more and more capability to an organization. In other words, the year-on-year influence of the GIS program can be modified dynamically, and the predicted returns can be immediately calculated since the GIS case for the input is adjusted accordingly. The cumulative impact of a change in the benefit realization percentage can also be seen under the "Yearly Values" section of a benefits summary worksheet (see figure 7.10).

7.3.5 Sum the benefit

In order to complete the totals and describe a benefit, a few formulas and descriptive labels will also need to be entered (figure 7.9). These will be entered into the "Benefits" area at the bottom of a benefits worksheet. In the case of the truck delivery example, the total for the base case is the following:

((Total fleet mileage per day / Average truck miles per gallon) × Average fuel price per gallon) × Average number of delivery days per year

All the resulting units will be in dollars. The following descriptions also need to be entered: Base—"Total Fleet Cost per Year"; GIS case—"Total Fleet Cost per Year with GIS"; claimed benefit (total)—"Tot. Year on Year Reduction in Fleet Cost"; and claimed benefit (cumulative)— "Cum. Tot. Reduction in Fleet Cost per Year."

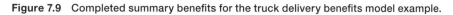

Benefits

		Unit	Base Case
Base Case	Total Fleet Cost per Year	$	$ 93,000.00
GIS Case	Total Fleet Cost per Year with GIS		
Claimed	Tot. Year on Year Reduction in Fleet Cost		
Benefit	Cum. Tot. Reduction in Fleet Cost per Year		

Figure 7.9 Completed summary benefits for the truck delivery benefits model example.

The formula used to calculate the base case can be copied and pasted into the fields in the "Yearly Values Benefits" section (figure 7.10). The appropriate formula will also need to be entered to calculate the GIS case totals for the yearly values. In the case of the truck delivery example, this means substituting the miles in the GIS case for the miles in the base case.

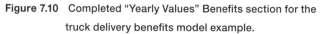

Yearly Values							
2008	2009	2010	2011	2012	2013	2014	2015
$ 93,000.00	$ 98,170.80	$ 103,629.10	$109,390.87	$ 115,473.01	$ 121,893.31	$128,670.57	$135,824.66
$ 84,281.25	$ 87,126.59	$ 90,675.46	$ 95,717.01	$ 101,038.88	$106,656.64	$ 112,586.75	$ 118,846.58
$ (8,718.75)	$ (11,044.22)	$(12,953.64)	$(13,673.86)	$ (14,434.13)	$(15,236.66)	$(16,083.82)	$(16,978.08)
$ (8,718.75)	$(19,762.97)	$(32,716.60)	$(46,390.46)	$(60,824.59)	$(76,061.25)	$(92,145.07)	$(109,123.15)

Figure 7.10 Completed "Yearly Values" Benefits section for the truck delivery benefits model example.

Using the forecasted values calculated from the input metrics and variables entered in tasks 7.3.2 and 7.3.3, the total truck operating cost per year continues to decrease, year-on-year, since the GIS case values are propagated from the "Average Truck Mileage Per Day," which was the primary input declared as changed by the GIS.

7.3.6 Confidence in the overall estimates

Although every effort has been made to estimate as closely as possible, based on information from stakeholders about their best "educated estimate" of success that a GIS would have for their area of business, it must be recognized that this is not an exact science. One way to factor in a measure of confidence in benefits estimates is to reduce the final overall figure based on some analysis of the methodology and the benefit problem domain.

Accordingly, the benefits model allows a confidence level to be set as a percentage (figure 7.11). The value populated in this cell is used to dynamically recalculate the claimed benefits figures, factoring in the confidence number as a percentage of the base and GIS case figures from the previous task (figure 7.9) to arrive at a more accurate annual claimed benefit value. Setting the confidence level to 100 percent will result in no changes to the model values. In this way, any changes in confidence level can quickly be incorporated into model results for yearly claimed benefit.

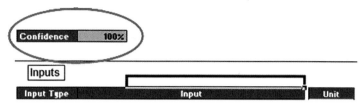

Figure 7.11 An example of the confidence level set to 100 percent for the overall business benefits model.

✔ 7.4 Total the benefits

In the case of the truck delivery example, the focus has been on just a single benefit. In a complete project, there will be multiple benefits, and these should be totaled to present the overall picture. Accessible from the benefits model template main menu, the benefit summary worksheet is used to total the benefits. The benefits should be grouped into the three basic categories that will be used in later financial calculations in chapter 9: revenue growth, assurance, and protection; operating expenditure cost savings and avoidance; and ongoing changes in capital expenditure, either negative or positive. Figure 7.12 shows the truck delivery benefit, along with some other benefits that have been totaled into these three benefit categories.

For the benefits modeled, the yearly totals for the claimed benefit (total) and claimed benefit (cumulative) rows at the bottom of benefit spreadsheets will need to be copied and then pasted into the benefit summary worksheet. Note that to get the correct result, use the "Paste Special" option in Excel to paste just "Values." Remember to enter the name into the yellow input field to the left so that each benefit can be identified. Once all the benefit yearly totals have been copied, they can be summed into the three categories outlined previously. A simple formula will need to be entered in order to sum the various benefits.

Insight: Consider benefit value drivers

As you build your benefits model by collecting metrics about your organization's business processes and common workflows, you may identify follow-on quantifiable benefits from intangible benefits. That is, a first benefit may foster a second benefit, which may result in a third quantifiable benefit, and so on. These benefit value drivers should be recognized and considered when modeling your total business benefits.

		2008	2009	2010	2011	2012	2013	2014	2015
						Yearly Values			
Truck Delivery Savings									
	Yearly Total	(8,719)	(11,044)	(12,954)	(13,674)	(14,434)	(15,237)	(16,084)	(16,978)
	Cumulative Total	(8,719)	(19,763)	(32,717)	(46,390)	(60,825)	(76,061)	(92,145)	(109,123)
Parcel Maintenance Savings:									
	Yearly Total	(30,000)	(30,000)	(30,000)	(30,000)	(30,000)	(30,000)	(30,000)	(30,000)
	Cumulative Total	(30,000)	(60,000)	(90,000)	(120,000)	(150,000)	(180,000)	(210,000)	(240,000)
Services Revenue									
	Yearly Total	23,402	51,454	97,666	137,799	199,960	235,339	291,886	350,695
	Cumulative Total	23,402	74,857	172,522	310,322	510,282	745,621	1,037,507	1,388,202
Reduced Capital Expenditure									
	Yearly Total	(125,000)	(70,000)						
	Cumulative Total	(125,000)	(195,000)	(195,000)	(195,000)	(195,000)	(195,000)	(195,000)	(195,000)
Total Benefit Savings									
	Yearly Total	(38,719)	(41,044)	(42,954)	(43,674)	(44,434)	(45,237)	(46,084)	(46,978)
	Cumulative Total	(38,719)	(79,763)	(122,717)	(166,390)	(210,825)	(256,061)	(302,145)	(349,123)
Total Benefit Revenue									
	Yearly Total	23,402	51,454	97,666	137,799	199,960	235,339	291,886	350,695
	Cumulative Total	23,402	74,857	172,522	310,322	510,282	745,621	1,037,507	1,388,202
Total Benefit Capital									
	Yearly Total	(125,000)	(70,000)						
	Cumulative Total	(125,000)	(195,000)	(195,000)	(195,000)	(195,000)	(195,000)	(195,000)	(195,000)

Figure 7.12   Completed benefits summary worksheet example from a benefits model template.

OUTCOME

Completing the tasks in this chapter provides a much better understanding of the elements that comprise the business processes within an organization. This work results in a model of each of the tangible benefits that affect revenue and costs, and which can be used to justify GIS expenditures within an organization. Additionally, details of some intangible benefits that also impact an organization, albeit in a lesser way, such as improved organizational image and staff well-being, are also created. This benefits information, along with the costs defined in chapter 6, will be used in the financial calculations later in chapter 9.

Case Study

ESTIMATE BENEFITS

In this step of the ROI methodology, Brian Sobers and his ROI team create an updated list of benefits for the City of Springfield and then estimate the value of the benefits of a key selection of the projects defined in chapter 4 and budgeted in chapter 6.

C7.1   List of benefits

The ROI team at the City of Springfield builds a list of benefits by revisiting the original list created during the interviews in chapter 2 and prioritized in chapter 3 (figure C3.1), the portfolio of work defined in chapter 4 (figure C4.1), and by examining case studies from organizations similar to Springfield. Figure C7.1 shows the list of benefits compiled for the City of Springfield. These have been adapted from figure C3.1 in several ways: the benefits that no longer apply or were shown not to be real benefits have been deleted, and the benefits have been expressed in a different way to make them clearer.

C7.2   Springfield's tangible benefits

The template for this task in the methodology is called "GIS Benefits Model Template.xls," and it is available on the supporting Web site (http://gis.esri.com/roi). The files containing the benefits estimates for three of the Springfield projects for which benefits were estimated are also on the Web site:

- Inward investment:
  Springfield Benefits Example P4 Eco Dev.xls

- Tree cover assessment:
  Springfield Benefits Example P5 Federal Highway Grant.xls

- GASB 34 regulatory mandate inventory:
  Springfield Benefits Example P6 Fire Hydrant.xls

Benefits were estimated for only three projects because this was thought sufficient to make a compelling ROI case. It also turns out that the two projects not selected overlap in terms of scope with two of those chosen.

The ROI team begins by creating a short, succinct definition of each of the benefits that they are going to model using the spreadsheet template provided. Then the relevant information is gathered, translated into a measurable form, and entered into spreadsheet documents based on the template provided. Next, any additional data and formulas are entered. Finally, the summary values are copied into the benefits summary sheet.

Opportunity	Benefits
Tree Cover Assessment: Baseline inventory of the city trees.	The City Manager wants to improve general appearance of the City. A Tree Cover Assessment will establish a base-line and allow future trends in afforestation/deforestation to be observed.
	Obtain Federal Highway Funding grant of $60,000/yr for 3 years if reduced pollution keeps air quality above critical level.
GASB 34 Regulatory Mandate Inventory: Create inventory and perform inspection and maintenance of City fire hydrants	Asset inventory data not only provide sound financial accountability, but the information necessary for obtaining bonding, grants and loans, recalculating impact fees and utility rates, estimating the cost of development, annexation costs and many other applications.
	Meet regulatory requirement as defined by GASB 34 legislation which applies to the City.
	An inventory of City fire hydrants will be a useful first stage to creating a database of all Public Works outside plant assets.
Brownfield Site Development: Identify brownfield sites suitable for redevelopment	Meet City's goal of reducing development of greenfield sites to 80% of current year total
	Obtain federal funding (EPA grant of $95,000) for brownfield site assessment.
Inward Investment: Use new application to attract new businesses	City is facing increasing regional competition for inward investment, new jobs and other regional activities.
	New businesses will generate revenue from business licenses, income tax and sales tax.
	New businesses will help to raise the educational attainment standards of schools.
Enterprise GIS: Create enterprise-wide GIS	Encourages collaboration, and sharing of data and other resources that will create a type of 'joined up" local government (this is one of the City Manager's goals).
	Provide better services to citizens by sharing more information, putting information and other services on-line.

Figure C7.1 List of benefits compiled for the City of Springfield

(yellow = intangible, orange = tangible).

P4 Economic development—Inward investment

The rationalization behind the inward investment economic development project benefits estimation is that new businesses attracted to the city will generate revenue for the city in the form of business licenses, property taxes, and income taxes. The estimation process treats small and medium businesses differently given the greater difficulty of attracting medium-sized businesses (there are fewer of them and they are typically less mobile), and the different levels of revenue that they will contribute to the city. It was felt unlikely, given Springfield's size, that large businesses would relocate to the city.

The base case revenue values on the "Inputs" tab were obtained from the Economic Development Department's historical data, and these values were simply adjusted for inflation for future years (figure C7.2). Historical values were also used for the number of new businesses without GIS (No GIS). The estimates for the number of businesses that could be attracted with GIS were decided by the Economic Development staff, following extensive discussion of the possible applications of GIS in the department. The analysis, as shown in figure C7.3, proceeds by calculating the estimated revenue without and with GIS, and then subtracting the former from the latter (GIS Case – Base in figure C7.3). Even allowing for the fact that it will take several years for the GIS-based economic development process to reach maximum potential (see "Benefits Realization Curve on the Benefit Tab for Small Businesses and Medium Businesses"), and that the confidence estimate is only 75 percent, the benefit yearly values are very large (medium businesses: $21,000– $120,000 per year; small businesses: $7,000– $71,000). Over eight years, the total (cumulative) benefit for this project is estimated at over $1.38m (see benefit summary sheet).

Input Name	Unit	Base Case	2008	2009
Small Biz Property Tax	$	$ 667.00	$ 667.00	$ 1,360.68
Small Biz Business License	$	$ 120.00	$ 120.00	$ 244.80
Small Biz Income Tax	$	$ 7,000.00	$ 7,000.00	$ 14,280.00
Medium Biz Property Tax	$	$ 474.00	$ 474.30	$ 493.27
Medium Biz Business License	$	$ 180.00	$ 180.00	$ 187.20
Medium Biz Income Tax	$		$ 105,000.00	$ 109,200.00
Small Business per Year Av No GIS	#	1.00		
Medium Business per Year Av No GIS	#	0.20		
Small Business per Year Av With GIS	#	5.00		
Medium Business per Year Av No GIS	#	0.50		

Figure C7.2   Economic development benefit input, City of Springfield.

P5 Federal highway funding grant (tree cover assessment)

The principal tangible benefit for the tree cover assessment project is receipt of a federal highway funding grant for three years due to the attainment of clean air standards in the city and surrounding areas (hence the name of the benefit is different from the project name).

The benefits estimation process is very simple for this project. It only requires the value of the clean air attainment grant to be entered in the "Input" tab and the "Benefit" tab, along with the respective benefit realization curve and confidence values. Following consultation with senior staff in the Parks and Recreation Department, Brian and his team elected to use values of 100 percent for the benefit realization curve, and 50 percent for the overall confidence. The benefit estimated for this project is $90,000 over eight years (actually all the benefit is achieved after the maximum three consecutive years of grants).

P6 Fire hydrant inspection and maintenance

The city fire hydrant inspection and maintenance project has been undertaken to meet statutory obligations under the GASB 34 regulation. The benefit estimation for the project is predicated on the assumption that travel time to fire hydrants will be reduced, and that once at the hydrants data entry will be faster and more accurate (electronic entry will be guided by interactive forms and will not have to be redone back in the office). The "Input" tab shows all the "with and without GIS" figures. The benefits sheet is shown in figure C7.4. This benefit is a little different from the earlier examples because the benefit is the cost saved and not the revenue generated, and hence the figures are negative (over seven years, $83,000 is saved by using GIS). Again, because of ramp-up time the benefits yield curve is set at 10 percent and 80 percent in years one and two. Also, due to some uncertainty in the efficacy of the field methods, the overall confidence value is 90 percent.

2010		2011		2012		2013		2014	
$	2,082.11	$	2,832.39	$	3,612.69	$	4,424.19	$	5,268.16
$	374.59	$	509.58	$	649.96	$	795.96	$	947.80
$	21,851.20	$	29,725.25	$	37,914.26	$	46,430.83	$	55,288.06
$	987.30	$	1,026.79	$	1,542.17	$	1,603.85	$	2,142.31
$	374.69	$	389.68	$	585.26	$	608.67	$	813.02
$	218,568.00	$	227,310.72	$	341,403.15	$	355,059.27	$	474,261.65

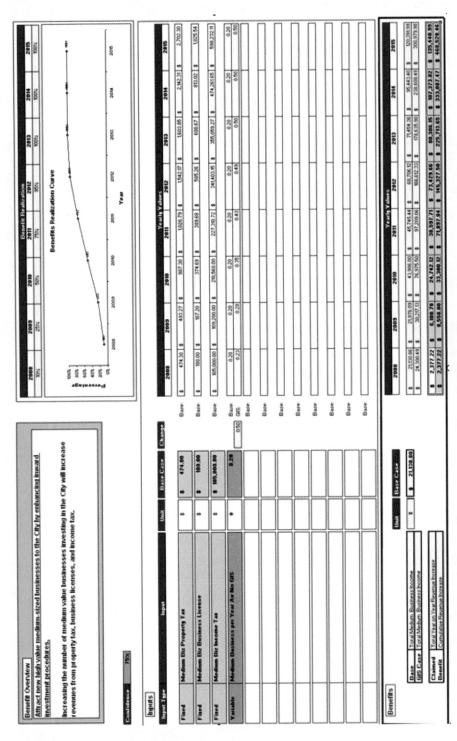

Figure C7.3   Benefit sheet for P4 inward investment, medium businesses, City of Springfield.

Benefit Overview

Conduct inspection and maintenance of City fire hydrants to minimize cost of compliance with GASB 34 regulation and to ensure correct operation.

Using GIS will be a more efficient and accurate method of data entry. It will avoid re-entry of data in office by data entry staff, and reduce time for field data entry because existing data will be provided in electronic forms on hand-held devices. GIS routing software will be used to optimize routes and provide driving directions.

Confidence: 99%

Inputs:

Input Type	Input	Unit	Base Case	Change
Variable	Average labor cost per inspection	$	15.05	$ 11.61
Variable	Average transportation cost per inspection	$	4.00	$ 3.50
Variable	Office data re-entry per inspection	$	1.00	0.36
Derived	Average Total Cost per Inspection	$	20.05	$ 0.36
Fixed	Total number Hydrants	#	2,492.00	

Benefits Realization Curve (Percentage vs. Year, 2008–2015)

Benefit Realization (2008–2015: 0%, 30%, 100%, 100%, 100%, 100%, 100%, 100%)

Benefits

	Unit	Base Case
Base	GIS Case	$ 50,064.85

Benefits		2008	2009	2010	2011	2012	2013	2014	2015
Base — Total Cost of Inspections	$	50,064.85	50,862.33	54,356.69	56,631.96	59,054.00	61,576.02	64,172.90	66,898.60
GIS Case — Total Cost of Inspections	$	48,928.72	42,700.60	42,046.63	43,098.56	45,080.36	47,440.28	49,050.23	51,770.18
Claimed — Reduction in Total Cost of Inspection	$	(1,022.52)	(8,515.55)	(11,081.75)	(11,932.46)	(12,029.23)	(12,542.17)	(13,070.49)	(13,633.91)
Benefit — Reduction in Total Cost of Inspection	$	(1,022.52)	(3,538.07)	(20,619.83)	(32,051.89)	(44,081.10)	(56,723.27)	(63,793.67)	(83,427.58)

Figure C7.4   Benefit sheet for P5 fire hydrant maintenance and inspection project, City of Springfield.

C7.3 Discussion of chapter 7 case study

The benefits estimation process is perhaps the most difficult part of the overall methodology because every project is unique and it often takes a while to work out how to model the form of benefits in a project. Indeed, Brian and his team spent a long time talking about the best way to model the benefits for the three projects they worked on. They also looked at a number of other possible benefits (for example, starting a business to sell geographic data and consulting services to other regional organizations), before settling on the three benefits presented here.

Even with just three projects, the ROI team was able to confidently predict a value of GIS to the City of Springfield of $232k in three years, $600k in five years, and $1.478m in eight years (see bottom line in figure C7.5).

	Yearly Values							
	2008	2009	2010	2011	2012	2013	2014	2015
Fire Hydrant Inspection:								
Yearly Total	(1,023)	(8,516)	(11,082)	(11,532)	(12,029)	(12,542)	(13,070)	(13,634)
Cumulative Total	(1,023)	(9,538)	(20,620)	(32,152)	(44,181)	(56,723)	(69,794)	(83,428)
Highway Funding Grant								
Yearly Total		$30,000	$30,000	$30,000				
Cumulative Total		$30,000	$60,000	$90,000	$90,000	$90,000	$90,000	$90,000
Total Businesses:								
Yearly Total	$23,402	$51,454	$97,666	$137,799	$199,960	$235,339	$291,886	$350,695
Cumulative Total	$23,402	$74,857	$172,522	$310,322	$510,282	$745,621	$1,037,507	$1,388,202
Total Revenue Benefits:								
Yearly Total	$23,402	$81,454	$127,666	$167,799	$199,960	$235,339	$291,886	$350,695
Cumulative Total	$23,402	$104,857	$232,522	$400,322	$600,282	$835,621	$1,127,507	$1,478,202
Total Operating Expenditure Benfits:								
Yearly Total	(1,023)	(8,516)	(11,082)	(11,532)	(12,029)	(12,542)	(13,070)	(13,634)
Cumulative Total	(1,023)	(9,538)	(20,620)	(32,152)	(44,181)	(56,723)	(69,794)	(83,428)

Figure C7.5 Benefits summary for three City of Springfield projects.

A few useful conclusions can be drawn from this benefits value modeling exercise. The best benefits are those that provide value each year and not just for a few years (for example, inward investment and highway funding grant). When modeling benefit values, concentrate on the most expensive or most valuable elements. For example, the impact of avoiding data reentry in the fire hydrant inspection example is quite small given the hourly costs of data entry labor, whereas each inspection costs a lot of money because of the hourly costs of inspectors. Finally, it is worth repeating that given the open-ended nature of the benefit value modeling process it is possible to be overzealous when building possible benefits. The hard realization, however, is that the assumptions made and the numbers generated will need to be sufficiently robust to stand up to detailed scrutiny by a panel of experts.

Endnotes

1. Halsing, D., K. Theissen, and R. Bernknoft. *A cost-benefit analysis of The National Map* (U.S. Department of the Interior and U.S. Geological Survey, Circular 1271 USGS, Denver 1–3, 2004); GITA and AWWA, *Building a business case for geospatial information technology: A practitioners guide to financial and strategic analysis* (GITA and AWWA, 2007).

2. Antenucci, J. C., K. Brown, P. L. Croswell, and M. J. Kevany. *Geographic information systems: A guide to the technology* (New York: Van Nostrand Reinhold, 1991).; Bernhardsen, T., *Geographic information systems: An introduction,* 2nd ed. (New York: John Wiley & Sons, Inc., 1999); Grimshaw, D. J., *Bringing geographical information systems into business,* 2nd ed. (New York: John Wiley & Sons, Inc., 2000); Tomlinson, R., *Thinking about GIS: Geographic information system planning for managers,* 3rd ed. (Redlands, Calif. ESRI Press, 2007); Thomas, C., and M. Ospina, *Measuring up: The business case for GIS* (Redlands, Calif.: ESRI Press, 2004); GITA and AWWA, *Building a business case.*; Pick, J. B., *Geo-Business: GIS in the Digital Organization* (Hoboken, New Jersey: John Wiley & Sons, Inc., 2008).

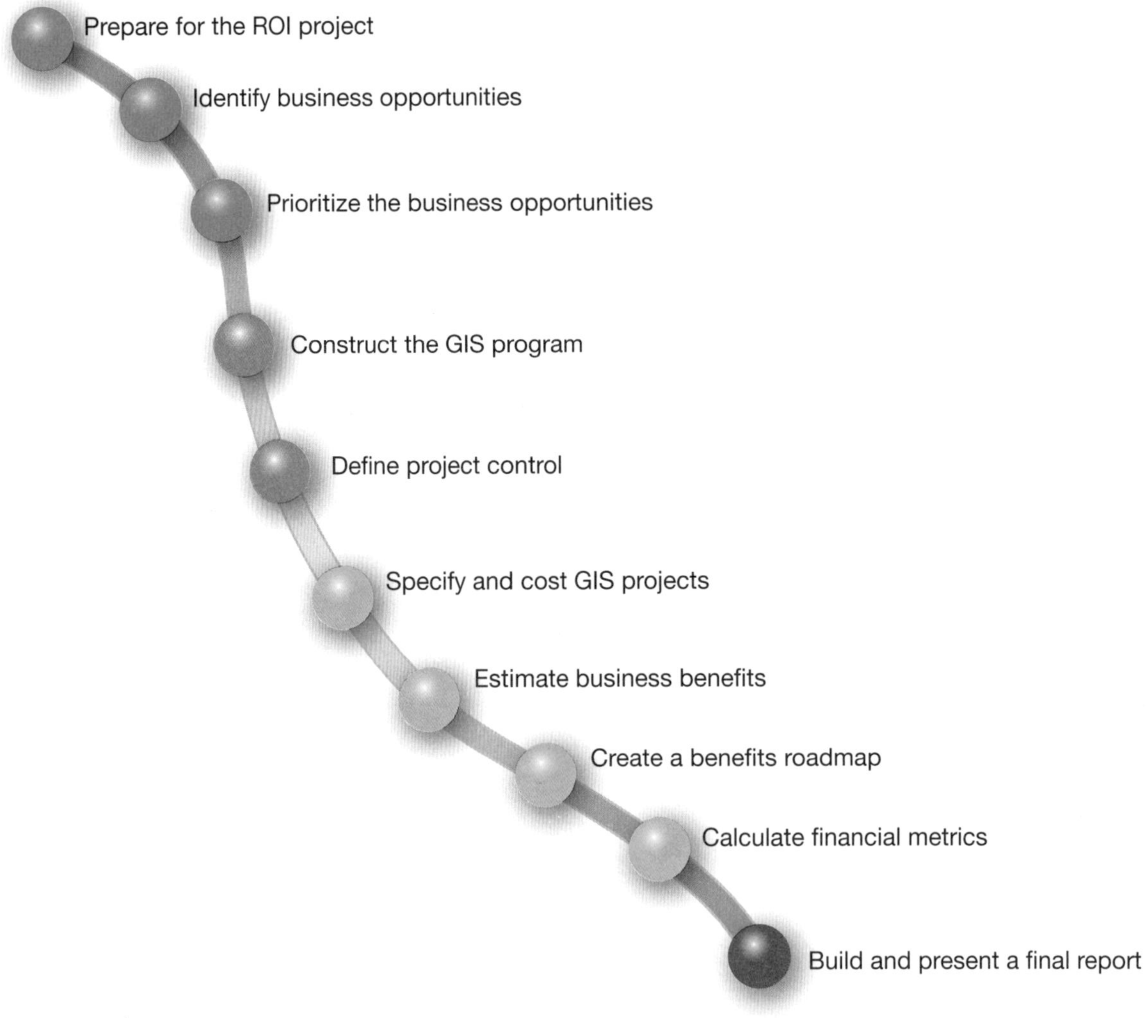

Prepare for the ROI project

Identify business opportunities

Prioritize the business opportunities

Construct the GIS program

Define project control

Specify and cost GIS projects

Estimate business benefits

Create a benefits roadmap

Calculate financial metrics

Build and present a final report

8

 Create a benefits roadmap

In addition to understanding the costs and benefits of large-scale investments, senior executives will also want a clear picture as to when the benefits of a GIS program will be realized within an organization. This chapter focuses on creating a timeline for delivery of benefits that shows major milestones and realized deliverables. In the case study, the creation of the benefits roadmap is discussed.

The previous two chapters have looked at the scale of GIS investment required, as defined through a budget, and quantified the value added to an organization using a benefits estimation process. This chapter uses inputs from the costs and benefits chapters to construct a high-level timeline for benefit delivery. This benefits roadmap is required to provide and communicate the delivery "pathway" for a GIS program over the next three or more years. It is not a project plan but rather a means to express what benefits a program will deliver on a quarter basis. The roadmap will also provide a useful means of communicating the overall scope and timing of events to executives and other relevant teams and individuals.

OBJECTIVES

The objective of this chapter is to construct a simple but communicative GIS benefits roadmap. The required inputs to do this are already available: the project timeline found in the budget document, created as part of the tasks in chapter 6; and the benefits summary sheet, created as part of the tasks in chapter 7.

There are a number of considerations that come into play when building a roadmap that may require revision of both a budget and estimated benefits. For example, when creating a roadmap it may be determined that the pace of investment needs to be evened out because it is too aggressive, or that there is a need to focus more on delivering one project benefit earlier in order to show quick results or because it is more important than another project benefit. Consider, for example, a case where a GIS project is being delivered that provides new capabilities to the Customer Service Department. Another project that has been identified may deliver improved capability to the Engineering Department. If it is known that an organization is under pressure to improve customer service quality, perhaps due to some bad publicity about service quality, then it may be best to choose to deliver the benefits associated with the Customer Service Department project ahead of those for the Engineering Department.

Consider the roadmap a communications tool for explaining benefits delivery to an organization as well as an operational tool to help a program manager or team stay focused and on track. Executives are unlikely to be interested in the specific details of a project plan; rather they will likely be more interested in the outputs from activities that impact the business in a positive way.

TASKS

Using the structured template available for download from the Web site, the main activity is to build a GIS program benefits roadmap. Projects will need to be grouped into logical themes to enable explanation about how all the projects in a program fit together and collectively deliver the final benefits that will be identified in the ROI financial calculations (chapter 9). Visualizing when the benefits will be delivered will make it easier to communicate the GIS program objectives to senior executives and other interested parties.

Tools: Benefits roadmap template

Documents created from the benefits roadmap template (figure 8.1), allow you to articulate and effectively communicate the value of the GIS projects and when your organization will realize the value of a portfolio of GIS projects. The digital file can be found under step 8 on the supporting Web site at http://gis. esri.com/roi.

There are four main tasks in this chapter: categorize projects into themes, construct the roadmap, add value-delivery milestones, and reconcile the roadmap with organizational expectations.

✔ 8.1 Categorize projects into themes

In chapter 4, the concept of the GIS project definition pyramid was introduced (figure 4.1), which helped to identify the discrete elements of each project (hardware, software, data, training, etc.). In this chapter, the projects that have been identified will be placed into key themes that help convey their importance to the overall program in more business, rather than technical project, terms.

Although there are no specific themes that must be used, there are some rules that will help when grouping projects. These thematic categories are used on the roadmap to demonstrate that each individual project plays its part in delivering an overall set of benefits.

When grouping projects, there are generally four themes that should be considered: foundation, governance, process, and technology solutions. On the roadmap and when articulating a plan to executives, these themes are necessary to help show that benefits are only delivered to the organization when a *collection* of projects has been completed. For instance, although a data consolidation project may not immediately or directly deliver benefits to the organization, it is still a fundamental element on the roadmap, and one that is a necessary prerequisite for other projects. For GIS professionals, the benefits of a data-aggregation project may seem obvious. However, for senior executives, without further related specific information, this explanation could be interpreted as late delivery of a new mapping application because there are a series of "other things to do that relate to data." If a roadmap is presented that visually illustrates how successive building blocks lead to the delivery of an application, stakeholders are more inclined to understand that the steps to a successful business return are not completed in a vacuum, but often have dependencies on the completion of preceding or succeeding activities.

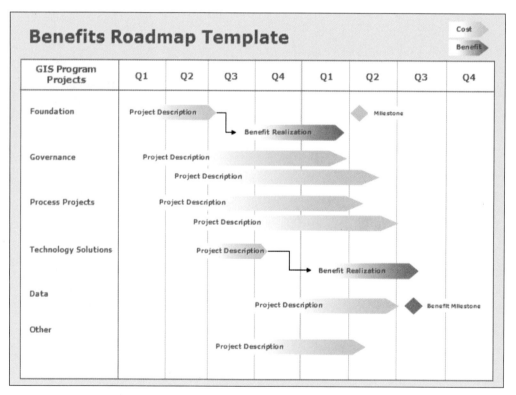

Figure 8.1   Benefits roadmap template.

As mentioned above, the key themes for categorizing projects are as follows:

Foundation: These are projects required to lay the right basis or foundation for building applications and capabilities that will deliver new or improved benefits/value to an organization. These can include establishing a GIS hardware and software base infrastructure upon which applications can be built; and creating base datasets that are required to support multiple applications (e.g., base mapping).

Insight: Data is an important foundational project

GIS are data-centric systems, and a significant portion of your GIS program budget is likely to be spent on data. Executives often don't understand the complexities of data conversion and legacy data alignment and integration, so you will need to make sure that the necessity of having high-quality data in your GIS program is clear, by showing it as a building block that is foundational to delivery of other benefits.

Governance: If a GIS program is of sufficient size and complexity, it may well be appropriate to define a project that sets up an organizational structure or program management office (PMO) to support the program. Chapter 5 discusses the details of an optimal organizational project control group.

Process: GIS programs will likely be modifying or implementing new work practices within an organization. It is important to give confidence to executives that a GIS program will not only capture/convert and align data but that once an investment has been made, it will not be diluted through the lack of suitable processes for keeping databases up to date.

Others: This category is provided to add any projects that do not fit into the other categories.

Technology solutions: Ultimately, the benefits that will be realized by an organization will be via technical application solutions that people interact with to drive better and more efficient and effective operations and decision making. Many GIS projects focus on the technology without sufficient attention to the other nontechnical categories, and as a result the benefits delivered to an organization are weakened or not realized at all. Applications that can be shown in action are more tangible to executives than the other categories, but the goal will be to convince executives that all of the projects are equally important for both delivering the benefit and sustaining it cost effectively.

After grouping GIS projects into these four themes, begin populating the roadmap document.

✔ 8.2   Use the budget Gantt chart to construct a roadmap

The process of creating a benefits roadmap document begins by transposing the Gantt chart view of a budget (figure 8.2) from chapter 6, into a document created from the benefits roadmap template. A budget document Gantt chart can be accessed from the budget main menu by selecting the "Gantt Chart" button.

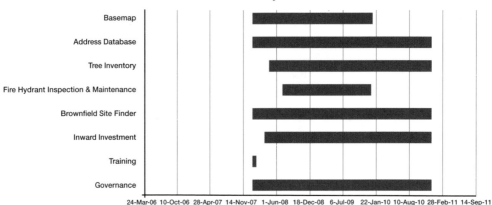

Figure 8.2   An example Gantt chart from a budget document.

There is no single formula for creating benefits roadmaps, given the diversity of GIS programs, so the template provided here is quite flexible. All aspects of a benefits roadmap document can be edited, including the title, timeline dates (in the template two sets of four quarters are shown), and the project categories. To begin creating a roadmap document, the title of the GIS program should be entered into the template at the top and the timeline set to that of the GIS program. At this point it is a good idea to create a new document under a new name to avoid overwriting the template.

On the left side of a roadmap document the default project categories are provided for use, but these can be changed if they do not meet the specific requirements of a GIS program. On the right side there is space to enter information about the specific projects. Details about specific projects are added using arrows to indicate activities and diamonds for milestones, as is shown in figure 8.3. Project dependencies can be added using the black arrow symbols. In this way, any project dependencies, and the cost and benefit parts of a project, can be linked together. For example, in figure 8.3 it can clearly be seen that a foundational project of address matching starts in Q1 and is estimated to be finished in mid-Q3. Once completed, both the dependent integrating workflow and enable service-oriented architecture projects can begin.

There may be quite complex relationships between projects and their benefits. For example, in figure 8.3, the benefit for Address Matching and Enable Service-Oriented Architecture is the same as the codependent Airport Facilities Management Project.

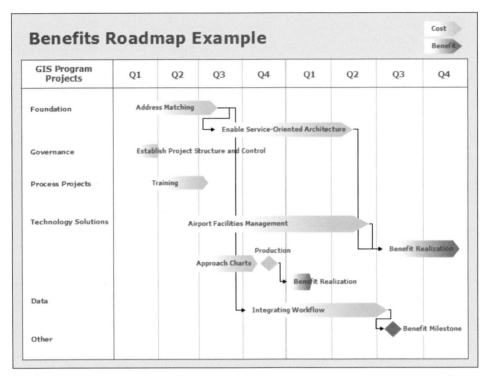

Figure 8.3 Example benefits roadmap.

Insight: Use the template only as a guide

Your benefits roadmap can take many forms, so do not be limited by this simple template, since it is intended only as a guide. For example, you may choose to add some text under each project for explanation, or perhaps balloon callouts to reference key milestones and provide more detail about their deliverables. It is also recommended that you use a poster-size plot of your roadmap, to be displayed on a wall or other large visible surface, to provide a "walk-through" for people.

✔ 8.3 Add milestones to represent "value drops"

Once all the details about costs and benefits have been added, the next task is to provide specific details of any key benefits milestones. Using the benefits model completed in chapter 7, "value drop" (benefit) milestones should be added that represent when major benefits will be delivered to an organization. Generally, it is only important to show when benefits delivery starts, rather than trying to show each benefit increment over a period of time. Recall in chapter 7 a benefits realization curve was used to recognize that all of a benefit may not be realized instantly but instead gradually.

Insight: Use familiar and standard organizational approaches

You may find that your executives don't respond well to poster-size roadmaps. Sometimes a list of quarterly milestones that clearly outline the benefits to be delivered each quarter—sometimes called "value drops"—will be sufficient (see task 8.3). Be conscious of the manner in which your executives like to receive and consume information and have concepts and objectives explained.

✔ 8.4 Reconcile the benefits delivery roadmap with expectations

Executives typically look for quick wins for their organization, and this is a useful guiding principle for creating benefit roadmaps. After building a benefits delivery roadmap, it is sometimes the case that no benefits are actually being delivered to an organization for a year or even longer. This might be a result of the manner in which foundational projects have been structured, which can often have a long upfront duration. In such cases, it is important to consider how benefit delivery can be moved forward on a roadmap. For example, rather than delivering 100 percent of the benefits in Q3, it might be possible to release version 1.0 of an application that delivers 80 percent of the value to the business in Q1, and the remaining 20 percent by Q3. Incremental wins that build upon each other are extremely powerful to strengthen momentum for a program. It is important to show results early and often.

OUTCOME

Once the four tasks described here have been completed, the benefits roadmap can be used to convey to executives and colleagues *when* benefits will be received by an organization. Here the focus should not be on the *details* of what will be happening from an activity perspective—since most executives won't be interested in the details of a data conversion project, for example—but rather *when* they will see benefit to the organization in business terms.

Case Study

CREATE BENEFITS ROADMAP

Having completed the costs (chapter 6) and the benefits (chapter 7) steps in the ROI methodology, the next step for Brian Sobers and the ROI team at the City of Springfield is to establish the timeline roadmap for delivering the benefits. The team used the benefits roadmap template "Benefits_Roadmap_Template.ppt," which is available on the supporting Web site (http://gis.esri.com/roi) to create a timeline for the City of Springfield ROI project.

The team categorizes the projects defined in chapter 4 (see section C4.2) into "themes" for the purposes of defining a roadmap and enters the data on projects and benefits into a new document derived from the benefits roadmap template. They then add milestones that indicate significant benefit delivery points. Lastly, they adjust the timeline to match overall organizational goals and expectations for the GIS projects.

C8.1   Benefits roadmap

Figure C8.1 shows the benefits timeline for the City of Springfield projects, as completed by Brian and the rest of the ROI team. The basemap and address database projects have been defined as foundation projects because they are building blocks for later projects. The diagram also shows governance (structure and control) and process (training) projects. There are four technology solution projects, as defined and discussed in earlier chapters. Some of the benefits begin gradually as intangible, shown as graduated colored bar arrows, before transitioning to tangible benefits. Specific milestones are shown as diamonds. In the case of figure C8.1, the main benefit milestones are the awards of government grants and completion of the fire hydrant inspection project.

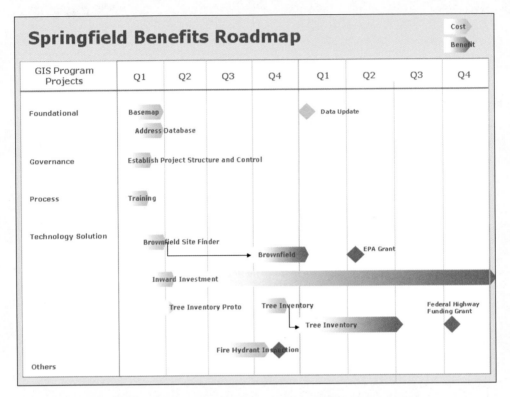

Figure C8.1 Benefits roadmap for the City of Springfield ROI projects.

C8.2 Discussion of chapter 8 case study

Creating the benefits roadmap is an effective approach to visualizing the timing of projects and the accordant benefit deliveries. A single diagram can be a useful way to summarize an ROI project and provides an easy way to explain the overall plan for deliverables. It also helps to identify project overlaps and resource conflicts, and to determine if the projects will meet overall organizational goals (i.e., if the projects are too long, if there is a regular sequence of deliverables, or if there is a lot of risk associated with all the deliverables arriving at the end of a long project). The benefits roadmap is a living document that will need to be updated on many occasions as the focus and timing of projects change.

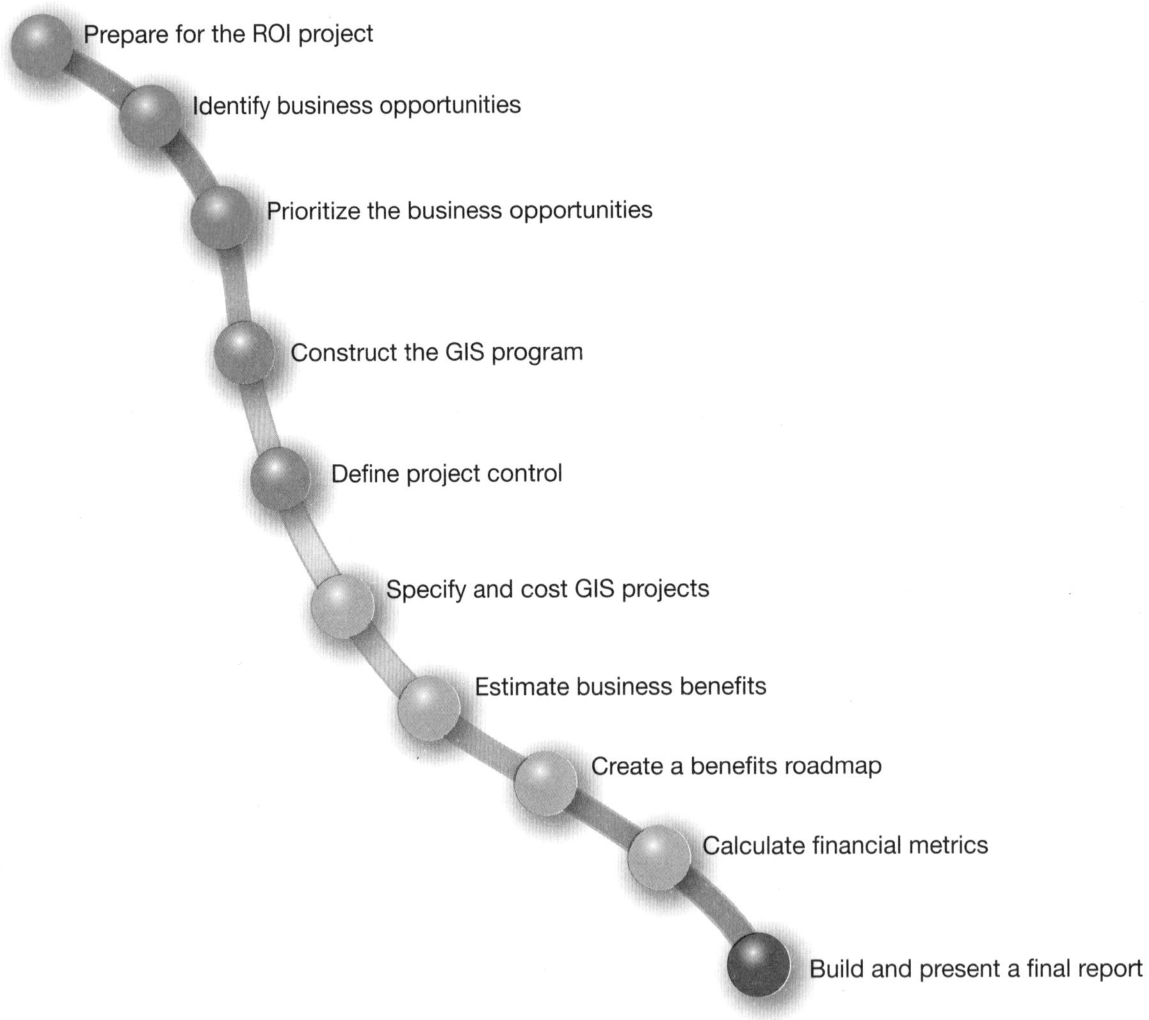

Prepare for the ROI project

Identify business opportunities

Prioritize the business opportunities

Construct the GIS program

Define project control

Specify and cost GIS projects

Estimate business benefits

Create a benefits roadmap

Calculate financial metrics

Build and present a final report

9

Calculate financial metrics

This chapter contains the last set of analytical tasks. Using input from the previous work undertaken to create a budget (costs) and assess the value of benefits, the next task is to perform the required financial analysis to calculate the real value of a proposed GIS program to an organization. A series of financial measures that compare costs and benefits to provide contrasting assessments of the expected overall value of a proposed GIS program is recommended.

INTRODUCTION

The previous chapters of this book detailed the creation of a budget for a program of GIS projects and estimates of the benefits for several of the key projects. Now it is time to use the budget and benefits data as input for financial analyses that will calculate the expected financial impact of a GIS program on an organization.

The financial analysis used here introduces some new terms that may not be familiar to many people who work in the GIS field. This chapter therefore begins with a definition of the key terms and financial metrics used as the basis for GIS return on investment analysis in an organization. Next, the budget and benefit data are used to calculate the recommended metrics. Some insights into how to interpret and use the various metrics are then provided. Finally, the analyses are undertaken on the case study data.

DEFINITIONS

"Return on investment" has been used in this book as a measure of the general success or failure of a GIS project or program of work. In this chapter, a very precise formulaic definition of "Return on Investment" (note capitalization) is also introduced into the discussion.

There are many financial measures of project efficiency in use today in the wider IT and business communities. Each evaluates something a little bit different, and each has advantages and disadvantages, depending of the nature of the project being measured and the goals of the measurement exercise. Of the many different metrics available, the most useful for ROI studies such as those described here are "Net Present Value" (NPV), "Internal Rate of Return" (IRR), "Payback Period–Discounted," and "Return on Investment" (ROI). For completeness, the phrase "cost-benefit analysis" is also defined, even though it is not recommended for use in GIS programs. The definition of these terms takes a high-level approach of explaining what each term means, how it is calculated, and how it can be interpreted and applied. More detailed discussion can be found in any good corporate financial analysis text or on the Web (see, for example, www.wikipedia.org). It is also recommended that the topic of financial performance metrics is discussed with key people in an organization's finance department who should be able to provide more in-depth understanding in an organization-specific context.

Time value of money. This is an important concept that needs to be understood in order to fully grasp some of the financial metrics presented here. With all things being equal, would you rather receive a fixed payment today or a promise of the same fixed payment in the future? If you received the payment today, then you could invest it, for example, in a bank, and accrue interest on it. Therefore, the *present value* of a given sum of money is actually greater than the promise of a given sum at some point in the future.

Net Present Value (NPV). How much is a project worth in today's money? Executives are usually interested in multiyear financial assessments of future programs of work. It is necessary, therefore, to take into consideration the "value" of money when forecasting potential returns. In simple terms, the money used to fund a GIS program could alternatively be used to fund other activities, or it could earn interest if invested elsewhere. NPV is a representation of the value of a project in today's money. In other words, future costs and benefits need to be discounted so that they can be expressed in today's value. An organization's finance department will generally have a set discount rate that it uses for financial analysis, and this is normally the number that should be used in ROI financial analyses. The *discount rate* is often referred to as the "opportunity cost of capital"—that is, the expected rate of return foregone by investing in a project. The discount rate is generally a little less than the prime rate, which is the interest rate a bank will charge to its most creditworthy customers (on November 5, 2007, the U.S. prime rate was 7.5 percent, and the European Central Bank rate was 4 percent). Net Present Value represents the cumulative value of the expected return of a project over a specified period of time minus the initial costs of the project (required investment), expressed in present terms. Represented as a simple formula, this can be viewed as the following:

Net Present Value = Value of Expected Return – Required Investment

NPV shows the magnitude of a project and if a project generates a profit and should, therefore, be undertaken. It is generally regarded as the best way to assess if investors will get their money back. NPV provides an indication as to whether or not an investment is worth it. A positive NPV means that a project will yield positive returns over and above the investors' expectations. A negative NPV is a red flag for investors, who should rethink a project's configuration (or perhaps cancel it all together), as it is not expected to deliver value in its existing form.

Internal Rate of Return (IRR). If the financial benefits of a project were restated as an interest rate, what would the rate be? Is the return higher or lower than the opportunity cost of capital? IRR is a similar indicator to NPV; however, where NPV is expressed as a dollar amount, the IRR is a percentage of a return over an investment. The IRR is the annualized effective compounded return rate that can be earned on an investment, i.e., the yield on an investment. Because IRR is expressed as a percentage, it can be a useful way to compare projects; however, NPV is generally considered a better overall measure because it defines the total added value in today's (present day) money, even though the project may run for several years.

The Internal Rate of Return should be compared with the discount rate of a project. If the IRR is above the discount rate, then a project creates value for an organization and its investors. An IRR below the discount rate is generally a sign that a project will destroy value. Executives will usually retool or abandon projects with an IRR below their discount rate. However, this is not always the case, as there are other criteria that come into play, such as strategic positioning.

IRR gives a good indication of the percentage of business impact of a project, and is especially useful for large multiyear investments, but provides no indication of the size or timing of benefits. IRR is often considered a "hurdle rate" used to compare many different types of projects (IT and non-IT), where the hurdle rate represents the minimum return required for a particular class of project. Typically organizations involved in GIS projects seek an IRR of between 8 and 30 percent, with an appropriate balance of risk.

Payback Period–Discounted. How quickly does a project pay for itself? How long must a project last in order to offer a positive net present value? The payback period represents the amount of time (usually number of years) required for an organization and its investors to get their money back from a particular project. For example, if an organization invests $1m in a GIS program, and receives $250k per year in benefits, then the payback period will be four years. Some organizations set a maximum payback period, e.g., an organization can choose to reject systematically any project with a payback greater than, say, five years. Payback Period–Discounted is more sophisticated than simple payback because Payback Period–Discounted takes *the time value of money* into account, in a similar way to NPV and IRR. Therefore, it provides a better representation of the payback period of a project.

Although evaluating the payback period may appear to be the simplest way to communicate the idea of whether or not a project should be pursued, be cautious that any cash flows that arrive after the payback period are typically not considered.

Finally, where the NPV and the IRR provide a view of how much value a project provides and returns, respectively, the Payback Period–Discounted shows *when* a project will provide a return on investment, if any.

Free Cash Flow (FCF) subsidy. How much cash will an organization need to find to put into a project? Executives, especially those in publicly-traded companies also want to know how much cash a program will require to "get it off the ground." The FCF subsidy is the maximum amount that will need to be invested by an organization before a project starts self-funding (becomes total cash flow positive). Ideally the FCF subsidy will be at its cumulative maximum early in a project. Then, as benefits are realized, the project will start to self-fund and reduce the amount of subsidy by the organization. Although not as widely discussed in the literature as some of the other metrics used here, it is felt that this is a useful measure of the status and success of a GIS program.

Return on Investment (ROI). ROI is a ratio of the expected gains (net benefits) divided by the total costs, both expressed in cash terms. The net benefits are calculated as the total benefits minus the total costs. ROI is normally expressed as a percentage either on an annual basis (annual ROI) or for the duration of a project/program (classic ROI). The classic ROI calculation, as used in this methodology, is defined as the following:

%ROI = (Total Net Benefits / Total Costs) × 100

ROI is a simple way of assessing whether benefits provide returns over and above the costs (capital and operational expenditures) of the GIS investment.

There are both advantages and disadvantages to using ROI as a financial measure of expected project return. The main advantages of the ROI metric are that it is simple enough to calculate and interpret, and that it is in widespread use. The main disadvantages are that ROI doesn't measure absolute value added (NPV measures this), doesn't explicitly specify the period of return (Payback Period is one measure of this), and there are several subtle calculation variations that can lead to different estimates of projected project return. Because of its popularity and widespread use by many project managers and other executives eager to get a feel for the return on investment from projects, it is included in the spreadsheet templates of this methodology. The other metrics discussed previously are also included in this methodology.

Insight: Capital budget planning

Remember, even if calculated financial figures show a positive return for an organization from a GIS investment, executives will be looking at a bigger picture. In a process known as "capital budget planning," they will be determining how best to allocate limited resources (money, IT, people, etc.) between competing programs of work. Therefore, it is important not only to demonstrate that GIS projects will add value but also that the level of investment, timing of returns, and predictability of future cash flows stemming from a GIS program are greater than other competing programs. Indeed this is the purpose of the roadmap, organizational design/governance, and GIS project selection of the methodology.

A note on cost-benefit analysis (CBA). Cost-benefit analysis is a straight ratio of total benefits divided by total costs. The terms CBA and ROI are sometimes mistakenly used interchangeably. Occasionally, it is suggested that CBA is more comprehensive than ROI because it includes both intangible and tangible benefits (see, for example, NSGIC[1]). Although in the comprehensive methodology used here, it is certainly recommended that both tangible and intangible benefits are considered, the ROI calculations only use tangible benefits—that is, those that are measurable.

OBJECTIVES

The objectives of the tasks in this chapter are to calculate a series of financial metrics or indicators, by completing a financial calculations document based on a spreadsheet template provided on the accompanying Web site (http://gis.esri.com/roi). The results are then interpreted, using guidance provided by the discussion in this chapter, to assess the strength of a financial case for implementing or expanding a GIS program.

TASKS

✔ 9.1 Reengage with the finance department

In order to help perform financial analysis, this chapter provides a typical financial calculation template that has all the most commonly used financial measures, as defined previously, for assessing the expected returns of programs. After reading this chapter completely, the first task is to take the template to someone in the organization's finance department and work with them to ensure they understand and agree with the overall approach. Fortunately, all but the smallest organizations have finance and accounting departments that perform financial analysis on a regular basis. The individuals in these teams are allies in the quest to calculate and interpret the financial results of ROI work. They will know the details and inner workings of the equations, but on the whole GIS professionals just need to know the basis of the metrics, the meaning of the results, and how to apply them within an organization.

Conferring with finance experts in an organization will have the added advantage of gaining buy-in from finance department managers for return on investment results. This is particularly important because executives most likely will rely on the judgment of senior people in a finance department as to whether any analysis is reliable and robust.

✔ 9.2 Populate the financial calculations template—General assumptions

This chapter provides a financial calculations spreadsheet that allows the results of the work in chapter 6, where the cost (budget) of the GIS program was estimated, and chapter 7, where the expected year-on-year benefits from that investment were estimated, to be comprehensively analyzed.

The financial metrics template spreadsheet (figure 9.1) maintains the same familiar main menu structure of the other templates, with Inputs, Outputs, and Setup. The name of the project should be entered first by clicking the field at the top labeled "<Enter Project Name>." A new document should then be created under a new name to avoid overwriting the template.

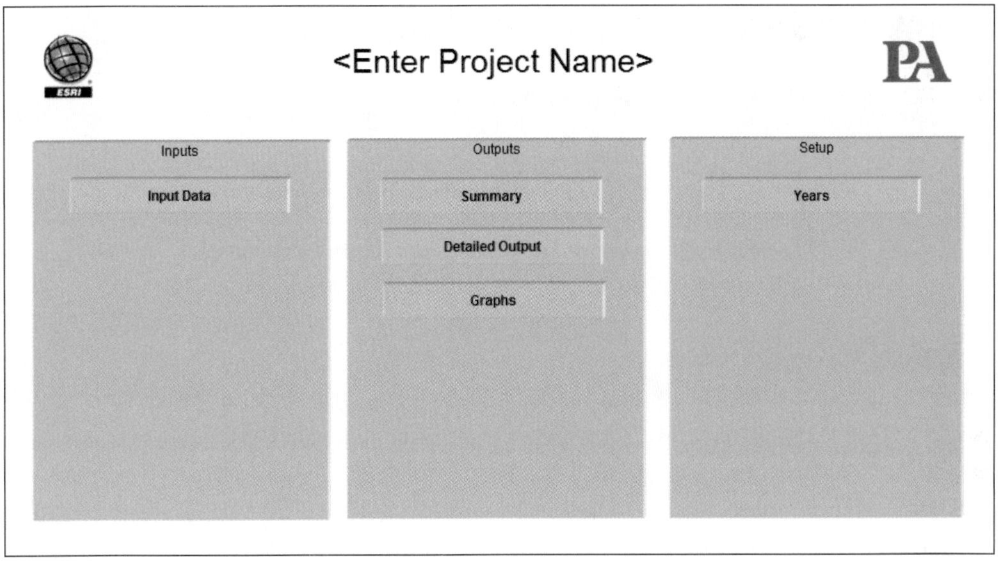

Figure 9.1 Main menu from the financial metrics template.

The first pieces of data that need to be entered relate to the duration of the financial model being created. Clicking the "Years" button on the opening menu will show the "Setup" screen (figure 9.2). The start year (the current year) and the number of years that the financial model will run should be entered here. The "Number of Years" represents the period of time over which the return will be modeled. In other words, over what period of time is it reasonable to expect a return on the initial investment? Many organizations have different planning horizons, even sometimes across different divisions of the same company. It is important, therefore, to agree on the review period for this potential GIS investment with the finance department and possibly with the key stakeholders. The typical range is 4–7 years, but this is only a guide. The template allows for modeling the return up to 10 years.

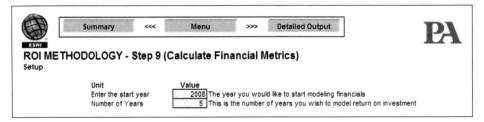

Figure 9.2   Setup from an example financial metrics document.

Next, the financial information should be entered by clicking the "Input Data" button. Figure 9.3 shows the input sheet that needs to be populated. Fortunately, most of this information is accessible from the work completed in earlier chapters. It is now simply a task of entering or transferring (copy/paste) the requisite data in the correct manner.

Some of the information required can be obtained from the financial department and then entered into the "General assumptions" section at the top of the "Input Data" screen in the model being created (figure 9.3).

ROI METHODOLOGY - Step 9 (Calculate Financial Metrics)
Input data

General assumptions

Source	Variable	Unit of measure	Value	Comments
1 Finance	Number of years to model	years	5	10 years max
2 Finance	Tax rate	%	39%	Enter tax rate on Corporate Earnings
3 Finance	Discount rate	%	10%	Consult your finance department

Time-sensitive assumptions

Source	Variable	Unit of measure	Start Year 2008	2009	2010	2011	2012
	Timeline						
4 Budget	Capital Expenditure (decrease in CapEx)	$					
5 Budget	Operating expenditure (savings)	$					
6 Budget	Depreciation (savings)	$					
7 Benefits	Revenue (loss)	$					
8 Benefits	Operating expenditure (savings)	$					
9 Benefits	On-going change in Capital Expenditure (savings)	$					

Figure 9.3 An input sheet from an example financial metrics document.

Tax rate–Line 2. In order to accurately capture the complete financial picture and obtain a bottom-line view of the impact of a GIS program, the value for the amount of corporate income taxation that the organization will have to pay on any earnings will need to be entered. For some organizations this figure may be a standard corporate tax rate of 39 percent; for other organizations it may be 0 percent (e.g., nonprofit or charitable organizations). Again, advice about the right number for analysis should be sought from someone in a finance department.

Discount rate – Line 3. This is effectively the cost of financing a project for an organization's stakeholders (for example, banks and shareholders), or the opportunity cost of not investing the money. The discount rate is applied to cash flows and is a function of risk and time. For instance, a cash flow expected in 5 years would be more discounted than a cash flow expected in 2 years (see earlier discussion on the time value of money). Also, a project with a higher risk profile may have a higher discount rate than a less risky initiative. For a project to be value-generating, its Internal Rate of Return (IRR) should exceed the discount rate, which is essentially the minimum rate of return required by an organization for any investment. Calculating the exact discount rate of a project, or for an organization, is a complex exercise. Again, there is a need to obtain this figure from someone in an organization's finance department. If a placeholder is needed in the meantime, then 10 percent is a good default to choose. However, this number is likely to change and can have a strong impact on the result of the analysis, especially if a project barely breaks even.

✔ 9.3 Populate the financial calculations template—budget (costs)

After completing the "General assumptions" part of a financial metrics document, the costs should be entered next into lines 4–6.

Capital expenditure (decrease in CapEx)—Line 4. Back in chapter 6, a 3-year capital and operational budget was created, the results of which are summarized on the "Financial Figures for ROI" tab off the main menu in a budget document (figure 9.4).

YEARLY TOTALS

	2008	2009	2010
Capital Expenditure	1,232,900	403,020	603,430
Operating Expenditure	78,000	82,000	84,000

Use these figures to populate the Financial Calculations template

Figure 9.4   An example of "Financial Figures for ROI" from a budget document.

The figure 9.4 example shows that there is an initial capital investment in 2008 of approximately $1.2m dollars, $403k in 2009, and $600k in 2010. This type of cost profile is to be expected for capital expenses, since GIS programs typically have large up-front investments in hardware, software, data, and so on, which decrease in the subsequent years (but not always because, for example, hardware and software could be leased). The Capital expenditure figures have been copied from the budget and pasted into the financial metrics model as shown in figure 9.5.

Input data

General assumptions

Source	Variable	Unit of measure	Value	Comments
1 Finance	Number of years to model	years	5	10 years max
2 Finance	Tax rate	%	39%	Enter tax rate on Corporate Earnings
3 Finance	Discount rate	%	10%	Consult your finance department

Time-sensitive assumptions

Source	Variable	Unit of measure	Start Year				
	Timeline		2008	2009	2010	2011	2012
4 Budget	Capital Expenditure (decrease in CapEx)	$	1,232,900	403,020	603,430		
5 Budget	Operating expenditure (savings)	$	78,000	82,000	84,000	88,200	92,610
6 Budget	Depreciation (savings)	$					
7 Benefits	Revenue (loss)	$					
8 Benefits	Operating expenditure (savings)	$					
9 Benefits	On-going change in Capital Expenditure (savings)	$					

Figure 9.5   Example of financial metrics model populated with data from a budget.

Insight: Increases to CapEx budget after year 3

The reality is, as a budget is recast year on year, there will be a need to modify the capital expenditure (CapEx) projections to reflect changing business priorities, new technologies, changes in an organization's business environment, and so on. However, generally increasing capital expenditure profile over the years should be avoided. This is not an attractive view for executives, since effectively, they are being told that each year they should expect to invest more and more funds, rather than less and less, in GIS. The budget must convey a clear sense of when something will finish.

Operating expenditure (savings)—Line 5. Figure 9.5 also shows the operational expenditure pasted from a budget. These figures relate to such items as ongoing support, running a help desk, and license maintenance. These effectively represent the cost of yearly ownership and operation of the GIS. In general terms, the operational expenses should not increase significantly unless there are new capital projects that also change the size or breadth of the GIS. Only three years of figures can be obtained from a budget, and so in cases where the goal is to evaluate the financial case for a GIS program over more than three years, the additional values must be extrapolated. The easiest way to complete the spreadsheet is simply to use values for preceding years, allowing for increases in inflation (generally only 3 to 10 percent increases), as has been done in figure 9.5 for years 2011 and 2012.

Depreciation (savings)—Line 6. Depreciation is a method of allocating a fixed asset's cost over its useful life. By avoiding a large lump-sum expense, a financial department is able to apportion expenses into smaller increments over several years, which smoothes out the bottom-line summary figures for an organization (and helps with taxation liabilities). In order to calculate depreciation, the following information is required: whether a given asset is eligible to be depreciated, the original valuation, and the rate of depreciation (the timeline for spreading the value). While there are many ways to calculate depreciation, most organizations are usually driven by income tax purposes, and the government will produce guidelines for how different types of assets can be depreciated. Most commonly, three methods are used to calculate depreciation: straight line, double declining balance, or some variation or combination of the first two (e.g., 150 percent declining balance). Straight-line depreciation is calculated by first subtracting the salvage value—the value after depreciation—from the current value of an asset, and then dividing by the number of years of useful life. Double declining balance involves first calculating the straight-line depreciation and then doubling the total percentage of the asset that is depreciated. In subsequent years, that same percentage is multiplied by the remaining balance until the value is lower than the straight-line value, at which point the straight-line method is used for the remainder of the asset's useful life. A large number of variations of these two methods exist, including using 150 percent (instead of 200 percent, that is, double) for the declining balance.

All three of these methods are calculated by the depreciation template provided as part of this methodology (depreciation.xls, see figure 9.6), and so it is simply a question of picking the one recommended by finance department policies for how an organization depreciates assets.

Depreciation Sample Worksheet

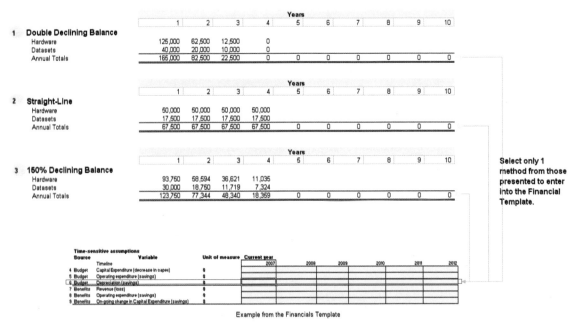

Figure 9.6 An example of depreciation calculations in the template provided. The table snapshot at the bottom shows where the depreciation values should be pasted into a financial metrics spreadsheet.

The depreciation spreadsheet template provided to assist with calculating the depreciation of assets included in a GIS program, takes input values from the "Analysis by Category" tab off the main menu of a budget document (see chapter 6). Budget documents automatically separate hardware and data—which can usually be depreciated—from software, outside labor, inside labor, and so on, which usually cannot. The depreciation spreadsheet template has three tabs: "Summary," "Hardware," and "Datasets." The "Hardware" and "Datasets" tabs have input cells for three values: initial cost, salvage value, and useful life (years). In the case of the example here, the input values are hardware initial cost: $105,000, salvage value: $0, useful life: 5 years, dataset initial cost: $30,000, salvage value: $0, useful life: 5 years. Once values have been entered into the depreciation spreadsheet, the three methods of calculating depreciation are presented automatically (figure 9.7). Figure 9.7 shows the depreciation calculations for the example being followed in this chapter. It is then simply a task of copying the values for the preferred methods and pasting them into the financial metrics spreadsheet. Figure 9.7 includes the double-declining balance depreciation calculations for the worked example.

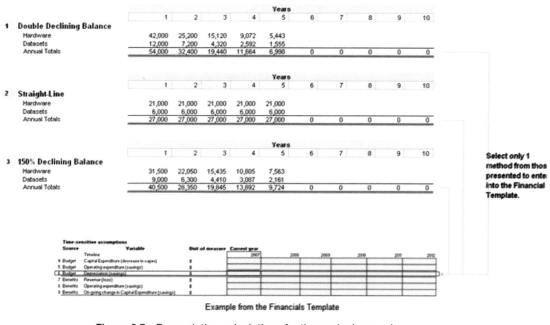

Figure 9.7 Depreciation calculations for the worked example.

Input data

General assumptions

Source	Variable	Unit of measure	Value	Comments
1 Finance	Number of years to model	years	5	10 years max
2 Finance	Tax rate	%	39%	Enter tax rate on Corporate Earnings
3 Finance	Discount rate	%	10%	Consult your finance department

Time-sensitive assumptions

Source	Variable	Unit of measure	Start Year 2008	2009	2010	2011	2012
	Timeline						
4 Budget	Capital Expenditure (decrease in CapEx)	$	1,232,900	403,020	603,430		
5 Budget	Operating expenditure (savings)	$	78,000	82,000	84,000	88,200	92,610
6 Budget	Depreciation (savings)	$	54,000	32,400	19,440	11,664	6,998
7 Benefits	Revenue (loss)	$					
8 Benefits	Operating expenditure (savings)	$					
9 Benefits	On-going change in Capital Expenditure (savings)	$					

Figure 9.8   Example of a financial metrics document populated with data
from a budget and depreciation calculations.

✔ 9.4   Populate the financial calculations template—Benefits

Task 9.3 addressed the first half of the ROI equation—the investment (cost or budget) portion. This section is concerned with the second half—the benefits.

In chapter 7, a benefits model was created with a summary page that showed all of the individually calculated benefits. Some of these related to making money, while others were concerned with saving money (figure 9.9).

	Yearly Values					
	2008	**2009**	**2010**	**2011**	**2012**	**2013**
Benefit 1: Revenue Growth						
Yearly Total	154,339	277,810	500,058	900,105	1,620,189	625,987
Cumulative Total	154,339	432,149	932,208	1,832,313	3,452,502	4,078,489
Benefit 2: Cost Savings						
Yearly Total	(134,898)	(242,816)	(437,070)	(786,725)	(1,416,105)	(400,351)
Cumulative Total	(134,898)	(377,714)	(814,784)	(1,601,509)	(3,017,614)	(3,417,965)
Benefit 3: Capital Savings						
Yearly Total		(410,345)			(225,000)	
Cumulative Total						

Figure 9.9   Parts of a benefits summary sheet from a chapter 7 benefits model.

Revenue (loss)—Line 7. This line in a financial metrics document includes projects that grow, protect, or assure revenue. The sum total of all the benefits of this type included in the benefits template summary sheet should be copied and pasted into the financials model at line 7 (figure 9.10). In some years it is possible that revenue numbers will be negative, perhaps as a project is ramping up.

Operating expenditure (savings)—Line 8. This includes projects that relate to saving money, that is, cost reduction or avoidance. The sum total of all the benefits of this type included in the benefits template summary sheet should be copied and pasted into the financials model at line 8.

Ongoing change in capital expenditure (savings)—Line 9. This represents changes to capital spending that have not already been included in the benefits calculations, which could be either positive or negative. For example, a field services department may have an increase in planned capital expenditure because of the need to buy more trucks, or hire more people in order to accommodate an increase in the number of new customers as a result of a GIS project that targets new customers more effectively based upon their lifestyle characteristics. It is possible that capital expenditure does not occur in every year; this is especially the case for large expenses, which tend to be irregular. Once again, the relevant figures should be pasted into the financial metrics model.

Figure 9.10 shows the financial model with all the inputs completed. There are two major capital expenses in 2009 and 2012 (both updates to a trucking fleet).

Input data

General assumptions

Source	Variable	Unit of measure	Value	Comments
1 Finance	Number of years to model	years	5	10 years max
2 Finance	Tax rate	%	39%	Enter tax rate on Corporate Earnings
3 Finance	Discount rate	%	10%	Consult your finance department

Time-sensitive assumptions

Source	Variable	Unit of measure	Start Year				
	Timeline		2008	2009	2010	2011	2012
4 Budget	Capital Expenditure (decrease in CapEx)	$	1,232,900	403,020	603,430		
5 Budget	Operating expenditure (savings)	$	78,000	82,000	84,000	88,200	92,610
6 Budget	Depreciation (savings)	$	54,000	32,400	19,440	11,664	6,998
7 Benefits	Revenue (loss)	$	154,339	277,810	500,058	900,105	1,620,189
8 Benefits	Operating expenditure (savings)	$	(134,898)	(242,816)	(437,070)	(786,725)	(1,416,105)
9 Benefits	On-going change in Capital Expenditure (savings)	$		(410,345)			(225,000)

Figure 9.10   Example of a financial metrics document with all input completed.

✔ 9.5 Interpreting the results

Once all the steps in the previous three sections have been completed (9.2–9.4), a series of financial calculations is performed automatically by the financial metrics spreadsheet macros. The results are available for interpretation on the "Summary" and "Detailed Output" screens accessible off the main menu.

The summary is an executive overview of the financial metrics (figure 9.11). All the terms used here were defined in the "Definitions" section at the start of this chapter. The metrics presented in the summary are the typical figures that executives rely on to determine whether a particular program of work is worthwhile or not for an organization.

ROI METHODOLOGY - Step 9 (Calculate Financial Metrics)
Executive summary

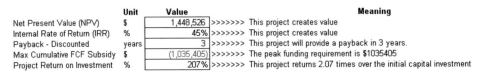

	Unit	Value		Meaning
Net Present Value (NPV)	$	1,448,526	>>>>>>>	This project creates value
Internal Rate of Return (IRR)	%	45%	>>>>>>>	This project creates value
Payback - Discounted	years	3	>>>>>>>	This project will provide a payback in 3 years.
Max Cumulative FCF Subsidy	$	(1,035,405)	>>>>>>>	The peak funding requirement is $1035405
Project Return on Investment	%	207%	>>>>>>>	This project returns 2.07 times over the initial capital investment

Figure 9.11 Example of the executive summary view of a financial metrics document.

Using the case of the example that has been followed in the earlier sections of this chapter, figure 9.11 shows not only the summary metrics, but also an interpretation of the meaning of the results. The NPV of $1,448,526 is the total amount of value that the GIS program will generate over 5 years (the time frame chosen for the analysis review period). The IRR at 45 percent is well above both current discount rates and the 8–30 percent range usually considered the minimum acceptable value (see earlier discussion in the "Definitions" section). The Payback-Discounted period shows that the investments in the GIS program will be recovered within 3 years. The maximum amount of cash that will be needed to fund the GIS program will be $1,035,405, which, although a lot of money, is probably acceptable given the NPV, IRR, FCF, and ROI values. Finally, the ROI of 207 percent indicates that the return will be a little over double the net investment, which virtually every executive will find impressive and will almost certainly be willing to fund on this basis, other things (such as alignment with the organization's overall strategy, generally sound finances, lack of competing programs, etc.) being equal.

Although this summary is a very useful overview of how much value the GIS program will deliver to an organization, it is often necessary to provide additional financial detail as backup to these figures. Finance departments in particular will want to understand how the calculations were arrived at, and so more detailed measures are also automatically calculated by the spreadsheet; these are accessible via the "Detailed Output" screen off the main menu (figure 9.12).

Detailed output

	Unit	2008	2009	2010	2011	2012
Pre-tax Operating Cash Flows						
Revenue (loss)	$	154,339	277,810	500,058	900,105	1,620,189
Operating expenditure (savings)	$	134,898	242,816	437,070	786,725	1,416,105
Pre-Tax Operating Cash Flows	$	289,237	520,627	937,128	1,686,830	3,036,294
Post-tax Operating Cash Flows						
Depreciation	$	(54,000)	(32,400)	(19,440)	(11,664)	(6,998)
Earnings Before Tax	$	235,237	488,227	917,688	1,675,166	3,029,296
Tax charge	$	(91,742)	(190,408)	(357,898)	(653,315)	(1,181,425)
Depreciation Add Back	$	54,000	32,400	19,440	11,664	6,998
Post-tax Operating Cash Flows	$	197,495	330,218	579,230	1,033,515	1,854,869
Free Cash Flows						
Capital Expenditure (decrease in CapEx)	$	(1,232,900)	(403,020)	(603,430)	0	0
On-going change in Capital Expenditure (savings)	$	0	410,345	0	0	225,000
Free Cash Flows	$	(1,035,405)	337,543	(24,200)	1,033,515	2,079,869
Ratio factors						
Discount multiplier	Discount multiplier	0	1	2	3	4
Discounted FCF	$	(1,035,405)	306,857	(20,000)	776,495	1,420,578
Cumul Discounted FCF	$	(1,035,405)	(728,548)	(748,548)	27,947	1,448,526
Payback years	Years				3	

Summary output				
	Unit	Value		Meaning
Net Present Value (NPV)	$	1,448,526	>>>>>>>	This project creates value
Internal Rate of Return (IRR)	%	45%	>>>>>>>	This project creates value
Payback - Discounted	years	3	>>>>>>>	This project will provide a payback in 3 years.
Max Cumulative FCF Subsidy	$	(1,035,405)	>>>>>>>	The peak funding requirement is $1035405
Project Return on Investment	%	207%	>>>>>>>	This project returns 2.07 times over the initial capital investment.

Figure 9.12   Example of detailed output from a financial metrics document.

Values in parentheses and red are negative.

Table 9.1 provides a brief summary of each of the line items listed in figure 9.12.

Pre-tax Operating Cash Flows	
Revenue (loss)	Revenue or loss before tax as entered in line 7 on the Input page.
Operating expenditure (savings)	Operating expenditure or savings before tax as entered in line 8 on the Input page.
Pre-tax operating cash flows	This is the sum of Revenue (loss) + Operating Expenditure (savings) before taxes are applied.
Post-tax Operating Cash Flows	
Depreciation	Depreciation is shown here as entered on the Input page on line 6.
Earnings before tax	Pre-tax operating cash flows summed with depreciation.
Tax charge	The amount of tax charged against earnings before tax, using the tax rate as entered on the Input page on line 2.
Depreciation add back	Depreciation is not taxable, so it is added back into the cash flow calculations. This is just a positive figure used from line 6 on the Input page.
Post-tax operating cash flows	This is a sum of earnings before tax, the tax charge, and depreciation add back; representing post-tax operating cash flows.
Free cash flows	
GIS start-up investment (decrease in CapEx)	Initial capital investment from line 4 of the Input page of the template.
On-going change in capital expenditure (savings)	Ongoing capital expenditure (savings) from line 9 of the Input page of the template.
Free cash flows	This is a sum of the post-tax operating cash flows, GIS start-up investment (decrease in CapEx), and ongoing change in capital expenditure (savings).
Ratio factors	
Discount multiplier	Used to apply the appropriate discount rate to each year.
Discounted FCF	Discounted free cash flow based on the discount rate (from line 3 on the Input page) as applied and the number of years to discount.
Cumulative discounted FCF	Cumulative discounted free cash flow based on the discount rate (from line 3 on the Input page) as applied and the number of years to discount.
Payback years	The payback period.

Table 9.1   Summary of financial metrics.

The results can also be viewed using the "Graphs" option off the main menu (figure 9.13). These graphs allow the impact of cash flow and other measures to be visualized. It is often useful to include some of these graphs in a final report or presentation to executives (see chapter 10). As figure 9.13 shows, for this example, there is initially a negative cash flow, but this becomes positive in year 2, decreases in year 3 (due to one-time capital expenditure outlays), before again becoming positive. Capital expenditure is restricted to the first three years, while revenue, operating expenditure (OpEx), and earnings rise throughout the five-year life cycle of the program.

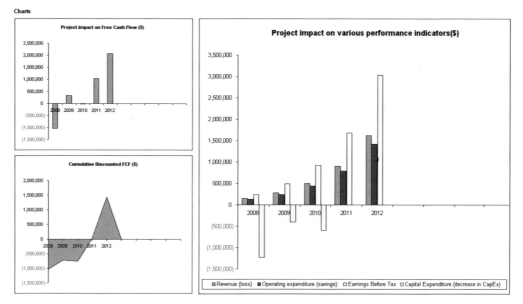

Figure 9.13 Example graphical view from a financial metrics document.

OUTCOME

As a result of entering the budget figures and benefit estimates, it is possible to analyze the return on investment using a number of financial measures. Based on the results of the analysis in this chapter, it may be necessary to adjust the budget or seek additional examples of quantitative benefits that can be modeled in order to make a strong argument for GIS. When this analysis has been completed, it is time to move on to the final chapter, which is concerned with creating a report that summarizes the results of the ROI project.

CALCULATE FINANCIAL METRICS

This is the penultimate step of the ROI methodology. Here Brian Sobers, GIS manager at the City of Springfield, and the ROI team that he leads calculate a series of financial metrics that provide a summary of the ROI case for GIS at the City of Springfield.

The team first met with a financial officer in the city's Finance Department to go over the metrics that will be used in the ROI study to ensure that they are consistent with the city's best practices. Next they created a financial metrics model by populating the financial metrics spreadsheet template, called "Financials Template.xls," that is provided on the accompanying Web site (http://gis.esri.com/roi). The completed financials model document for the City of Springfield is also on the accompanying Web site; it is called "Springfield Financials.xls." The depreciation calculations that were used to create the financial model are in the spreadsheet "Springfield Depreciation.xls."

C9.1 Springfield financial metrics

The inputs for the general assumptions part of the input data sheet were obtained from the city Finance Department (figure C9.1). The values for the budget and benefits parts were simply copied out of the spreadsheets prepared in earlier chapters (see figures C6.2 and C7.4), as described earlier in the text of this chapter. Since the budget only runs from 2008 to 2010, the values for 2011 and 2012 were extrapolated for these years using an annual inflation rate of 3 percent in the case of operational expenditures (for simplicity, the 2010 capital values were used for 2011 and 2012 without an increase). An additional "Ongoing change to Capital Expenditure" charge of $75,000 was added for 2010 to cover the capital cost of replacing two of the vehicles used to route inspectors to sites. Although outside the benefits calculations discussed in chapter 7, this charge is included here to give a complete financial picture, and also because without it the probability of success for the GIS program will be diminished.

ROI METHODOLOGY - Step 9 (Calculate Financial Metrics)
Input data

General assumptions

Source	Variable	Unit of measure	Value	Comments
1 Finance	Number of years to model	years	5	10 years max
2 Finance	Tax rate	%	0%	Enter tax rate on Corporate Earnings
3 Finance	Discount rate	%	6%	Consult your finance department

Time-sensitive assumptions

Source	Variable	Unit of measure	Start Year 2008	2009	2010	2011	2012
	Timeline		2008	2009	2010	2011	2012
4 Budget	Capital Expenditure (decrease in capex)	$	243,460	5,199	4,889	4,889	4,889
5 Budget	Operating expenditure (savings)	$	34,245	35,274	32,851	33,837	34,852
6 Budget	Depreciation (savings)	$	5,700	5,700	5,700	5,700	5,700
7 Benefits	Revenue (loss)	$	23,402	81,454	127,666	167,799	199,960
8 Benefits	Operating expenditure (savings)	$	(1,023)	(8,516)	(11,082)	(11,532)	(12,029)
9 Benefits	On-going change in Capital Expenditure (savings)	$	0	0	75,000	0	0

Figure C9.1   Input values used to calculate financial metrics for the City of Springfield.

The input values for the depreciation calculations were obtained from the Springfield budget, and the parameters used (salvage value and time) were defined by the city Finance Department. The city uses straight-line depreciation for all its projects, and so this was used here (figure C9.2).

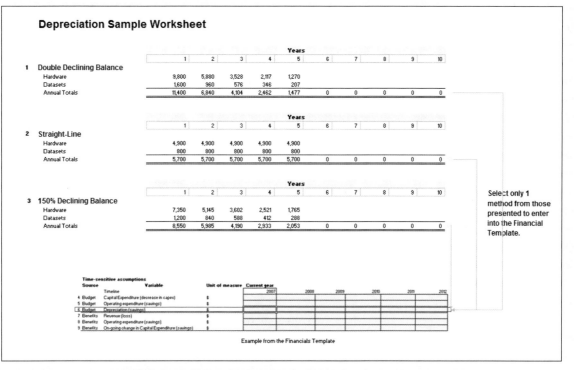

Figure C9.2   Depreciation calculations for City of Springfield.

The summary sheet for the Springfield financial metrics model shows the metrics that are automatically calculated by the macros in the spreadsheet (figure C9.3). As can clearly be seen, this program of GIS work will be very beneficial in financial terms to the City of Springfield. Taken together, the projects will add $223k in value over a five year period, and will require a maximum cash injection of a similar amount ($220k). This investment will provide a financial payback within three years. The IRR of 37 percent and ROI of 216 percent are well in excess of generally accepted public sector values. The patterns of income and expenditure shown in the table (figure C9.3) and the graphs (figure C9.4) also provide an acceptable pattern of monetary flows (generally decreasing expenditure and increasing cash flows).

ROI METHODOLOGY - Step 9 (Calculate Financial Metrics)
Detailed output

	Unit	2008	2009	2010	2011	2012
Pre-tax Operating Cash Flows						
Revenue (loss)	$	23,402	81,454	127,666	167,799	199,360
Operating expenditure (savings)	$	1,023	8,516	11,082	11,532	12,029
Pre-Tax Operating Cash Flows	$	24,425	89,970	138,748	179,331	211,390
Post-tax Operating Cash Flows						
Depreciation	$	(5,700)	(5,700)	(5,700)	(5,700)	(5,700)
Earnings Before Tax	$	18,725	84,270	133,048	173,631	206,290
Tax charge	$	0	0	0	0	0
Depreciation Add Back	$	5,700	5,700	5,700	5,700	5,700
Post-tax Operating Cash Flows	$	24,425	89,970	138,748	179,331	211,990
Free Cash Flows						
Capital Expenditure (decrease in capex)	$	(243,460)	(5,199)	(4,889)	(4,889)	(4,889)
On-going change in Capital Expenditure (savings)	$	0	0	(75,000)	0	0
Free Cash Flows	$	(219,035)	84,771	58,859	174,442	207,101
Ratio factors						
Discount multiplier	Discount multiplier	0	1	2	3	4
Discounted FCF	$	(219,035)	79,973	52,384	146,465	164,043
Cumul Discounted FCF	$	(219,035)	(139,063)	(86,679)	59,786	223,829
Payback years	Years				3	

Summary output

	Unit	Value		Meaning
Net Present Value (NPV)	$	223,829	>>>>>>>	This project creates value
Internal Rate of Return (IRR)	%	37%	>>>>>>>	This project creates value
Payback - Discounted	years	3	>>>>>>>	This project will provide a payback in 3 years.
Max Cumulative FCF Subsidy	$	(219,035)	>>>>>>>	The peak funding requirement is $219035
Project Return on Investment	%	216%	>>>>>>>	This project returns 2.16 times over the initial capital investment.

Figure C9.3 Summary output from City of Springfield financial metrics model.

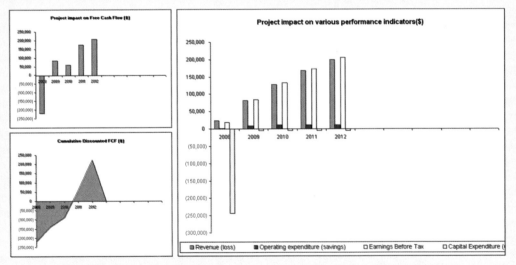

Figure C9.4 Graphical output from City of Springfield financial metrics model.

C9.2 Discussion of chapter 9 case study

The City of Springfield financial metrics model presents a very favorable view of the proposed GIS program and makes a compelling case for investment. With relatively little additional work, the budget and benefits figures have been integrated to create a comprehensive picture of the financial viability of the GIS program. All parameters are within general public (and private) sector acceptance ranges, and indeed some are extremely positive (for example, IRR and ROI).

The only task remaining for the City of Springfield ROI team is to consolidate and document the work in the form of a report to city stakeholders, and this is the basis of the next chapter.

Endnote

1. NSGIC, *Economic justification: Measuring return on investment (ROI) and cost benefit analysis* (CBA) (NSGIC for FGDC, 2006) http://www.nsgic.org/hottopics/return_on_investment.pdf.

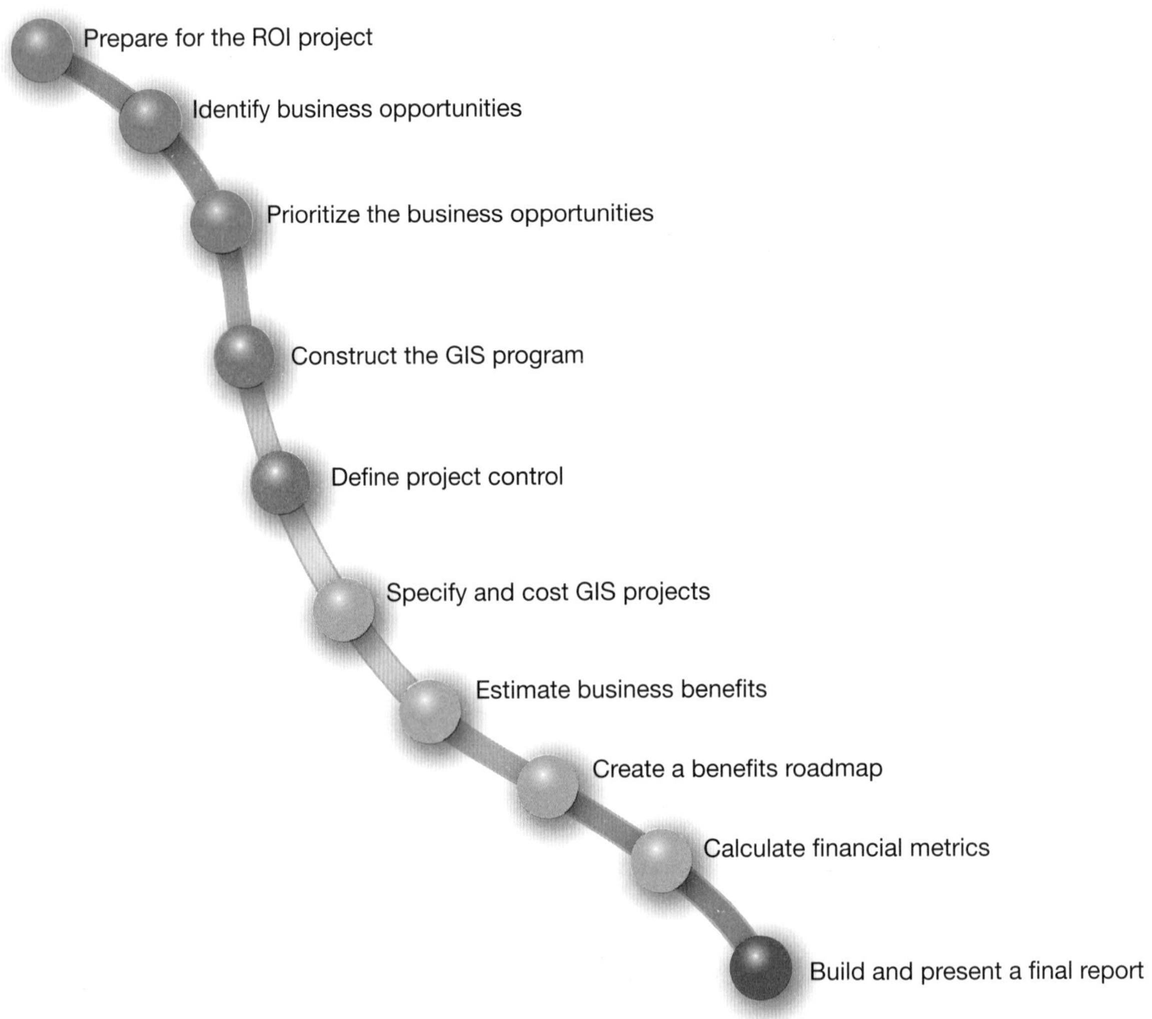

Prepare for the ROI project

Identify business opportunities

Prioritize the business opportunities

Construct the GIS program

Define project control

Specify and cost GIS projects

Estimate business benefits

Create a benefits roadmap

Calculate financial metrics

Build and present a final report

10

 **Build and present a final report**

The ROI methodology concludes with the final tasks of authoring and presenting a compelling executive report with the purpose of convincing budget decision makers of the value of funding a program of GIS projects within an organization. This chapter provides discussion on the key issues of a report's objective, audience, style, and content. It describes how to generate an effective written proposal by simply completing and elaborating upon the sections in a report template.

As the last chapter in the ROI methodology, the goal here is to create a compelling business proposition that will receive funding from an evaluation body. This proposal should take the form of a report that summarizes all of the key information that has been created during an ROI project.

There are two main tasks in this final chapter: write a report, and then present the report to interested parties. Effective report-writing is an acquired skill based upon a few key tenets, articulated in the first part of the discussion. The case study section presents a complete report for the City of Springfield ROI study that has been followed throughout this book.

BUSINESS REPORT WRITING

Before launching into specific details about the structure and content of an ROI report, it is worth reviewing some of the key principles of effective business report writing; however, this is not a complete primer on how to write reports.

A good ROI report should encompass four key considerations: objective, audience, style, and content. Each of these will be discussed in turn in the next paragraphs of this section.

There is a single and simple objective for an ROI report: to convince a funding body to finance a proposed program of work. It is important to remember this at all times when writing an ROI report because it will focus the discussion, guide the structure, and ensure the exclusion of unnecessary material. Consider closely the criteria that an evaluation group will use to make a decision on funding. The scope of a report then becomes collecting, organizing, and presenting the information necessary to meet these criteria.

An ROI report should be written with a specific audience in mind. A different type of report will be required for a lay council of elected officials, a group of financially-aware business executives, or a group of technical engineers. Before starting on a report, a small piece of investigation into the characteristics of an audience will pay dividends later. It will allow the correct message to be tailored to the expectations of the recipients. A key issue to be faced here is the degree to which the technology of GIS is exposed or hidden beneath business objectives and solutions. Usually, executive technologists, engineers, and scientists will want to know about such things as technical architectures, transaction processing, and key features and functions. On the other hand, elected officials and nontechnical business executives will often not be interested and, indeed may be put off, by too much exposure to technology and technical terms. A report prepared for an evaluation group composed of nontechnical people will be better received if GIS is presented as an enabling technology that is embedded within business solutions.

Insight: The report completes the circle

Sometimes the final report will be seen by the evaluation body for the first time during the evaluation process. This will be the case, for example, where organizations have very formal, quasi-independent review bodies (e.g., a council of elected officials or a government grant awarding authority). A key tenet of this methodology is to win the hearts and minds of key decision makers early in the process and then work to build their trust throughout the whole process. Over the period of this methodology a number of influencers and decision makers will have been engaged—after all it was they who provided the input on what benefits the program should deliver for the business (chapter 2). These are the individuals that need to be kept abreast of progress on assembling the report. The final report is simply a formal summary that articulates the program's intent—it is the socialization of the content prior to the budget evaluation that will determine whether the GIS program's funding needs are met.

There is no escaping the fact that in the twenty-first century style is almost as important as substance. It is vitally important that an ROI report is presented in a way that is consistent with the norms of an organization and that it is attractive, well written and, most importantly, free from errors. There is no universal reporting style or format that works for every occasion, but some guiding principles will be covered below. Strict adherence to these principles is by no means necessary, and indeed tailoring to local standards and circumstances is generally welcomed. If possible, it is a good idea to obtain and emulate examples of other reports that have been evaluated successfully by a funding body.

One of the major benefits of using the ROI methodology presented in this book is that most of the content for a final report will be created as each task is finalized. The main task in the report, therefore, is to extract the relevant material, organize it in a suitable way, format it for presentation, and write a commentary. Generally, a short business or technical format is advocated for ROI reports, but this may need to be adapted to the specific needs of an organization. A short business composition should include the following sections: title page, report history, glossary of terms, executive summary, purpose and scope, background and history, methodology employed, business challenges and opportunities, proposed program, program costs, time frame, governance, business analysis, and conclusions. Each of these will be discussed.

The length of a report is a topic that is often debated. A report should be long enough to cover all the main topics and evaluation criteria that an evaluation group will expect, but not so lengthy that the reader cannot find the necessary information or loses interest. As a guide, 10–15 pages are usually sufficient for a report of this nature. Additional, supporting information can be provided as appendixes or a separate supplement.

Finally, the report writing process should be considered. Even a moderately complex business paper, such as the one under consideration here, will need to go through a series of editing and review cycles. Once a final draft has been completed, it may need to be presented for "sign off" by a senior project sponsor or key authorities (e.g., a finance officer, chief technical officer, or division head). Only then should it be submitted to a funding body for evaluation. Organizations often have strict protocols for reports that must be followed completely.

TASKS

The two main tasks are to build and then present a successful report. Although there is no single, universally applicable format to produce ROI study reports, an example report template is provided as part of this methodology. A report is built by copying relevant material from earlier documents completed as part of other tasks and then pasting it into the template provided. The material may need to be reformatted for presentation, and a commentary will need to be created that discusses the material.

Tools: ROI report template

A suggested ROI template Microsoft Word document can be found on the supporting Web site at http://gis.esri.com/roi. This file contains a document outline and some draft text that you can use as the basis for your ROI report. Areas requiring input are enclosed in angled brackets (< >).

✔ 10.1 Build the final report

The task of building a convincing ROI report can be quite daunting at first. To assist in the process, a template is provided on the accompanying Web site (see Tools box). This report template contains a suggested structure for a report and some boilerplate text that acts as a stub for a report document derived from the template. This report template is an example of a short business report. If an ROI project or an organization requires a more extensive report, then a long business report format should be used. A long business report will have longer sections, a formal table of contents page, extended content (e.g., more data and charts) and, possibly, appendixes that provide greater details about, for example, the proposed program, program costs, and financial analyses.

Although there is no set way to write good reports; it is a good idea to begin with an outline and then work from the "inside out," that is, first fill in all the detailed sections with information from chapters in the ROI methodology, then write the commentary and, lastly write the conclusions and executive summary.

The following discussion reviews each of the main sections that should be in a report and offers some comments on what content to include and how it should be presented. As each section is reviewed, the appropriate material should be entered into a document based on the template provided (or some other suitable substitute).

Title page

The title page should contain the report title and the author's name; optionally an organization's logo can also be added. Choosing the title is a vital decision, not least because the title is the first thing evaluators will read. Generally, a title should be short, succinct, and descriptive. It should also set the tone for what is to be communicated in the report. For example, if the report will focus on business issues, then the words "business" or "financial" could be in the title; whereas, if the report is to be technically focused, then "GIS" or "information system" might be used. Generally-speaking, it is a good idea to try to link the title to a business performance improvement theme that is embodied in the benefits that will be delivered, for example, "Standardization Initiative" or "Bridging the Functional Divide."

Report history

It is important to show who has contributed to an ROI report and that it has been reviewed and signed-off by all the required people in an organization. Aside from the ROI team involved in the study, a report should also be reviewed by at least one senior executive (for example, a senior project sponsor) to ensure that it is consistent with overall organizational goals and standards for report writing. Additionally, sign-off may be required by a senior finance and technical person to confirm to evaluators that it is consistent with an organization's overall business and IT strategies. The second page of the ROI report template contains a block for recording author and revision (version control) information (figure 10.1).

Report History

Project Name:	< Study Name >
Division:	< Division Name >
Focus Area:	< Name of Area within Organization >
Product/Process: GIS	

Prepared By

Document Owner(s)	Project/Organization Role
< Owner Name >	< Owner Department >

Report Version Control

Version	Date	Author	Change Description
< Version Number >	< Date >	< Author Name >	< Brief Description of Edits >

Figure 10.1   Report history section from the ROI report template.

Glossary of terms

The readers of an ROI report may appreciate a definition of all key business and technical terms. A glossary of terms at the start of a report is a good place to provide definitions. The definitions should be quite high level and capable of being understood by general readers. If there is a need to provide detailed, specific definitions, then these would be placed in an appendix or supplement. A glossary is less likely to be necessary if a report is being presented to executives that have been closely involved in the overall process and are actively engaged in the general field.

Executive summary

The executive summary is perhaps the most important part of any report; it is certainly the part which will be most frequently read, and it will probably be the most influential. As a consequence, it is critical to put as much effort as possible into writing a clear, concise, and correct description of the overall case for funding a program of work. Since this is a summary for executives only, the most important points need to be covered at a high level. A good executive summary should cover the following topics: background to the project, the challenges and opportunities (the problem), the solution proposed (the answer), the benefits that will accrue, how much it will cost (a summary of the budget), and the business case for funding the work (the ROI metrics). An executive summary should not be too long; ideally it should be kept to a single page. It is essential to get an executive summary thoroughly reviewed by at least one, preferably two or three executives prior to submission of a report for evaluation. Figure 10.2 shows the executive summary section from the ROI report template. This presents a structure as described above and some stubs (text enclosed within < >) for writing project-specific content.

Executive Summary

This report to < Evaluation Body > was commissioned by < Name of Person who Commissioned ROI Study>; it sets out the business case for a program of work that will deliver significant business value to < Name of Organization >. The program was designed specifically to meet a series of challenges and opportunities that were highlighted by a cross-section of executive managers. Collectively the program will contribute value to < Name of Organization >:

- < List Key Reasons For Funding The Program, Focusing On Tangible (Measurable And Fact-Based) Benefits. Explain The Benefits In The Context Of The Mission Of The Organization, And Use Non-Technical, Non-Financial Language. >

The initiatives proposed will be completed within < Years > years (the majority of capital expenditure will be within the first year). Benefits will begin in the first year and will continue to flow for at least five years. All the necessary resource requirements, both internal and external, have been identified and are included in budget calculations. A program delivery organization has been defined that will ensure successful business, technical and financial outcomes.

The program of work will **cost** < **Cost** > over five years. It will collectively generate a **Net Present Value of** < **NPV** > and an **Internal Rate of Return of** < **IRR** > for the < Name of Organization > over five years. The investment will provide a **Pay Back within** < **Pay Back Period** > **years** and will provide a < **ROI** > **Return on Investment**. Finally, a maximum of < **FCF** > **in Free Cash Flow** will be required to finance the program. These values are all well within accepted < Name of Organization > guidelines.

It is recommended that the < Name of Organization > **agrees to fund the program of work defined by this study and described in this report.**

Figure 10.2 Executive summary section from the ROI report template.

Purpose and scope

This section is the real start of the report, and its purpose is to introduce the report, explain the context of why it was created, and provide an outline of the contents. Evaluators will want to know why and how a report came about, that is to say what the justification was for creating it. It might have arisen from an internal review of processes and capabilities, been proposed by external consultants, or have been the directive from an influential executive, for example. To introduce the ROI report, it is often a good idea to go back to the six basic issues that interest executives as introduced in the preface of this book: show the real business value, determine the specific costs, estimate the time frame for benefits, understand the resource requirements, define the governance and management structure, and calculate the return on investment. If the evaluators are unfamiliar with GIS, this would be a good place to provide a short description. The purpose and scope section should be no more than about one page in length.

Background and history

Before tackling the substantive parts of a study, a little history will provide a useful foundation for evaluators and demonstrate that the authors have a complete understanding of events that have transpired in an organization. All the material for this discussion can be summarized from that collected in chapter 1, task 1.3. This section should be no more than a half page in length.

Methodology employed

It is useful to build credibility for a report by stating that the ROI study used a well-proven and recognized methodology from reputable sources with extensive experience of management consultancy and information technology projects. This section should be no more than a paragraph in length.

Business challenges and opportunities

This is the section that sets out the problems that an organization needs to solve and the benefits that will arise from resolving them. To begin, the sources of information (the business opportunities) should be cited—that is, the names of the executives interviewed should be listed. To assist with arrangement of the material in this section, a table is provided in the final report template (figure 10.3) to enter information about each opportunity and its value or benefit potential for a business unit. The contents for this table can be based on information in the business opportunities spreadsheet document created in chapter 3. In this section it is important not to include too much detail but to remain specific, fact-based, and benefit-focused. Even though the title of this section is "Business challenges and opportunities," the emphasis should remain positive and focus on solutions, not problems. This section should be one to two pages in length and will be one of the most substantial sections of the report.

Group	Opportunity	Value / Benefit Potential
< Name of Group >	< Name of Business Opportunity >	< Describe each benefit and the value that it will bring to the organization. Be specific, application focused and concentrate on the facts. >

Figure 10.3 Table for describing business opportunities in the ROI report template.

Proposed program

Next, the solutions to the problems outlined in the previous section should be presented. By way of introduction and as an organizational instrument, begin with the benefits roadmap diagram created in chapter 8. This will provide a useful summary of all the projects, their timeline, and the expected delivery schedule. Each of the proposed projects should then be briefly described. Again, executives are not looking for extensive detail here, just the salient points that describe what is proposed. As before, the emphasis should not be on technology or the mechanics of projects, but the purpose and benefits that will arise. Executive evaluators will be asking the question, why should the organization fund this (instead of another proposed program/project)? The projects should not be presented individually, but as a complete portfolio or program of work. The purpose of this approach is to avoid discussion of the possibility of partial funding or picking and choosing projects.

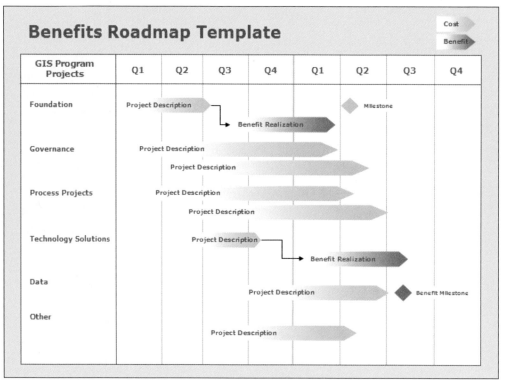

Figure 10.4   Benefits roadmap template from the ROI report template.

Program costs

Having outlined the proposed program of activity, the next step is to present the costs of the program. The main figures that executive evaluators will be interested in are the total cost that will need to be budgeted, the net additional expenditure (i.e., the total less any expenditure that is already committed, such as inside labor), the breakdown of capital and operational expenditure, and the expenditure by major category. All this information is available in a budget document as created in chapter 6 (in particular, see the "Financial Figures for ROI" and "Analysis By Category" screens that are accessible off the main menu in a budget document). Beyond these summary figures, only a little additional commentary is needed.

The budget information will need to be reformatted so that it is suitable for inclusion in a final report. A simple spreadsheet template "Chptr 10 Reformat Calc.xls" is provided on the accompanying Web site (http://gis.esri.com/roi) to assist with additional calculations and reformatting (figure 10.5). The relevant data from the budget should be copied and then pasted into this spreadsheet. The data can then be manipulated using the standard functions using Microsoft Excel software to obtain the final values required.

Financials - from Chapter 9 Financial Metrics

	2008	2009	2010	2011	2012	5-Year Total
Capital Expenditure (decrease in capex)						
Operating expenditure (savings)						
Depreciation (savings)						
Revenue (loss)						
Operating expenditure (savings)						
On-going change in Capital Expenditure (savings)						
Total Cost						
Total Revenue						

Figure R3: GIS Program Expenditure - from Chapter 6 Budget

	2008	2009	2010	2011	2012	5-Year Total
Capital Expenditure						
Operational Expenditure						
Total Expenditure						

Figure R4: GIS Program Expenditure By Category - from Chapter 6 Budget

	2008	2009	2010	2011	2012	5-Year Total
Dataset						
Hardware						
InsideLabor						
Maintenance						
Miscellaneous						
OutsideLabor						
Software						
Total						

Total Less Inside Labor

	2008	2009	2010	2011	2012	5-Year Total
Dataset						
Hardware						
InsideLabor						
Maintenance						
Miscellaneous						
OutsideLabor						
Software						
Total						
Total Less Inside Labor						

Figure 10.5   Template for reformatting data for inclusion in the ROI report.

It is recommended that the following tables and chart are placed in the ROI report: GIS Program Expenditure, and GIS Program Expenditure By Category (both table and bar chart).

Time frame

The focus in this section should mainly be on the roadmap for benefits delivery. The benefits roadmap document already included in the proposed program section described previously (figure 10.4) can be referenced here. A short commentary can be used to describe the major events and milestones for the implementation and production phases of the program.

Governance

Since lack of appropriate governance and management control is often identified as one of the main reasons why projects fail, executive evaluators will be concerned that a program is being governed in an appropriate way. The program delivery organization chart created in chapter 5 should be included in a final report (figure 10.6). It may also be appropriate to discuss the formation of a project management office, a steering committee, or a set of standard program management competencies and approaches.

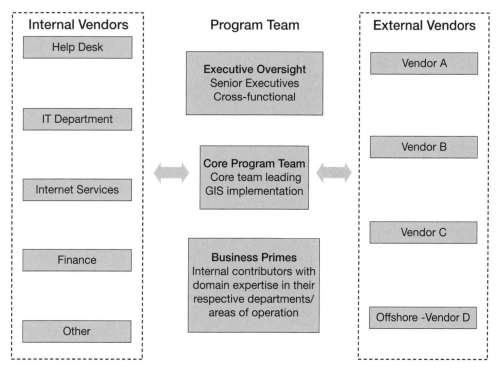

Figure 10.6   Governance template from the ROI report template (see also figure 5.3).

Business analysis

The results of the financial metrics calculations should be presented next. All the data needed for this section is on the "Detailed Output" screen accessible from the main menu of a financial metrics spreadsheet document. An image of this screen can simply be pasted into this section of an ROI report (figure 10.7). The key metrics—NPV, IRR, Payback Period, ROI, and Free Cash Flow (FCF)—should be highlighted in the commentary that accompanies a copy of the detailed output screen. Again, the tone of the discussion here should be that of the financial benefits that an organization will receive from the proposed program of work. In a separate paragraph, the intangible benefits should also be listed, since they will provide backup support for the tangible benefits already discussed in summary form.

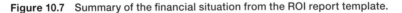

Input Data	<<<	Menu	>>>	Graphs	

PA

ROI METHODOLOGY - Step 9 (Calculate Financial Metrics)
Detailed output

	Unit	2008	2009	2010	2011	2012
Pre-tax Operating Cash Flows						
Revenue (loss)	$	0	0	0	0	0
Operating expenditure (savings)	$	0	0	0	0	0
Pre-Tax Operating Cash Flows	$	0	0	0	0	0
Post-tax Operating Cash Flows						
Depreciation	$	0	0	0	0	0
Earnings Before Tax	$	0	0	0	0	0
Tax charge	$	0	0	0	0	0
Depreciation Add Back	$	0	0	0	0	0
Post-tax Operating Cash Flows	$	0	0	0	0	0
Free Cash Flows						
Capital Expenditure (decrease in capex)	$	0	0	0	0	0
On-going change in Capital Expenditure (savings)	$	0	0	0	0	0
Free Cash Flows	$	0	0	0	0	0
Ratio factors						
Discount multiplier	Discount multiplier	0	1	2	3	4
Discounted FCF	$	0	0	0	0	0
Cumul Discounted FCF	$	0	0	0	0	0
Payback years	Years					

Summary output	Unit	Value		Meaning
Net Present Value (NPV)	$	0	>>>>>>>	This project is value-neutral
Internal Rate of Return (IRR)	%	N/A	>>>>>>>	This project creates value
Payback - Discounted	years	no payback	>>>>>>>	This project does not provide any payback within the considered period.
Max Cumulative FCF Subsidy	$	0	>>>>>>>	The peak funding requirement is $0
Project Return on Investment	%	N/A	>>>>>>>	Cannot calculate ROI as the investment is either equal or below zero

The cash flows are so negative or positive that the project does not have an IRR, as the NPV is negative or positive independently of the selected discount rate.

Figure 10.7   Summary of the financial situation from the ROI report template.

Conclusions

The purpose of the final section is to summarize the results and make a recommendation to the evaluators that the program should be funded as proposed in the report. This final section should be very focused on the key arguments advanced and should be no more than a few paragraphs. Like the executive summary, this section should be reviewed by one or more senior advisors prior to submission for evaluation.

✔ 10.2 Present a final report

Once a report has been completed, it may be necessary to present it to one or more groups of people. It is recommended that a slide presentation (e.g., PowerPoint) be created from the material in the report. Like all presentations, this should be tailored to the specific needs of an audience, and should highlight only the salient points. Virtually all of the recommendations made earlier for the written report also apply to a digital slide presentation.

Insight: Prepare the ground before giving a presentation

Wherever possible it is a good idea not to go into a presentation situation "cold" but to socialize a report beforehand with people who will be in attendance. It is very difficult to present something that executives have no knowledge about. A Microsoft PowerPoint presentation can be sent ahead of time to key participants with a note such as "please let me know prior to the meeting if you'd like to discuss specific issues."

OUTCOME

A successful outcome of this final step, and the methodology as a whole, will be continued and expanded support and funding for a portfolio of GIS projects. The material created throughout the course of implementing this ROI methodology will provide a benchmark for later GIS projects and, potentially, other ROI studies in an organization. Although funding is not a foregone conclusion, by employing this methodology, the chances of fostering broad ownership of a GIS mission among key members of an organization should be significantly enhanced.

Receiving funding for a GIS program is, of course, only a milestone and not the end of the matter. Next the projects will move into an implementation life-cycle phase that will also raise a number of ROI-related issues. During this phase the costs and benefits should be tracked so that when it is time to seek a new round of funding approval, there will be real, concrete evidence of the value and return on investment of GIS. Benefits can be tracked using a number of the tools presented here (especially those in chapter 7). Good project documentation is also an important aspect of tracking: for example, who is using GIS, where is it deployed, what value has been created, and what are the key performance indicators that can be used to measure future benefits?

BUILD AND PRESENT THE FINAL REPORT

In this final step of the ROI methodology, Brian Sobers and the ROI team at the City of Springfield will create a final report that will be presented to the city's executive evaluators, which in this case means a city council of elected officials. The city council meets on a monthly basis, and the report will need to be tabled for discussion by the city manager, Bob James. Thus, the report that the team creates will need to be written with the specific interests of this group in mind.

Before writing the report, Brian talks to his division head, Sue Coldfield, to get her opinion on the scope, content, and presentation of the report. She confirms that the report should be about a dozen pages in length and that it could be in any generally accepted business format. She cautions that because the elected officials have a predominantly business focus, the report should not be overly technical in nature.

C10.1 Build the final report

Brian Sobers uses the ROI final report template to create a report suitable for submission to the next city council meeting. He incorporates the relevant materials from the various documents completed as tasks during the ROI study, and then adds a written commentary to link the material together and explain the rationale for the work that was done. The calculations for the ROI report are saved in a document called "Springfield Chptr 10 Calc.xls" that is available on the Web site that accompanies this book. The report is then reviewed by each member of the ROI team. When all their comments have been incorporated and a final draft of the report completed, following general city practices, the report is sent first for general executive review to Sue Coldfield, head of the Community Development Division at the City of Springfield (and Brian's boss), and then for financial review to Anita Williams, city clerk, for financial review. Brian saw this as part of socializing the report with senior executives, which should improve the chances of funding success.

The final report was submitted to the city council on March 28, 2008, and received unanimous approval at a council meeting on April 10, 2008.

A full version of the final report submitted to the city council is included on the following pages.

City of Springfield

Business Case for GIS Expansion

Brian Sobers, GIS Manager
March 28, 2008

Report history

Project name: Business case for GIS expansion
Division: Community development
Focus area: Business capability expansion
Product/Process: GIS

Prepared by

Document owner(s)	Project/Organization role
Brian Sobers	GIS Manager, Planning Department
Contributions from: Scott Chapman, Engineering; Bartholemew Simpson, Library; Zak Wildmore, Information System; and Ernest Shi, Finance	ROI project team, City of Springfield

Report version control

Version	Date	Author	Change description
1.1.1	March 21, 2008	Anita Williams, City Clerk	Financial approval
1.1	March 17, 2008	Sue Coldfield, Community Development	Revision to match Springfield corporate standards
1.0	March 15, 2008	Brian Sobers and team	Original document

Glossary of terms

Free Cash Flow (FCF): The maximum amount of cash needed to fund a program of work.

Geographic Information System (GIS): A geographic problem-solving methodology and technology.

Internal Rate of Return (IRR): The percentage received from an investment. For comparison, the current rate of return from investing money in a bank is 3 to 5 percent.

Net Present Value (NPV): The total value in dollars that a program will generate over an assessment period (5 years in this case).

Return on Investment (ROI): The percentage received over and above an investment (Net Benefits/Total Costs) during the assessment period (5 years in this case).

Payback Period: The number of years before an investment is paid back by the benefits received.

Executive summary

This report to the council was commissioned by the city manager; it sets out the business case for a program of work that will deliver significant business improvement and value to the City of Springfield and its residents. The program was designed specifically to meet a series of challenges and opportunities that were highlighted by a cross-section of division managers. Collectively the program will contribute value to the city by substantially improving the following city activities:

- **Increasing revenues** from property tax, business licenses, and income tax by attracting new high value businesses to the city.

- **Retaining and improving the attractiveness of the city** by maintaining tree coverage at current levels. Trees help to keep the city green; they reduce pollution, provide shade, and improve civic pride, as well as make Springfield a desirable place to live and work.

- **Reducing urban sprawl** by redeveloping "brownfield" sites instead of new "greenfield" sites at the urban fringe. Cleaning up brownfield sites within the city boundary will further improve the scenic character of Springfield.

- **Enabling the City to comply with government regulations** that govern the inspection and maintenance of key physical assets. Inspecting and maintaining city fire hydrants could save lives and alleviate or minimize damage to property in the event of a fire.

- **Enhancing citizen services** by providing online access to maps and data.

Currently these activities are ineffective due to a combination of some out-of-date manual processes, poor information, unreliable and slow IT systems, and lack of collaboration across functional groups. The initiatives proposed will be completed within two years (the majority of capital expenditure will be within the first year). Benefits will begin in the first year and will continue to flow for at least five years. All the necessary resource requirements, both internal and external, have been identified and are included in budget calculations.

The program of work will **cost $509,384** over five years. It will collectively generate a **NPV of $223,829** and an **IRR of 37 percent** for the city over five years. The investment will provide a **Payback within three years** and will provide an **ROI of 216 percent.** Finally, a maximum of **$220,000 in Free Cash Flow** will be required to finance the program. These values are all well within accepted city guidelines.

It is recommended that the city agrees to fund the program of work defined by this study and described in this report.

Purpose and scope

This report was prepared by Brian Sobers, GIS manager for the City of Springfield, and a small team, who worked with a cross-section of key executives and many employees throughout the city. The report covers a study commissioned by the city manager, Bob James, who requested that the city should examine "the ways in which GIS could add value by contributing to the key strategic initiatives of improving services and reducing costs through the use of new technology."

This is the final report of the study that was undertaken in the first quarter of 2008. It sets out the background and history of GIS at the City of Springfield, discusses the methodology employed, describes a proposed GIS program of work, and reports on the business analysis undertaken. This report is only a summary of a considerable amount of detailed analysis, and there is a substantial amount of supporting documentation (spreadsheets, graphics, and text) that is available upon request.

The City of Springfield is at a pivotal point in its development. The city's traditional economic base of agriculture and mining industries is being superseded by service-based industries. The unique historic position held by the city because of its geographic location no longer provides competitive advantage. Increasingly, the city is competing for inward investment, new jobs, and other regional activities. At the same time, low-density development is reducing the number of trees in and around the urban area, and is changing the character of the city. The city council has observed that neighboring cities are making extensive use of new technologies to reduce costs and increase services to citizens.

Geographic information system (GIS) solutions are used by many cities (and other organizations) throughout the world to generate revenue, reduce costs, and improve service efficiency and effectiveness. This report describes a program of proposed projects that will leverage GIS methods and technology and bring tangible benefits to the city and our citizens. The report covers the following topics:

- Areas where GIS will contribute **business value**

- The initial and ongoing **costs**

- How long it will take to fully realize the **benefits**

- The **resources** required

- A proposed project **governance** and **management** structure

- The **return on the investment (ROI)** case

Background and history of GIS at the City of Springfield

Like many municipalities, the City of Springfield has been involved in GIS for several years. However, recent developments in the field have largely passed the city by, primarily because of a lack awareness of the potential for GIS to add value to city activities.

To date, a series of uncoordinated projects in the Library, Planning, and Police departments, together with the use of CAD systems in Engineering, has resulted in a set of digital maps and some good examples of how GIS can benefit the city. A notable example of a good project is the digital zoning maps available online from the city Web site (maintained by the city library). Unfortunately, the initiative in the Planning Department that produced the zoning map and some other useful products came to a halt a few months ago when the GIS manager retired. There has never been a citywide GIS plan and no attempt to quantify the value of GIS-enabled business functions. Presently, the city has old and outdated GIS resources (e.g., hardware, software, and data) in the following departments: Library, Planning, Police, and Engineering.

Methodology employed

The methodology employed was originally developed by PA Consulting Group, Inc., an international firm of management consultants, in collaboration with ESRI, the major global GIS company, and has been widely employed in many organizations around the world. Both PA Consulting Group and ESRI are leaders in their respective fields and have impeccable reputations for work in this area. The PA–ESRI methodology is unique because it is a GIS-specific ROI methodology grounded in sound management science principles.

Business challenges and opportunities

At the start of the methodology implementation process, the following City of Springfield executives were interviewed to establish their business priorities for their departments:

- Community Services manager, Andrew Jones

- Public Works manager, Phillip Stott

- Community Development manager, Sue Coldfield

- Economic Development manager, Arthur Spaliceck

- City manager, Bob James

After analyzing their structured interview responses, the following opportunities and challenges were identified:

Division	Opportunity	Value / Benefit Potential
Community Services	The division is seeking to reduce pollution levels and maintain Springfield's green city image by establishing a baseline tree coverage inventory that will allow it to monitor change over time.	The head of the Parks and Recreation Department has established that the city will be able to obtain a $60,000 federal highway funding clean air attainment grant for each of three years ($180,000 total) if a tree coverage assessment is undertaken and positive results are reported to the federal government. Enabling this activity with GIS will meet this need more effectively than other alternatives.
Public Works	The division needs to meet mandatory regulatory obligations under the GASB 34 directive that requires the development of complete inventories of assets and liabilities for all infrastructure and facilities with maintenance and operational costs, as well as revenues and expenditures. The division is seeking to minimize the costs of adhering to this directive by first undertaking a fire hydrant inventory.	GIS technology is the most cost-effective way to design inspection routes and to improve the speed and accuracy of inspections. Using GIS, more inspections can be completed per day and the overall cost will be reduced when compared to a manual approach. Safe and code-compliant infrastructure also reduces citizen litigation against the city.
Community Development	In keeping with state policy, the division wishes to reduce the amount of greenfield site development by shifting construction to brownfield sites within the city.	The Planning Department has identified the opportunity to apply for an EPA federal funding grant of $95,000 for brownfield site assessment. GIS is needed to identify suitable brownfield sites for development. This is too time-consuming to do by manual means.
Economic Development	The division has identified increasing the number of new businesses in the city as their major challenge and opportunity for the next five years.	They propose to use GIS to build a Web site that will attract new high-tech businesses to the city. These businesses will contribute several forms of revenue to the city (business licenses, income tax, and property tax), as well as help to raise the general educational attainment levels within city schools.

Figure R1: Summary of business opportunities identified by division managers.

A rigorous business analysis methodology was used to determine the specific projects needed to address these opportunities and challenges. This methodology allowed definition of the exact costs, benefits, and the return on investment that the city will gain if it implements this program of projects.

Proposed program

Based on the objectives outlined by the city's division managers (figure R1), a program of projects was identified that will allow the city to use GIS methods and technology to reduce costs and improve services. Figure R2 highlights the GIS program, when the individual projects will be completed, and the time frame for realizing the projected benefits.

By way of summary, it can be said that the proposed initiatives comprise a collection of eight interlinked projects: two are foundational, four are technology solution focused, and two are associated supporting projects that address governance and control, and training.

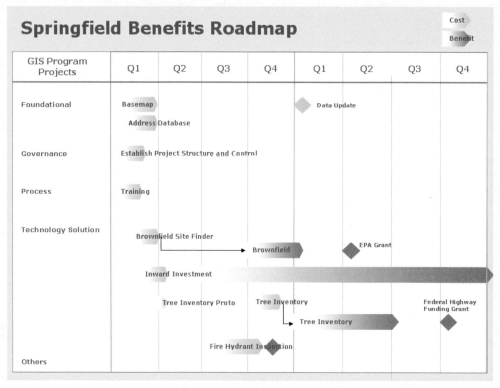

Figure R2: Proposed GIS program projects, timeline, and benefits roadmap.

Foundation projects—these are building block projects for later projects:

- Citywide basemap Web service: Enhance the existing map files by using GIS to create an online, integrated, continuous basemap comprising key layers that will be a centrally managed foundation for multiple city applications. The maps and associated data will be made available for citizens via the city's e-government portal using GIS.

- Citywide address database: Create a standardized, integrated GIS-based, citywide address database that will be Web accessible, centrally managed, and used in multiple applications. City employees and citizens will be able to locate services and data based on their address.

Technology solutions—these will provide the main measurable benefits:

- Tree Inventory: Control air pollution and maintain and improve the attractiveness of the city by maintaining tree coverage at current levels. A tree coverage inventory using GIS will qualify for a federal highway funding grant and will allow long-term monitoring of tree levels.

- Fire Hydrant Inspection and Maintenance: Conduct inspection and maintenance of city fire hydrants using GIS to minimize the cost of compliance with the Governmental Accounting Standards Board (GASB) 34 regulation and to ensure correct operation.

- Brownfield Site Finder: Reduce urban sprawl by redeveloping brownfield sites instead of greenfield sites. A GIS-based application will be used to find suitable sites. A federal EPA grant can be obtained to cover the cost of GIS-based assessment.

- Inward Investment: Attract new high-value businesses to the city by enhancing inward investment procedures using GIS. Increasing the number of high-value businesses investing in the city will increase revenues from property tax, business licenses, and income tax.

Supporting projects—these enable the other projects:

- Establish project structure and control: Define the city governance structure and management team necessary for successful delivery of the proposed benefits.

- Training: Educate and train city staff in the principles, applications, and operations of GIS and the applications being deployed.

Program costs

The full cost for the proposed GIS program is **$509,384**, as shown in figure R3, where the total is broken down by year, and capital (CapEx) and operational (OpEx) expenditures. As is to be expected, the majority of the cost falls in the first year and is CapEx-based. A second peak in capital expenditure in 2010 arises from the need to replace part of the inspection truck fleet.

	2008	2009	2010	2011	2012	5-Year Total
Capital Expenditure	$ 243,460	$ 5,199	$ 79,889	$ 4,889	$ 4,889	$ 338,326
Operational Expenditure	$ 34,245	$ 35,274	$ 32,851	$ 33,837	$ 34,852	$ 171,058
Total Expenditure	$ 277,705	$ 40,473	$ 112,740	$ 38,726	$ 39,741	$ 509,384

Figure R3: GIS program expenditure.

The total program expenditure includes all hardware, software, data, and outside (contractor) labor and the additional burdened inside labor required. The costs for the key types of expenditure are shown in figure R4; excluding inside labor, the cost over five years is **$241,499**—that is the additional finance required.

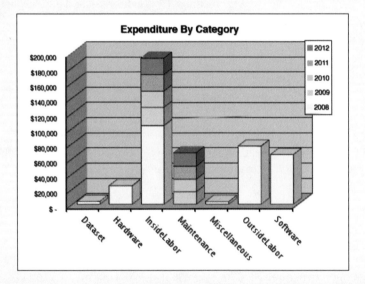

	2008	2009	2010	2011	2012	Total
Dataset	$ 4,000.00	$ -	$ -	$ -	$ -	$ 4,000.00
Hardware	$ 24,500.00	$ -	$ -	$ -	$ -	$ 24,500.00
InsideLabor	$ 103,704.83	$ 23,973.18	$ 21,240.00	$ 21,730.53	$ 21,730.53	$ 192,379.06
Maintenance	$ -	$ 16,500.00	$ 16,500.00	$ 16,995.00	$ 17,504.85	$ 67,499.85
Miscellaneous	$ 3,500.00	$ -	$ -	$ -	$ -	$ 3,500.00
OutsideLabor	$ 76,500.00	$ -	$ -	$ -	$ -	$ 76,500.00
Software	$ 65,500.00	$ -	$ -	$ -	$ -	$ 65,500.00
Total	$ 277,704.83	$ 40,473.18	$ 37,740.00	$ 38,725.53	$ 39,235.38	$ 433,878.91

Figure R4: GIS program expenditure by category: chart and table.

Time frame

As is shown in figure R2, the main implementation phase for of all the projects will be within the first year. The fire hydrant project will begin to return benefit by meeting GASB 34 regulatory requirements immediately upon completion at the end of Q4 2008. The inward investment project benefits will scale up gradually throughout 2008 and 2009 as awareness spreads and the impact of the new GIS-based approach is felt when new businesses set up operations in Springfield. Since the benefits of the tree inventory and brownfield site finder projects are contingent upon award of federal grants, their financial benefits will not be achieved until the second year. Even after the five-year business analysis review period, some of these projects will continue to generate benefits to the city.

Governance

Critical to the overall success of this program of work is proper project governance and control. All the key resources have been identified to oversee the successful business, technical, and financial outcomes discussed. Figure R5 shows the proposed management organization for the program. The names in this diagram are only proposed and will be confirmed if the program of work is given the go-ahead.

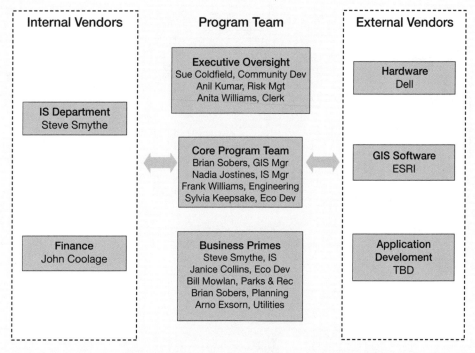

Figure R5: Proposed governance organization for proposed program of work.

Business analysis

Lastly, and most importantly, the financial analysis related to this proposed program of works is summarized in figure R6. The data presented show that the proposed program of work will generate a **Net Present Value of $223,829,** an **Internal Rate of Return of 37 percent,** and a **Return on Investment of 216 percent** for the city over five years. The investment **Payback Period will be three years,** and the program will require a maximum of **$220,000 in Free Cash Flow** subsidy. These values are all well within accepted City of Springfield guidelines for projects of this nature.

| Input Data | <<< | Menu | >>> | Graphs | | PA |

ROI METHODOLOGY - Step 9 (Calculate Financial Metrics)
Detailed output

	Unit	2008	2009	2010	2011	2012
Pre-tax Operating Cash Flows						
Revenue (loss)	$	23,402	81,454	127,666	167,799	199,960
Operating expenditure (savings)	$	1,023	8,516	11,082	11,532	12,029
Pre-Tax Operating Cash Flows	$	24,425	89,970	138,748	179,331	211,990
Post-tax Operating Cash Flows						
Depreciation	$	(5,700)	(5,700)	(5,700)	(5,700)	(5,700)
Earnings Before Tax	$	18,725	84,270	133,048	173,631	206,290
Tax charge	$	0	0	0	0	0
Depreciation Add Back	$	5,700	5,700	5,700	5,700	5,700
Post-tax Operating Cash Flows	$	24,425	89,970	138,748	179,331	211,990
Free Cash Flows						
Capital Expenditure (decrease in capex)	$	(243,460)	(5,199)	(4,889)	(4,889)	(4,889)
On-going change in Capital Expenditure (savings)	$	0	0	(75,000)	0	0
Free Cash Flows	$	(219,035)	84,771	58,859	174,442	207,101
Ratio factors						
Discount multiplier	Discount multiplier	0	1	2	3	4
Discounted FCF	$	(219,035)	79,973	52,384	146,465	164,043
Cumul Discounted FCF	$	(219,035)	(139,063)	(86,679)	59,786	223,829
Payback years	Years				3	

Summary output					
	Unit	Value		Meaning	
Net Present Value (NPV)	$	223,829	>>>>>>	This project creates value	
Internal Rate of Return (IRR)	%	37%	>>>>>>	This project creates value	
Payback - Discounted	years	3	>>>>>>	This project will provide a payback in 3 years.	
Max Cumulative FCF Subsidy	$	(219,035)	>>>>>>	The peak funding requirement is $219035	
Project Return on Investment	%	216%	>>>>>>	This project returns 2.16 times over the initial capital investment.	

Figure R6: Summary of the financial situation for the program.

In addition to the tangible benefits highlighted by the financial analysis, there are a number of important supporting intangible benefits that will accrue to the city if this program of work is carried out:

- Creating an inventory of tree cover is the first step in maintaining city tree coverage at the current level (and eventually returning it to historic levels). Trees help to keep the city green; they reduce pollution, provide shade, and improve civic pride, as well as make Springfield an attractive place to live and work.

- Inspecting and maintaining city fire hydrants, in addition to being mandated by the GASB 34 regulations, will ensure that in times of emergency the hydrants are able to function correctly. This will save lives and alleviate or minimize damage to property. Up-to-date asset inventories will also be required for future city bonding, loan, and grant applications.

- Constraining development to brownfield sites instead of greenfield sites will help reduce the amount of urban sprawl that has blighted a number of other cities in the region. This will further assist in maintaining the scenic character of Springfield.

- Attracting new high-value businesses to the city using inward investment procedures will not only increase city revenues, but will also help to raise educational attainment levels in schools, which are below regional averages.

- The new citywide basemap and address database projects will encourage collaboration between city departments, and the sharing of data and other resources that will create a type of "joined up" local government community, which has long been lacking. Furthermore, in the future, these projects will provide better services to citizens by sharing more information and services online, as part of the city's e-government initiative.

Conclusions

This study has used an externally developed and verified methodology to calculate the business case for a program of work at the City of Springfield. This approach has demonstrated that implementation of this program of work will yield major benefits to the city. The program will generate a net value of $223,829 with an Internal Rate of Return of 37 percent for the city by year 5. The investment will pay for itself within three years and will provide a 216 percent Return on Investment. These values are all well within accepted City of Springfield guidelines for projects of this nature.

In addition, this program of work would attract new high-tech firms, contribute meaningfully to maintaining the scenic character of the City of Springfield, and would enable the city to meet regulatory obligations. Collectively, these benefits are consistent with the City of Springfield strategic objectives of improving citizen services and reducing overall costs.

As a result of this analysis, it is recommended that the city fund this program of work.